IT'S ALIVE!

BRINGING NIGHTMARES TO LIFE

EDITED BY JOE MYNHARDT AND EUGENE JOHNSON

Let the world know:
#IGotMyCLPBook!

Crystal Lake Publishing
www.CrystalLakePub.com

WELCOME TO ANOTHER CRYSTAL LAKE PUBLISHING CREATION.

Thank you for supporting independent publishing and small presses. You rock, and hopefully you'll quickly realize why we've become one of the world's leading publishers of Dark and Speculative Fiction. We have some of the world's best fans for a reason, and hopefully we'll be able to add you to that list really soon. Be sure to sign up for our newsletter to receive three eBooks for free, as well as info on new releases, special offers, and so much more. To follow us behind the scenes while supporting independent publishing and our authors, be sure to follow us on Patreon.

You can also subscribe to Crystal Lake Classics where you'll receive fortnightly info on all our books, starting all the way back at the beginning, with personal notes on every release.

Welcome to Crystal Lake Publishing—Tales from the Darkest Depths.

COPYRIGHT ACKNOWLEDGEMENTS

Artwork by Luke Spooner

TABLE OF CONTENTS

Structure of the Plot:

Writing Your World

The Nitty Gritty

Now What

Artwork by Luke Spooner

INTRODUCTION

IF YOU'RE A writer and you're holding this book in your hands, you owe editors Joe Mynhardt and Eugene Johnson a huge helping of gratitude.

When I first started writing and submitting horror stories (this was back in the late 1980s when the Internet didn't yet exist and dinosaurs roamed the land) the only way to get this level of writing advice from established professionals was to attend genre conventions or writing conferences. There were panels to attend, speeches to listen to, personal conservations to eavesdrop on, and of course, there was the bar—where many mentorships and genuine friendships were born.

I still remember stiffly climbing out of the car in Rhode Island after a long drive north from Maryland and finding myself, within mere minutes, engaged in a *is-this-really-happening?* conversation with legends Charlie Grant, Rick Hautala, and Doug Winter. Talk about a dream come true for a twenty-two-year-old rookie.

But attending conventions took time and money, neither of which I had much of in those days. It was a rare and special occurrence.

So, what was left for the eager, new writer looking

to learn the inside tricks of the trade? Let's see. There was always, *Writer's Digest* magazine and their annual Market Report books, but you were lucky if you could find one or maybe two articles related to horror or genre fiction within those hallowed pages. Most of the essays were devoted to romance fiction (red hot at the time), science fiction, non-fiction, and writing the Great American Novel.

For us fans of the dark, new information and advice was pretty scarce.

The next rung down the ladder you had small press market guides, publications such as Janet Fox's, *Scavenger's Newsletter,* and Kathy Ptacek's, *Gila Queen's Guide.* These monthly newsletters were invaluable resources for marketing information, featuring everything from detailed writers' guidelines for new and established genre markets, average response times for submissions (remember, this was pre-Internet, so you had to stuff your printed story in an envelope and actually snail-mail it), current news and reviews, and even a fun column devoted to authors listing their recent sales—all of this goodness focused on horror, sci-fi, and fantasy fiction.

I devoured these publications religiously and learned to view them as a kind of writer's bible—hell, I still have a box of *Scavenger's* tucked away somewhere in my office, but the one thing that was missing? Solid advice from writers who had paid their dues and "made it."

Hopefully, you're getting the picture by now, folks. If you're an aspiring writer or even a semi-established author who has made some decent sales but are looking to improve your craft (this last group *should* include a whole lot of us currently working down here in the trenches!), *It's Alive: Bringing Nightmares to Life* is a veritable gold mine—and maybe the bargain of the decade.

Where else are you going to pull up a chair and catch authors like Joe R. Lansdale, F. Paul Wilson, Jonathan Maberry, Chuck Palahniuk, Ramsey Campbell, and Tom Monteleone (and so many others) all in the mood to talk shop?

And, my God, the topics being discussed around this shadowy corner table, everything from how to create new worlds and build suspense to writing sympathetic characters and unveiling theme through plot and creating effective dialogue. Talk about being in the right place at the right time!

One more brief aside before I step out of the way and let you get to the good stuff. For me, listening to (and/or reading) established authors discussing their craft has always been more than just about learning the nuts and bolts of writing and getting better.

Their voices and wisdom have always inspired and energized me to keep at it and believe in myself despite the doubts and rejection, to keep dreaming. I hope the heartfelt words in this volume from so many successful storytellers provide all of you with the some of the same tools and emotions I discussed above. Editors Mynhardt and Johnson have thrown one hell of a party here and we're all very fortunate to be on the invite list.

Okay, enough from me. It's time. Now open that desk drawer and pull out a pen or a highlighter (that's right, you not only have my permission to scribble inside this gorgeous edition—normally an act of

blasphemy, I know—you have my encouragement to do so). Turn the page, folks, and get to work. It's time.
   Time to listen.
   Time to learn.
   Time to dream.

—Richard Chizmar

Artwork by Luke Spooner

WRITING, STORYTELLING, AND HORROR, OH MY

CONFESSIONS OF A PROFESSIONAL DAYDREAMER

JONATHAN MABERRY

I HAVE A weird job.

I am, a professional daydreamer. I make stuff up for a living and get paid for it. My job is built around letting my mind wander down improbable hallways and to open the creakiest doors to see what jumps out. That's what I do. It's what people like me do.

Kind of.

Those of us who define ourselves as writers bring certain qualities to the game. We all have a natural gift for storytelling. We know how to shape tales and include an appreciation for drama and pacing, twists and dramatic beats, but that isn't what makes us good writers.

Writing doesn't rely too much on those natural gifts. They're absolutely necessary, but there is more to being a writer than having good ideas.

Let's unpack that.

If I were to use a Venn diagram the, 'natural storytelling ability,' would probably only count for a third of what it takes to be a successful writer, possibly less.

A bigger chunk of that is craft. Those are the skills we learn in school, in creative writing programs, in workshops at conventions, from mentors, in books and magazines, and so on. The skills and techniques of craft are typically divided into two categories: narrative elements and literary devices. Each set is important, and neither set can be completely mastered in a single lifetime. It's like the Japanese sword masters said of learning *kenjutsu*, "there is no end to the pursuit of perfection."

Let's pause there for a moment because perfection is an unattainable goal. It isn't required. Moving toward that point, however remote it might be, is the point. It is incumbent on us as writers to constantly improve our craft. Partly because we wish to be able to tell the story we have cooking in our minds, and do so in a what that allows it to be fully realized and to ensure that it says what we want it to say in a way that readers will be able to grasp.

The ideas that come into our heads, whether they are born there or pulled in by observation and will, are often amorphous. *We* understand them, but they are not necessarily framed in ways that would make sense to others. I remember being a little kid and trying to explain stories to adults. I rambled and rambled and often lost the thread. Patient adults listened with glazed eyes and patience faltered because what I was able to say was not sufficient for them to hear and understand. As I grew and went to school, I learned how to express myself. That was the beginning of applying craft to idea.

Narrative Elements help us build a cohesive structure around an idea, and they work as well in nonfiction as in fiction. They include setting, characters, point of view, theme, plot, conflict, and foreshadowing. Literary Devices are more specific and the reliance on them varies from writer to writer and often from story to story. They include: metaphor, simile, irony, parallel structure, alliteration, dramatic beats, paragraph and sentence structure, hyperbole, personification, allusion, understatement, and even onomatopoeia.

Collectively these elements of craft fill another big chunk of the Venn diagram. Other elements in that mix are: social media savvy, an understanding of how the publishing industry works, business etiquette, and networking. The heart and soul of this is something that blends natural storytelling with a solid understanding of the function and potential of elements of craft. That last element is story development.

Many writers new to the business make the completely understandable rookie error of thinking that a good idea is the same thing as having a story that's ready to be written. Ideas are concepts; stories are structured things that have a beginning, middle and an end.

When I was a kid I was lucky enough to be introduced to several of America's greatest science fiction, fantasy and horror writers. Not just to their works, but to them. My middle school librarian was a secretary for several clubs of professional writers, and all through seventh, eighth and ninth grades I got to meet literary gunslingers like, Ray Bradbury, Richard Matheson, Harlan Ellison, Avram Davidson, Robert Bloch, Robert Sheckley, L. Sprague de Camp, Lin

Carter, and others. For a poor kid from the inner city this was pure magic.

Of those writers, two, in particular, took time to tutor me on how to develop a story. Richard Matheson and Ray Bradbury, my literary godfathers, walked me through the process. I was twelve or thirteen at the time, but the lessons stuck.

We were at the lavish apartment of some writer (and, sadly for the life of me I can't remember *whose* place it was), with maybe forty writers and a couple of dozen other folks from the TV world and publishing. Bradbury and Matheson were seated in big chairs by a fireplace and I was sitting on the floor, very much like an apprentice to a pair of sorcerers. It was winter and although the party was in the afternoon, it was getting dark. There were some pigeons on the ledge outside of the window, four of them looking down at the street, but the fourth was looking in at us.

Bradbury pointed to that bird. "Why is he looking at us?"

Matheson asked, "Who is he looking at in here?"

I gave some kind of answer, and they kept hitting me with questions.

What will happen if the person the bird is looking for sees it?

Why is that this particular bird has darker feathers than the others?

What would happen if someone opened a window? Would the bird come in?

It was my answer to those last two questions that made both men smile. "No, the person he's here to find would jump out of the window."

They liked that answer.

Matheson said, "Sure . . . but why?"

Before I could answer Bradbury asked, "And what will happen if that person doesn't jump out of the window?"

I came up with an answer to that, and they countered with more questions, and I had to concoct more answers. Bradbury and Matheson were teaching me a story development exercise they called the, 'What if,' game.

The idea of that bird story is the fact that a bird is looking for a specific person at a party and that person feels compelled to open the window. It's a good concept. Most concepts feel so damn right, and they can be so exciting that it's easy to be caught up in the delight of a cool, creepy idea. It's easy to think you have a story.

The, "What If," game is about taking that idea and developing it, exploring it, unlocking its potential, and then chasing the cause-and-effect implied by each question to an end point that makes sense and tells a complete story. (Side note, in short fiction, the ending does not have to be as revelatory or fully realized as in a novel.) Short fiction has within it the potential for some rule-breaking, for the disruption of the three-act structure. Novels, on the other hand, generally require a bit more payoff, largely because of their complexity, a larger cast of characters, more subplots, bigger central crisis, and because of the time a reader has been asked to invest in reading. This is not an absolute, but it's true more often than not.

The, "What If," game takes idea and transforms it into a workable story. I've taught it in writing programs to adults and teens and one of the things I most love about the exercise is that no two writers will come up with the same answers. That's why I smile and shake my head whenever some unenlightened person says something like, "Vampires? Oh, that genre's totally played out." They say the same about zombies, ghosts, werewolves, demons, and all of the other subgenres of horror, and they are never correct.

Prior to World War II vampires, mummies and werewolves were pretty damn scary. The rise of Hitler and Nazi Germany deflated that by presenting a much, much bigger threat. It's hard, after all, to be scared of a pale Eastern European nobleman in an opera cloak who kills three or four people in the course of a movie, or maybe a dozen in a novel when you have tens of millions of people being herded into gas chambers at concentration camps. So, during the war the standard monsters faded, and people thought they were, pardon the pun, dead.

After the war, in the era directly following the dropping of the atomic bombs on Hiroshima and Nagasaki we suddenly had a new kind of horror. Writers could have written a slew of novels and movie scripts about what happened to those islands, and there were some, but the 'idea' of something as large and destructive as nuclear weapons and radiation suggested new thoughts. Out of that atomic age were born brand new monster stories because writers, knowing that radiation caused mutation, began to ask themselves, "what if?"

What if radioactivity made things grown large? What if those blasts awakened creatures long forgotten? And so on, and by developing those ideas from cause (radiation/nuclear power) to effect (the cost to society and the rise of dangerous mutations) we got Godzilla, Them, The Beast from Twenty Thousand Fathoms, Deadly Mantis and the Amazing Colossal Man.

By asking, "what if?" humans kept dropping bombs writers gave birth to apocalyptic and post-apocalyptic fiction. Other writers took that idea of an apocalypse and played the same game with other kinds of causes, still ending the world, but shifting the blame for it from atomic energy to bacteria and viruses. This brings us back to vampires. In 1954 Richard Matheson wrote *I Am Legend*, which was a post-apocalyptic science fiction story told as a horror novel. It breathed new life into the vampire genre. Pun intended that time.

By the end of that decade, Hammer Films, in England was releasing brand new takes on Dracula, werewolves, Frankenstein, the Mummy, and other familiar horrors. Not retreads, but new visions of them. Playing the game to ask, "What if these were in color?"

What if there was strong adult content that tapped into lust and connected that more overtly to the implied rape in vampire fiction? What if the good guys didn't always win? What if the monsters were not explicitly evil? And so on.

What if, what if, what if?

I came to fiction rather late. For the first twenty-five years of my career, I focused on nonfiction. Lots of articles about martial arts and self-defense, about science and travel, about theater and sports; and from there to writing textbooks for the courses I taught at Temple University, and then mass-market nonfiction books on everything from a history of sparring to the folklore of supernatural predators. I never really expected to write fiction, despite the mentoring from two of fictions' giants.

Then, while editing one of my books on supernatural folklore, I began playing that useful old game. While writing about vampire beliefs in various countries, and focusing on how radically different those vampires were from the versions in Hollywood and popular fiction, I wondered, *What if people encountered folkloric vampires, but all they knew about fighting vampires came from books and movies? What would happen?*

What if?

You see, in folklore, vampires are not afraid of the cross. The concept of holy items being used to ward off bloodsuckers was created by, Bram Stoker, an Irish Catholic. Same goes for the concept that a vampire can't enter a house unless invited. That was Stoker's way of keeping Dracula from simply killing everyone he met in London.

Stakes? Nope. Long-shafted stakes were only used to pin a vampire down while other people cut its head off and performed the full Ritual of Exorcism.

Sunlight? Not a factor at all until the 1922 silent film *Nosferatu*. Re-read *Dracula*—he walks around in sunlight.

And so on.

As I worked on the nonfiction book I kept playing with the idea, working out scenarios of cause and effect with ordinary people encountering monsters they *think* they understand, but really don't. What would be the effect? What's the learning curve? How do they find out how to stop this or that specific kind of vampire? How do they square the reality of a supernatural monster with their own logical worldview? How would they summon the courage or optimism to fight those creatures? What would it take to win? What would happen to the town if they lost?

On and on.

By the time the nonfiction book was done, I'd spent a considerable amount of time dragging hypothetical characters through my scenarios. I was not content to leave it at, "What if real people encountered vampires?"

I kept asking myself questions. I applied logic to the answers, and with each step, I asked, "What happens next?"

"What are the consequences?"

"How do you win that kind of fight?"

What I didn't know was that the game was working me through the logic, the cause and effect equation of plotting my first novel.

And then I thought: "What if I tried to write a novel?"

"What if that novel was about realistic people fighting vampires?"

Which is when I sat down to begin writing *Ghost Road Blues*.

Writing it took me over three years, and at no point during that process did I think it would be good enough to sell. It was just that I'd played the, "What if," game so long with the idea that writing the book was the only way to get it out of my head.

When it was done, I revised the ass off it. Eighteen drafts. I finished it in late 2004.

Then I asked myself, "What if it's good enough to sell?"

I had no yardstick for measuring its quality. I didn't know any novelists at that time, and hadn't spoken to Matheson or Bradbury since the 1970s. I had serious doubts about it because, after all, I was a nonfiction guy. What did I know about fiction? What made me think my stuff was worth submitting, let alone being sold?

On the other hand, what if it *was* good enough to submit? What if by spending so much time working through the cause and effect of my concept that I'd managed to build something believable enough to be frightening? What if I'd learned enough from my mentors, and from reading and re-reading the novels by my favorite authors, that I actually had a shot at becoming a novelist?

"What if?"

As it turns out, that book landed me an agent pretty quickly and she sold it to the second editor who read it. It was published in April of 2006, less than eighteen months from the end of my final draft. It went on to win the Bram Stoker Award for Best First Novel.

Who knew?

Ray Bradbury and Richard Matheson both gave me generous cover blurbs, among the last each of them would write, which appeared on the 10th anniversary editions of that book and its two sequels.

I sure as hell didn't *know*, but I played the, "What if," game, applying it not only to the original idea, but to a new genre for me, a new career path.

So that was 2006, and I write this in late summer 2018. I'm writing my 34th novel. I've also written six more nonfiction books, over a hundred short stories, and enough comic books to fill fifteen graphic novels.

One of my novels, also based on folkloric versions of vampires, is being filmed as a Netflix series. All because of asking myself, 'what if?'

And I still play that game.

Maybe a dozen times a day. It's where most of my stories come from. I goose the process along, too. Since a good chunk of my business these days is writing science-based horror (*Dead of Night, V-Wars*, etc.) and weird science thrillers (the Joe Ledger thrillers), I read a lot of science journals, articles and books. Ditto for world history, global politics, psychology, and so on. Any time I hit on something odd or interesting I start asking myself those questions.

What if the prion disease from *fatal familial insomnia* could be weaponized? Who would do that? Why would they do it? How would someone profit from that —financially or ideologically? These questions, followed by dozens of others that led me along the cause and effect path, became my novel *Patient Zero*.

What if a group secretly funded terrorists to make devastating strikes, such as 9-11, and then positioned themselves to profit from the ensuing radical shifts in the stock market? That became *The King of Plagues*.

What if parasites such as the green jewel wasp could be used as a bioweapon? Could it create a zombie-like pathogen? How? Who would I ask? Who would create it? Why? And what else could it be used for? That was the basis of my zombie apocalypse novels *Dead of Night* and *Fall of Night*. And the strong foundation of credible science so appealed to George A. Romero, writer-director of the landmark *Night of the Living Dead*, that he asked me to write a story officially connecting my books to his movie. That story, "Lone Gunman," appeared in the anthology we co-edited.

What if? On and on and on.

It isn't just about having good ideas. A lot of people have those, and in great quantity. No, what makes a *writer* is to take that idea and develop it, explore it, deconstruct it, and then follow it all the way to a killer conclusion. Do that and you're writing real stories. Do that, and you're probably writing your best stuff.

Do that, because Richard Matheson and Ray Bradbury once told a young kid that it was the secret to writing compelling and memorable stories.

So, yeah . . . do that.

WHAT IS WRITING &
WHY WRITE HORROR?

JOHN SKIPP

I LIVE IN Los Angeles, where every cockroach has a screenplay to hustle, and every studio executive is convinced that any moron could write a script, because *look at all these morons!*

Yet, in a town that publicly praises the writer while treating them as disposable as tampons, many stalwart souls remain inflamed with the desire to make magick out of nothing but words, and paint pictures in our skulls that will both matter and last.

So I was asked, for this book, to answer two simple questions:

1) What is writing?

2) Why write horror?

Let's tackle the first one first.

Writing is the process of slapping words down on paper, or the digital format of your choice (Word doc, Open Office, Final Draft and so on). Even texting is writing, albeit on the primitive/high-tech level of passing notes in class, and writers like Joe Hill have spun elaborate, gripping narratives out of nothing but tweets.

The purpose, of course, is to communicate something: a thought, a feeling, a story, a strategy. Words are great for that. That's why we replaced inarticulate growls and moans with them (although inarticulate growls and moans still have a place in the communicative pantheon). When I write songs, for example, I often start by singing melodies phonetically, making sounds that please me along the vowel spectrum, only later going back to figure out what those noises might be trying to say, then plug the words in retrospectively

Since I suspect we're mostly talking about fiction in this book: writing fiction is the process of telling stories, or delivering slices of life through the eyeballs of others, so that they land and rattle around said reader's braincase, and though there are many people who claim they are writing only for themselves, I think it's fair to say that most of them kinda hope someone else will read them, and respond to them. Hopefully well.

I love the nuts and bolts of writing. The structure of sentences, the dance of language, the remarkable precision and clarity that the right words, in the right order, can deliver: I find the process thrilling, and am delighted when some other writer brings those types of thrills to me. But without something to communicate, it's just word salad: even less useful than grunts or howls, because at least you know what the fuck those noises meant. So I don't love words for words' sake. I love them because they're such wonderful tools of expression, and I've got a lot to express.

Which leads to the second question.

Why write horror? Out of all the things you could hope to communicate, why would you want to deal with the most haunting, horrific, ugly, sinister, brutalizing subject matter on Earth?

Or, as my Mom used to ask, "Why can't you write about *nice* things?"

I've talked with hundreds of horror writers about this, over the last several decades. Everyone has their own particular reasons, and circumstances. It basically comes down to one or more of the following:

1) **"I'm a fundamentally haunted person**." In these cases, the writer usually discovered at an early age that they were tormented by frightening questions of mortality, of pain and injustice, of violence and madness and the existence of evil. They found themselves compelled to explore these questions, even if they never held out hope of actual answers. They were, in short, on a need-to-know basis with the darkness: either because of something traumatic that happened in their lives, or because they were just *born that way*, with no discernible cause. Which is, in some ways, even more haunting for its inexplicability.

2) **"I'm wrestling my demons**." This is similar to the first, but differs in that the writer is confronting those troublesome forces within themselves. Fighting their own madness, their own dark compulsions, their own rage and capacity for evil. Much of the most intense and intimate horror fiction comes directly from here.

3) **"I think monsters are awesome."** This is the

least-complicated way in, often rooted in childhoods where dinosaurs and sharks were the coolest things ever, and Halloween was the finest holiday on Earth. There's not a lot of deeper diving involved. It's just fun! And fun is more than enough for these folks.

4) **"I'm a sick fuck with a twisted sense of humor."** The great cartoonist Gahan Wilson and I had a swell time discussing how horror and humor were flip-sides of the same coin. Often, when confronted with unspeakable wrongness, laughter is the only remotely sane response. And because life confronts us with unspeakable wrongness on pretty much a daily basis, the appetite for black comedy is a hearty one indeed. From the first time you hear a dead baby joke in childhood, you know whether or not you are one of those people.

5) **"I like shocking and disturbing people."** Sometimes this translates as "I get a kick out of how your little eyes bug out when I make up my crazy shit." Sometimes it's more like "I'm in horrible pain, and I'm going to make you feel it." Sometimes the answer is, "I don't know why. I just do." And sometimes—although they'll rarely admit it—it comes down to "I'm a psychological sadist, and I hurt you because I can. You don't like it? *Good!*"

Important safety tip: those last people are bullies. Which is to say, assholes.

6) **"I'm writing survivalist horror."** Because horror is the fiction of worst-case scenarios, many writers are psychologically rehearsing for the worst

and positing possible heroic solutions. Training themselves mentally, spiritually, and emotionally to not just cope, but to win. This is particularly true when horror melds with action-adventure, but shows up in many surprising ways across the field.

7) "**I'm a social satirist and horror has many powerful symbols**." This is the place where horror becomes a fiction of ideas, exploring metaphors, delving into deeper meaning. This is horror at its most subversive, using tooth and nail to fight back against the Powers-That-Be, and the horrors of actual life. Sometimes it's funny. Sometimes it's not. But, to me, it's the fieriest of the forms; and one that is often integrated by writers who don't consider themselves genre-bound, with bigger cultural fish to fry.

I have, at various points in my life and career, fallen under each and every one of these categories. Yes, including bullying asshole.

I was a haunted child. I had demons within. I loved monster movies, had a sick sense of humor, loved to shock and disturb, wanted to learn how to survive, and was so pissed off at the monstrous injustice of the world that I would do anything to subvert it.

But that's just me!

I love to write because I love to explore the human condition, in all its dark and light. I love to communicate with people, to touch minds and souls with them, to pass along ideas, and share experience. To connect.

I also love writing for the sheer pleasure of the act. Sitting in the chair, and making shit up, to the best of my ability.

So the question becomes: why do *you* write horror?

TRIBAL LAYS

GENE O'NEILL

"There are nine and sixty ways of constructing tribal
lays, and every single one of them is right."
—Rudyard Kipling, "In Neolithic Age"

IN HIS RATHER long poem, "In Neolithic Age,"
Rudyard Kipling was reacting to the rigid literary
standards of the 19th Century. Specifically, he was
referring to the strict *rules* for the structure of a poem
or story. But he was also commenting in general on a
number of literary standards, like the proper education
and training of a writer. He was insisting that there
was more than one path to all of these literary
outcomes, and I agree wholeheartedly.

Below, I'm offering examples of two paths to
becoming a writer—one, traditional, like my
granddaughter is working on right now, and one not
so traditional, my winding route.

**One traditional way of acquiring and
demonstrating necessary skills, in becoming
a writer—**

Fiona

Early speech, speaking in fully constructed sentences, having a good ear for words:
The little girl, not quite two-years-old, grabbed her grandfather's hand and led him out the front door. "C'mon, Papa, let's go feed the goats."

When they got to the pasture around the corner, she handed her grandfather the clippers she'd brought along. "Papa, let's feed them some tree leaves." He clipped several short branches of leaves, hanging near the fence. Fiona noticed, during a previous visit, that the goats ate all kinds of things, but really loved the darkish-green live oak leaves.

So, part of developing early speech is also developing the power of observation, and being curious about the names and uses of the different things you spot.

Loves stories, both written and oral, even adding own stories to earliest drawings:
Fiona constructed a colorful drawing with her crayons, and brought it into the kitchen for her mother to put up on the side of the fridge. She pointed to two stick figures and told a story: "Once upon a time there were two kids, Jack and Jill . . . "

The oral stories may have plagiarized portions, but were always laced with original additions. Soon, even before school, she began to learn to read by following along when read to. She had sixteen DVDs and memorized every word, following along mouthing words under her breath.

Once Papa asked: "Fiona, are you going to college?"
She answered, "Do they have DVDs there?"

In elementary school demonstrates an appreciation for all the language arts:

Fiona loved story time, being read to by the teacher, telling her own stories, and was adept at early Spanish study. She brought home her homemade workbook full of stories and even some poems. She practiced her early Spanish orally when she came to visit her grandparents.

"Como se llama?"

Her grandmother answered, "Me llama es Mimi."

In high school excels in not only English, but all the Humanities:

Like other developing writers, Fiona became interested, almost obsessively, sometimes in a specific subject—like the African Bushmen and explored everything she could find about it. She read several articles on the Khoi-Khoi and his unusual *click* language. Fascinated, she checked out every book in her school library on the Bushmen and their home base in the Kalahari Desert. She extends her exploration to the city library, and read everything pertinent. She checked the internet, and then began her senior project, a fiction booklet, entitled: "Treasure of the Kalahari," about two Bushmen children tracking a wounded kudu, the spirit animal of their tribe. Her English teacher gave her an A on the project, and told her mother that Fiona is his best writing student ever. With good grades, demonstrated writing ability, and financial help from her grandparents, Fiona was accepted into the famed Stanford writing program.

In college, takes advantage of top instruction, developing her stories of magical realism:

As a freshman and sophomore, Fiona wrote, polished, and sent out several stories to various literary journals and the *Magazine of F & SF* and *Asimov's Science Fiction Magazine.* She received only rejection, but always personal encouraging notes. She eventually placed a short poem in *Ploughshares,* and another one in the *Kenyon Review.* But at the end of her sophomore year, her grandfather became terminally ill, requiring expensive healthcare, and she dropped out of her expensive degree program. She finished her undergraduate work at San Diego State, near her parent's home.

Fiona continued to write, and early in her senior year placed a short story in a good literary journal. She immediately phoned her grandmother, who held the phone up close to her bedridden grandfather's ear.

"Papa, McSweeny just bought, 'Ghost of a Chance,'!"

Months earlier, after workshopping the story and revising, she'd read it to her grandparents, who both loved the tale that was told from the viewpoint of an imaginary friend. The summer after graduation she was accepted with a full ride into the MFA in Writing Program at the University of Oregon in Eugene.

In graduate school, she places a few stories in genre magazines and begins her first novel:

After reading a draft of Fiona's first novel, "Flying with Radar Angels," the head of her department got her hooked up with a top NYC literary agent. She graduated with her MFA, and accepted a TA position for the next year at Oregon, while working on the revision and polishing of her novel.

"Flying with Radar Angels," is finally published, and has a serious movie inquiry:

Fiona's agent sold her magic realism novel, and received solid interest from Hollywood. They signed an option for the movie, the process dragged out for over a year before they exercised the option, while Fiona worked on her second novel, "Soulflash." But following early advice, she prepared herself to teach literature and writing as a necessary day job. She landed an assistant professor spot in the Creative Writing Department at the University of San Francisco, continuing her writing career in her spare time. After two years of teaching and the publication of "Soulflash," she proudly called her grandmother.

"Mimi, I'd love to take you and Mom to the premiere of 'Flying with Radar Angels' down in Hollywood."

After four more years, and the sale of another novel and a collection of her short stories, Fiona left teaching and becomes a full-time writer.

This is a fictionalized example of a traditional route to becoming a writer, my granddaughter is only in high school, and in fact, very few writers have this *fairly* smooth of a route. They experience many more ups and downs and *most* never become full-time writers.

Now, I'd like to spell out my own non-traditional route.

Acquiring the skills necessary to becoming a non-traditional instinctive writer

Gene

I was raised by my grandparents in a federal housing project (not called a ghetto back then) in the shadow of cranes at Mare Island Naval Shipyard in Vallejo, California. My grandparents had only 2nd and 3rd grade educations, but Gramps was a rigger at the shipyard, one of the blue-collar working-class, proud of his work. The housing project was a rough place to grow up. My brother and I were often exposed to bullying, racial strife, and crime, especially sexual assault. The teachers were tough disciplinarians, and expectations for most students were held low. Education was of little value to my classmates.

The emphasis was kept on sports. More than just a few outstanding athletes came out of the area; I had good motor skills, and boxed. I played basketball, and football, reaching a fairly high proficiency level at all three—playing basketball in junior college, but high school academic achievement was not so high. I did enough to pass.

Even though reading and books were not valued by most of my peers, I developed an early fascination with the big magazine rack at the cigar shop. The colorful illustrations caught my eye on a wide array of books. I equally liked the *Classic* comic books, like *Treasure Island*, and the science fiction magazines like *Imagination* with their more interesting covers, but had money to purchase only a few.

Was it likely a writer might develop from this kind of environment?

When I was six, I had polio. A year later I got released from the hospital. To celebrate, my grandfather took me to a little branch library near the project recreation center, a converted, old, two-story Victorian residence. A sign in front read:

Vallejo City Library

I couldn't read the sign because I had missed a significant portion of the 1st grade while in the hospital rehabilitating from my illness. I recovered relatively quickly, but fell behind in school.

On that first library visit, in his wonderfully expressive brogue, which I would learn to relish during family story time, Gramps said, "I wanted to show you this place, Gene, because this is where all the *right* words finally end up."

I looked at the shabby, poorly-maintained Victorian, needing at least a new roof and a fresh coat of paint. I frowned and bunched my face up at my grandfather. I wondered why the right words would all travel to this dilapidated building, and how they even discovered this out-of-the-way-place right in the heart of the federal housing project.

Gramps smiled and continued in what I recognized as a nearly reverent tone. "Aye, lad, all the right words. And when they have enough collected inside there, they are carefully assembled into a group. Now, if they have selected wisely, and if they have put those right words in exactly the correct order, something extraordinary happens. They create one of God's true magical gifts . . . a wonderful book. Let's go in and inspect some of the magic."

We stepped into that branch library, actually the entire bottom floor of the old residence, now mostly one undivided large room, but with floor to almost ceiling of rows of book shelving that seemed to extend forever. Nowhere had I seen so many books in one place.

I gazed about awestruck. "How many of these can I read, Gramps?"

"If you have the time, you can read them all."

We got my first library card that day, and I checked out three books, including one with wonderful illustrations and golden leaf bordering each page, "King Arthur and the Knights of the Round Table." I checked the book out three more times that year. Then, at Christmas time, my grandparents, who were just barely making ends meet, bought me that very expensive book.

So, I think that the cigar stand, the branch library, and the encouragement from my grandparents, stimulated an early love of books and reading. Gramps further stimulated my interest in stories, by telling oral ones from what I later learned were called *The Red Branch Tales*, many of them featuring the great Irish mythic hero: CuChullain. Outside of our home, though, I don't remember ever talking about books or stories with classmates or my sports team members.

Finishing high school, I didn't leave a particularly distinguished record behind in any subject. Looking back, I think even then I had been honing some early writing skills, a keen observation of what was transpiring around me. I knew early on that a fourteen-year-old classmate getting suddenly pregnant was a much bigger tragedy than a Stanford law student experiencing the same unexpected event. I truly honed the Irish love of the word, maintaining an ongoing interest in definitions and etymology. I eventually read all kinds of comics, magazines, and books, which both Grams and Gramps encouraged. Regardless of their lack of education, we engaged in interesting discussions on what I read. Both had very high recognition and speaking vocabularies.

After working a year or so out of high school, I enlisted in the Marines. I went overseas, saw and learned a lot in Southeast Asia (around that time, the area was known as French-Indo China), right before they declared the beginning of the Vietnam War, living in a tent in the jungle. I continued to read during my enlistment, mostly cheap paperbacks, which were readily abundant.

I returned home, worked a couple of years, saved up, and finally went to junior college, and then to a State college. I wanted to be a P.E. teacher, and took no extra English or any writing courses, but I took a better paying job than teaching when I graduated. Like many good readers, by this time I may have had some inkling that I wanted to try writing. But I took no coursework or prepared myself formally in any way.

Eventually, I did teach P.E. and coach after I got married and had two children. I worked a second job as a painter for a contractor, who had been a Marine colleague. By then, after reading a ton of books, including some science fiction, I tried my hand at a few stories. I got some personal feedback, but was always rejected. Then, after numerous trips to the library with my kids, and checking the children's section, we began reading the array of children's magazines. We even subscribed, but I realized many of the stories were heavy-handed with their moral lessons. It was only then that I found many of the magazines were published as an arm of some church.

I thought I could do better, and I wrote eight children's stories. I was right, sold four of them to the best kid's magazines. Based on this success, I decided to write adult material. But at thirty-eight, I realized that I needed some formal training, and applied for the Clarion Workshop in SF, taking place at Michigan State in 1979.

I was like a sponge during my six weeks at Clarion, soaking up everything, because I knew nothing about writing, including the typical story structure. Carol Emshwiller sat me down one day and privately taught me how to do more with less: Use the precise verb and you don't need modifiers. I was probably somewhere at the bottom of the class as far as *demonstrated* ability, but I made a good friend in Scott Edelman, our paths crossing many times in the future.

I also demonstrated something, so that Damon Knight and Kate Wilhelm invited me to attend private writerly gatherings/workshops monthly at their home in Eugene, Oregon. They also mentioned a young, promising writer who lived nearby to me, whom I should bring along.

That young writer was Kim Stanley Robinson, and my real education took place in those eight to ten eight-hour trips on weekends up to Eugene and back to Northern California. Stan had a formal education in writing, and would eventually go down to UCSD and get his PhD. We talked writing for a solid eight hours up and back, plus workshopping our stuff, at Damon and Kate's.

I heard the entire three-book Mars Trilogy outline

before it was written. The education wasn't entirely one way. I had lots of life experience to share with Stan, including stuff about the USMC rifle range at Camp Mathews, underneath part of the UCSD campus he would soon attend. He included some of that in fiction and non-fiction, which he would write.

Not too long after our trips, when Stan was a young SF star and I'd started selling stories to good markets, we both attended a Nebula dinner. He won the Nebula Award for his novelette, *"The Blind Geometer."* I'd read it and made a few suggestions based on working with blind P.E. students, and shared the most common prenatal cause of blindness. Stan recognized me as an influence on his writing, and his *favorite P.E. teacher.*

Unfortunately, I didn't feel I could write full time, working two jobs for several years. At this time, I was selling maybe three or four stories a year to good markets, which attracted NYC agent solicitations. I made the mistake of telling them that in my situation, holding two jobs and raising two kids, I had nothing to show them when they asked if I had a book they could market. I should have lied and tried to quickly write one then.

I also made a mistake early on with my short stories. I didn't write things that fell neatly into a genre category. I'd send something to Editor B. She'd say this is great but not clearly what I'm buying, but send it to Editor A. Of course, Editor A said the same thing, telling me to send it to Editor B. I was stubborn and continued to write mixed genre stories. But times change. Recently, I've been on panels discussing the value of mixed genre work.

A number of years ago, I was ready to begin writing

novels, and thought I'd quit my day job to do it. But my daughter, who graduated in pre-med, and was working in a clinic, wanted to go on to PA school. I thought about her great-grandparents, who never lived to see me published, and how proud they'd have been for Kaydee. I continued working.

But finally, I was able to write full time. And I've done pretty well. 170 short stories and novellas in good markets. Recently, I placed a two-novel series, which will total eight novels published. I've been a finalist for twelve Bram Stoker Awards, and won two of those haunted houses.

A meandering route, I agree, started way late at age thirty-eight.

In the past, I've been asked what I'd like to be, if I could choose anything. I answered, "A *writer!*" Very few people get the opportunity to be exactly what they want to be.

I'm a lucky man.

BAKE THAT CAKE
(ONE WRITER'S METHOD)

JOE R. LANSDALE: PASTRY CHEF

Recipe 1:

THERE ARE MORE ways than one to prepare and bake a cake, and only the ones that succeed and taste good count. The ones that fail you need to throw out and hope the birds and worms like it, hope they don't choke. That's the way writing works. Or at least something close to it. You throw out the words that don't do the story justice and hope the metaphorical birds and worms don't choke.

There is no exact rule for writing a story, except for the same one that is consistent with cake baking. You put the ingredients in a bowl, mix them, and then bake that sucker, or otherwise you lie dreaming with your unappeased sweet tooth while your cake remains unbaked.

To give an example of how I "bake my cakes", I'm going to give my methods for approaching a story, how I get geared up, what works for me, and then my daughter, who is a newer writer, will give examples of her approach.

The way a writer works can change with age. But

one thing is certain, if you are having trouble starting, then it's not a bad idea to consider the methods of others. The method I use I have used for over thirty-five years of my forty-five-year career, or some slight variation of it, and I see no reason to abandon it, but if I found it failing me, I would consider something else. I read other writer's methods when I started out, and through experiment, I found what works for me.

Let me start with this. I love writing. I don't enjoy only having written, I love the act itself. I wake up in the morning and when my feet hit the floor, I'm ready to go. Writing a scene that reads the way you imagine it can be difficult, but for me the attempt is always pleasurable. So, that's my first bit of advice. If you don't love it, or think real writing is about rolling around on the floor and crying and suffering for the right word, save the drama. Writing can be hard, but it beats jobs I used to have. Digging ditches, aluminum chair factory work, field work, janitor work, and the like. Do not confuse a hard day of writing for martyrdom. Compared to those things, it's a treat. It's all I ever wanted to do with my life, at least career-wise, and I feel like the luckiest person in the world every day I wake up. First, I woke up, and second, there's the work to look forward to.

Second, don't procrastinate. It doesn't get better as the day wears on. You may choose a different time of day to work, but whatever time you choose, be true to it. If you can go to a job you hate, or tolerate, and what you really want to do is write and you're not doing it, that's on you.

Quit waiting for inspiration. You are the inspiration. That's where it comes from, and the more you show up, the more it shows up, and in time you have yourself trained to not only sit down and start to work, but you have given your inner self permission to let the genie out of the bottle, and not just when you feel the mood. The mood is there waiting on you, instead of the other way around. I've found that if I'm feeling less than motivated, all I need to do is write one good sentence, and then if nothing follows, so be it. But, that one sentence nearly always opens the gates.

I wake up, have coffee and a small breakfast, and go to work. My goal is simple. I write at least three to five pages a day, and generally I achieve that within three hours. Now and again I'll work extra hours, but overall, for me, that's counterproductive.

I do better early on, and go downhill as the day wears on. Frequently, in those three hours, I end up writing a lot more than three to five, but that's my goal each day. I find that easy to achieve, and if I quit at three pages, then I feel like a hero all day long. If it's going well, it's possible those three pages will come in thirty minutes, and I continue if I so desire, but if not, I can quit with a clean conscience. I have my minimum.

I proof as I go. When I get about halfway through a story, or novel, or what I sense is the halfway point, I go back to the first, begin to read, and revise where I think it needs it, then lurching off that momentum, I write the rest of it, revising as I go, and then I give it a polish, but I avoid multiple drafts. I find that merely confuses me.

I don't plot. I might have an idea I'd like to see in a work, but I don't know how I'll arrive there. I like the sense of discovery. That way I'm as surprised as the reader, and it gives the work less of a clockwork-like feel. I like it to come together as organically as possible.

For me, the story needs to arrive by secret passage. I can't sit down and consciously think it out. My subconscious does that. The conscious mind worries too much and shops too hard for reasons, tries to determine who the characters are, where the subconscious knows these things, and reveals them to me as I create. I sit down, put my fingers on the keys, and generally the story is fed to me, digested, and distributed on the computer screen as if by magic.

I know it's working well when I hear the music. There's a beat, there's a pacing, a base line, all provided by the story's voice. It can't clank and clang, unless that's the nature of the story. The work must have soul, rhythm and blues, a country boogie, the depth and feeling of a sweeping ballad, sometimes all those things, which I suppose makes it more like freeform jazz. The story decides. The music must be right. It needs poetry without being a poem. When I feel the music, then the story is real. I show up, and the words, hopefully, sing.

Let your love for the story carry you along. If you don't have that love, find a story that you feel love for. Find that love, then you arrive at the point where you can feel the story loving you back; it's a phenomenal high.

Some days the work is magical, some days a little more work-a-day, but by showing up you soon reach a point where the work has a level it does not fall below. It's professional. At best, what we all strive for, of course, it's akin to designing a great architectural achievement, shiny glass, spirals of light that puncture the clouds. The other is like building a functional kitchen chair. Both do the job, but in different ways, but neither can be sloppy, because either can then collapse; failing to do what it was designed to do in the first place. A good chair, an architectural achievement, both should bring satisfaction.

Lastly. Keep the prose simple. Sure, there are exceptions, but a reader shouldn't feel they need a dictionary at their side to read your work. Write to be clear, not to impress. Can you try something experimental? Of course, I have, and I've enjoyed it, but your best bet is to write a story you want to read.

Characters are not things you write on five by ten cards and pull out of the bag when you need them. You let the stories grow out of your personal experiences, the depths of your thoughts, good and bad. Real characters are contradictions, and as has been said, "Everyone is the hero of their own story," which includes the villains. Walk-on characters should have something interesting to define them. Dialogue should sound like something someone would say. It might not be, but you should give the illusion that this is how real people talk. In the real world, we might be less witty and interesting, but the world you create should give you a feel of reality, but with all the boring stuff left out. If you write a scene where the character is bored, the reader shouldn't be. You should feel the character's boredom without the character boring you.

When you do decide to take a day off, know the difference between an honest day off, and goofing off. Play seriously when you work, as Bruce Lee said of martial arts, and when you goof off, feel like you deserve it, and enjoy the hell out of it.

Because tomorrow, you'll be back at it again. That's like having your cake and eating it too, every single day.

KASEY LANSDALE: PASTRY SOUS CHEF

Recipe 2:

I'm finding that my cake usually has the same ingredients as the chef, but the recipe is altered. Like when grandma refuses to write down the secret family recipe because even she doesn't know it. It's a dash of this and a pinch of that, and you know you're close, but try as you might, what comes out of the oven ain't Grandma's. I have a harder time being motivated than the chef, or staying motivated if you will. I usually toss everything in the mixer, and before I turn on the oven, I start cleaning up behind me. Wiping down the proverbial counters. I find that's when I begin to struggle. I just wanted to eat a piece of cake, not deep clean the whole kitchen. I'm learning the process of releasing the need to have a perfect dessert every time I sit down to work. It's easier said than done.

Unlike my dad, writing isn't the only thing I've ever wanted to do. Writing has been something that came about naturally because I do enjoy the process, and have grown up in that environment. Most of my writing, however, has been for songs.

I think, in truth, the best of what I've learned, most of it, has been by osmosis. I think finding people who are in similar stages of life and work as you are, who have the same career goals, and surrounding yourself with those people to keep you motivated, has been helpful for me. As a musician, you're always surrounded by other people when you work. As a writer, it's you and that laptop, and sometimes for me, since the habit hasn't been built in as long, it's easier to get off-track.

The best piece of advice I got from an editor was "show not tell." Actually, that's not exactly what she said, but I'll keep it PC, as that was the point. I tend to over-explain things, as I do in life. Finding a way to get to the point, and still inject it with the humor and irony that usually goes along with it is what I'm working towards now. I'm lucky. I grew up in a home where the idea of wanting to make a living being creative was seen as the norm, and I know that lots of folks didn't get that, but that's why finding your tribe is so important.

I don't think you should let everyone read your work and have an opinion on it all the time, that's a surefire way to get discouraged. I personally don't like to spread out the criticism week by week. Read it when it's done, then break my heart, just the once. But, if you're going to take someone's opinion, be sure they have some creds to back it up. Or at the very least, that they're on your team.

Oftentimes, people want to have an opinion to feel important, not because you really need it. Just like your wedding cake, you want references, samples.

Read the books that you like, that are reminiscent

of the things you want to write. I learned the rules of writing a long time ago in grade school. We all did. Now I'm trying to be sure that if I'm breaking them, it's with good reason. That I don't let the rules dictate what I am allowed or not allowed to do, and I hope that eventually I'll wake up and without thinking just put fingers to keys and unleash the way Chef does.

It might never happen, but I also think figuring out what my goals are for writing has been important. Maybe don't start out saying, "I want to be a bestseller and get reviewed in the NY Times." If that happens, awesome. Having a mental vision board of that is wonderful, but for me, setting mini goals is what helps me stay slightly more consistent. If I tell myself I have to write a bestseller I get overwhelmed and defeat myself before I get started. If I say, okay, I need to write five hundred words and hopefully they are good, that's a more manageable goal for one day.

I'm also discovering that like baking, it takes time. I really believe every time I write something, I learn something new—something important. Not just of the process of writing, but of my process. That's the fun part about being a newer writer. You're still discovering things. Like when I sing a song the same way a hundred times and suddenly, when I've gotten comfortable with it, I'm brave enough to take the melody somewhere new. I look forward to the day when I'm writing and that same feeling comes. Right now, I'm doing a lot of work with Chef, and that's like a crash course on steroids. If I don't take the initiative and get to work, I'll look up and he's baked forty-seven cakes and a batch of cookies. And there I am still mixing the dough. Now I want cookies.

Also, as a newer writer, I'm learning to let go of things. I'm learning that even if I put blood, sweat, and tears into fifty pages of something, if it's not getting better, then maybe I just need to move on from it, stop adding sugar and start fresh. That said, sometimes I toss the mix out too quick, which just a dash of something could save. If I am stuck at a place in a story, it's because inherently, I know the last section I wrote doesn't work. I may not know why, but I usually have to stop and come back to it another day. I have a certain amount in the tank, and when it's empty, it's empty.

I liken it to the gym. Sure, I could stay in there doing bicep curls for eight hours, but it won't really improve things. Better to call it and start fresh, so long as that's not an excuse to go play. Though at times, not thinking about it allows the subconscious to sort out the problem when you come back the next day. That's the real trick, though, coming back. I also find that like the gym, if I roll out of bed and get to it, I'm far more productive.

If I don't start until after lunch, then I'm already tired. I know some people who can only write at night, and bless 'em, but I'm not one of those people. That's something about my process I am sure of. It's easy to build up an arsenal of excuses by lunch. I'd much rather get to it and then have the rest of the day to hang, do errands, watch a movie, whatever I decide to do that day 'cause I already got my work done.

I do work longer than my father, because it takes me longer in general, but I also know that when I'm just staring at the screen for long periods, going for a walk or calling it is usually best. I have the joy of being able to put the fiction aside and work on something else. Though, not always, I usually have concurrent projects going in different fields, so when one stonewalls I flip to the other.

That might be a secret, too; not having all your eggs in one basket when you're starting out. Eventually, you can move all the eggs over and "watch that basket," but maybe you don't have to live off only cake for a while. You gotta build up that sugar tolerance. I wish I knew all the answers. I wish Chef knew them, 'cause I know he'd tell me at the very least, and then I'd tell you. But we don't. One can only hope that eventually the cream will rise to the top and all the excess will be seen as a beautiful mess that got you to where you want to be. At least, close to it, as I don't think we ever stop striving towards new goals, no matter what we have accomplished.

Living life, meeting people. Hearing their stories and feeling empathy. Showing kindness. That's where a lot of good stuff comes from. Take notes when something strikes you. Let it marinate. If you read it again the next day and it's still as poignant, use it. Be raw, be honest in the writing. I fight this a lot. My desire to show who I am and my desire to stay behind the veil. What I do know, is every time there's an honest moment, either in person or on the page, that's what people connect to time and time again.

The problem with advice and methods is that there's no one way. It's infuriating to hear, and I'm not sure where my process will land either, but I keep believing that one day I'll wake up and all the pieces of the puzzle will fit. And if they don't, well, then I guess they don't. I guess what I'll be left with is a modest body of work, some I got to do with Chef, some not.

That's been a great driving force for writing for me personally—being able to do something that stays in the family. Maybe help carry on the legacy just a bit. I'll never make the same cake he does, in the same way, and that's probably for the best. I can only hope I'll make one equally delicious.

AH-HA: BEGINNING TO END

CHUCK PALAHNIUK AND MICHAEL BAILEY DISCUSS THE SPARK OF CREATIVITY

ONE LIVES IN the Pacific Northwest and nearly lost his home in a wildfire the summer of 2017, while the other used to live in what is now a scorched part of Sonoma County from a wildfire the autumn of that same year. One's surname is often mispronounced[1], while the other's surname is often mistaken as having Irish heritage[2]. Both have been recently threatened by fire, both have problematic last names, and both have been nominated for the Bram Stoker Award® on five separate occasions[3] in a mix of categories.

Whether or not one believes in coincidence, these two magicians of creativity have been brought together, one thing leading to another thing leading to another, to discuss the spark of creativity from beginning to end. Something short and sweet.

---

[1] Pronounced *paula-nick*, for those stumbling over it.

[2] Bailey, in this case, is English.

[3] Chuck's nominations include *Lullaby* (2002, novel), "Guts" (2004, short fiction), *Haunted* (2005, fiction collection), *Beautiful You* (2014, novel), and *Burnt Tongues* (2014, anthology); Michael's nominations include "Primal Tongue" (2013, short fiction), *Qualia Nous* (2014, anthology), *The Library of the Dead* (2015, anthology winner), "Time is a Face on the Water" (2016, short fiction), and *Chiral Mad 3* (2016, anthology).

Imagine these two strange fellows sitting behind laptops, conversing from places not-so-far-apart—perhaps one sips coffee, while the other sips tea—to reveal some of their dark magic:

Michael Bailey: The first volume of *Where Nightmares Come From* focused on the art of storytelling in the horror genre, while this latest edition explores how storytellers transform ideas into finished products. Most writer interviews start with the obvious question: "Where do you get your ideas?" But let's not go there. Story origin has been done to death. Instead, how about: "What's the first thing you do after your mind sparks original concepts? In other words, what's the *very* first thing you do after that original *ah-ha!* moment?"

Chuck Palahniuk: Once an idea occurs I repeat it to other people to see how readily they engage with it. And to see if they can offer examples of it from their own lives. And to test whether others have seen the idea depicted elsewhere in popular culture. If they engage, if they expand upon the idea, and if they offer no recent examples of it in fiction or movies, then I proceed.

MB: What's your first-draft poison: dictation, pen and paper, pounding tired keys on an old typewriter, fancy computer/laptop, tapping tablets, cocktail napkin notes, or a combination of sorts? How do you release your words? And once released, do they live primarily on virtual paper, physical paper, or both?

CP: I make all my notes on paper. Only after I've collected several pages of notes do I keyboard the notes into a word processing file and begin organizing them by cut and paste. The next step is to look for plot holes and create the bridging scenes or moments to resolve those.

MB: I used to have an uncontrollable need to transcribe the noise from my head directly onto the page. Early drafts were perfect, of course, ready to sell without revision. I think most writers go through something similar at the beginning, before learning the stuff *not* to do. Early in my endeavors, I met Thomas F. Monteleone and F. Paul Wilson, and they fortunately set me right. They explained that writing/storytelling is a disease (if one *must* do it) . . . and like *all* diseases, one can't go untreated for long, lest they shrivel up and die. They took me under their wings and showed me the ropes, for *many* years. And they introduced me to Douglas E. Winter, who (also over the course of many years) taught me the art of self-editing (much more difficult than editing the work of others). He slashed and sliced that evil red pen of his until my manuscripts bled, severed them in *half*, typically. "Start here," he'd say, "*on page 13*." My writing has evolved, sure, and my writing has gotten slower because I can't help but edit along the way. With all that pre-loading, I guess my next question is this: How ugly (or pretty) is a Palahniuk first-draft?

CP: What you'd call my first draft is actually my third or fourth draft. In a story, each of the three or five acts gets its own draft, and each must work well before I tackle the climax of the story. That way my eventual finished first draft isn't too shabby.

MB: And a follow-up: How has your first draft evolved during your writing career? Do you binge and purge? Do you edit-on-the-go?

CP: My process has stayed essentially the same since 1992. I take long-hand notes. Then, transcribe the notes into a computer file. Then, print the draft and carry it with me on paper so I can read and revise it anywhere in the world. Then use those edits to revise the computer file, print it and repeat the process.

MB: Some writers set daily or weekly goals, whether it's word count or page count. Some try for 5,000 words a day, some 1,000. Some try for 5 pages a day, some 10. Some try to, at least, write *something* each day. And there are some oddballs, like me, who go for months without writing a single fucking word, sometimes as long as a year (although I'm always doing *something* creative), when suddenly the mind takes a laxative and dumps out 10,000- to 30,000-word chunks. What are your writing goals and/or habits?

CP: As a physically active person I hate to sit and keyboard. Notebook in hand, I'll go for weeks just jotting down details that might apply to a story. This used to be called "brain mapping" in the science of the 1990's. It takes a stretch of rainy weather before I'll settle down and begin to type. Often the typing takes place aboard an airplane or in a hotel room or some other stifling place where I have no other options. As for goals, each January 1st I decide what I will accomplish for the year.

MB: What's the most you've ever written at one time (not necessarily in a single sitting, but what you'd consider *all-at-once*)? And how long have you gone *without* writing?

CP: My greatest single sitting output was the eleven-page story "Guts." To be frank, that many keystrokes makes my elbows and wrists ache like you wouldn't believe. Years at the Freightliner Truck Plant have left me with carpal tunnel syndrome, and any kind of marathon typing now requires a Vicodin. Blame it on the drugs, but that short story just poured out.

MB: Writer's block: real news or fake news?

CP: Writer's block: Not my problem. As with any living thing, there are dormant and active phases. When I'm not actively writing, I still watch and listen, always trying to identify new patterns and ideas.

MB: 'Character' is arguably the most important part of a story. Some say 'plot' or 'conflict' or '*the message*' is most important, but they are wrong, no? Your fiction always breathes with the lives of diverse, colorful, incredibly memorable characters. Where do your *characters* come from? I realize that's sort of like asking the "Where do you get your ideas?" question, but since 'character' plays such an important part of the story, it seems to be an important question.

CP: My characters are always based on actual people. Their most memorable lines of dialog have already been said by real people. Even their dogs are real. Although I'm trained as a journalist, I find that there's more fun (and money) in passing off reality as fantasy.

MB: So you've spawned an idea, and created characters, and they converse through dialogue and navigate plots and traverse conflict, and the manuscript has maybe gone through a few drafts (or not) and all that other magic that happens during storytelling, and suddenly you find yourself with a completed manuscript—short story, novelette, novella, novel, comic/graphic adaptation . . . doesn't matter. This interview started with an *ah-ha!* moment—the original spark of creativity—but there's another *ah-ha!* moment to consider: the moment one realizes a story is *complete*. What next? Do you send it to beta-readers, let it marinate in a drawer somewhere, send it off to an editor?

CP: To date I've done my beta testing while I write. By testing each scene on my peers or fellow writers in a weekly group. This creates an informal collaboration and allows contributions from possibly hundreds of people. David Sedaris advised me to always test new material by reading it aloud on tours; that works well also. Nothing goes off to New York until it's made people laugh or cringe everywhere else in the country—or the world.

MB: We recently discussed the fires in California and in the Pacific Northwest, as well as some of our losses and scares. I was lucky and for some reason already had my laptop in the car before fleeing from one of these fires (and I habitually upload files to off-site storage), but the threat of losing creativity begs the question: What if it all burned down? Where do you keep your creations, in case a fire someday threatens (or accomplishes) turning them to ash?

CP: If you're talking about past notes, drafts, books, I don't keep them. I burn everything once the final book has been typeset.[44] Regarding on-going work, I back-up to flash drives and keep them separate from each other—in my car, with friends—and I always have a printed hard copy of the work in progress.

MB: And since this interview/discussion is about bringing nightmares to life, what is your nightmare, the thing that scares you most?

CP: Plenty of things scare me. These include driving over extremely high bridges or being buried alive. But nothing scares me the most.

MB: Over the last few years I have collaborated with writers for fiction and have sought out collaborative works for anthologies I've edited. My next anthology is composed entirely of collaborations, even. Collaborations are perhaps my new *ah-ha!* in this business, something of which I want to see more. I love the concept of multiple minds working together to create entirely new voices and visions. But I have yet to collaborate on: 1.) interview questions; and, 2.) with

[4] Something both writers now have in common after the fires.

49

Chuck Palahniuk. So, how about we spin things around? My freelance work is roughly 33% writer, 33% editor, 33% book designer, and now 1% interviewer. What question, in the broad scope of 'from concept to finished product,' would you like *me* to answer?

CP: My question to you is: Do you think piracy has damaged the viability of writing professionally? And if so, how do you bring yourself back to the task despite that threat?

MB: There's potential in book piracy eventually hurting the industry, but we're not there, at least not yet; we may *never* get there. I would argue that eBooks, in terms of sales, have caught up to printed books, perhaps even surpassed sales in some cases, but I would also argue that most eBooks go unread. It's easy to purchase digital books—a single-click sometimes. They are priced to move copies. It's easy to fill virtual shelves with digital books because they're not really *there* and don't take up physical space. They are simply strings of binary designed to mimic books, which is neat. But this also makes them easier to steal, sure, like music was easier to steal once it turned digital. How many digital books are read from start to finish? I'd guess 5-10%, if I'm being generous. A printed book, however, for now, is *there*, is something real, and harder *not* to read—if it's pretty enough and smells like a book and you can hold it in your hands—and likewise harder to steal.

Here's my confession, which might help explain what I'm trying to say. Before the fire (which took just about everything but our lives), I used to have a nice collection of Palahniuk on my shelves. I also used to have a Kindle with about a hundred titles, including your Kindle short story "*Phoenix*," released in 2013, which I bought for $1.99 (a steal!). I have read every book of yours (that I used to own), from start to finish . . . except for *one*—the title of which I now find ironic because it's the only book that still 'exists' somewhere in those 0's and 1's, and I could still read it on my laptop if I choose to. My physical books are gone, sure, but I'll get new ones going forward, and I'll probably read those before ever browsing my digital shelves.

My point: book piracy has the potential to hurt the industry monetarily, sure (as piracy did the music industry at first), but we'll always have books (like we'll always have music). Piracy will never hurt the creative process. Books will survive as they always have. I would argue that those doing the stealing aren't doing enough damage at this point, but someday (who knows?) they might, and the industry will adapt accordingly. Book pirates are most likely never going to read the books they steal, anyway, and neither are those taking them from wherever they take them, so who gives a shit? We'll adapt. We'll evolve. Musicians are still making music. Writers will continue to write, if they *must*, because writing's a disease, right? All creators will continue to create as they always have.

No matter the threat, professional writers should continue to write professionally. Books will always have a place in our world, however they—*and we*—evolve. All we can do as writers is to keep writing. All we can do as editors is to keep editing. All we can do as book designers is to keep designing beautiful books. And readers: must keep reading (purchased books only, please). It doesn't matter what tools we use to create, and it doesn't matter what tools we use to immerse ourselves in those creations. We simply need to keep doing what we're supposed to be doing.

Imagine the coffee and tea cups empty, or perhaps untouched this entire time and now lukewarm and undrinkable. Perhaps Chuck leans back in his chair, and Michael does the same. One stretches, while the other cracks his knuckles and winces. One looks to the blank wall and sets up the next scene, while the other looks off into the distance and listens for the voices. Both move on to the next project, for there are always next projects. There are stories that need to be written. There are deadlines that need to be met. There are books of various kinds in development.

THEY GROW IN SHADOWS: EXPLORING THE ROOTS OF A HORROR STORY

TODD KEISLING

THERE'S A POINT in every horror writer's career when he or she will be asked the most dreaded of questions from a reader, an interviewer, or maybe even someone who is morbidly curious. You probably know what I'm talking about. The interchangeable interrogatives of "why" and "how."

Why *do you write about such awful, terrible, gooey, gross, bloody things?*

How *do you write about such awful, terrible, gooey, gross, bloody things?*

The question of "why" is a topic for another day. I want to talk about the question of "how," and in a bit more detail than what you might be willing to explore in a random encounter. And, really, *how* do we as horror writers conjure such macabre tales? Do these horrid scenarios leap from our nightmares right onto the page? Perhaps it's the language we use to convey the anatomy of fear, a certain "necrolexicon" known to illicit chills in readers. I admit there's a certain magic in the act, a dark sort of magic channeled from that vacuous space of infinity we call our imagination.

But let's go deeper into the process itself—and to do so, we're going to need a few things. Some metaphors, for starters, so we can visualize these concepts in a concrete fashion. Maybe a hardhat of some kind. We'll need a knife, and a flashlight, too. There's something growing in this weird place I call my psyche, something that only grows in the shadows, and I have to show it to you.

I'm not an expert at this. I just know what works for me, and now I'm going to share it with you. I've got about twenty years of practice, and I still haven't got it figured out, so when we get to where we're going, remember this most ominous of warnings: *caveat lector.*

Ready? Good. Turn on your flashlight. It's dark down there.

I.
Demon Seed

We're at the bottom of the world. In a dank cavern that's never known light, is the center of this void, a mound of earth. Buried inside the little mound is a demon seed. Why is it called a demon seed? Because it's from this seed that your horror story will sprout. This seed represents your idea, and when it's ready, it's going to possess you. Before it sprouts, you need to nurture it first. The seed is already waiting in a cradle of earth. Now we wait with it.

While we're waiting, let's step back from our metaphorical cave and discuss the actual implications of what this seed really is. The seed is your idea, yes, but it's also representative of something I can only describe as pure magic. It's the transmutation of your collective senses and memories and creativity into a single concept. It's mental alchemy, boiling down any number of elements into a single and altogether different creation. Mental lead into gold. Magic, or something close to it, and it's happening inside your head even while you're not paying attention.

These ideas can come from anywhere, at any time. Maybe it's a bit of conversation you've had, a daydream of hypothetical scenarios, a news article you've read, or a personal experience you've endured. They could grow from a feeling, a memory, a dream or nightmare, a sensation. Ideas are infinite. They're everywhere, and they can take root anywhere. For me, it's in this dark place I'm calling a cavern of my psyche, blanketed with the fertile soil of my imagination. Maybe yours grow in a sunlit field or in the cracks of an urban sprawl. You're welcome to apply whatever metaphor you choose, but the point is that ideas are resilient little buggers. They don't need the dark or the light to grow. This demon seed of ours, nestled below a pile of earth, only requires a little nurturing on our part.

What this looks like to us in the real world is something as simple as writing down that idea. A single sentence, or even a fragment, can serve as the basis for something far greater. My first novel began with a sentence scribbled in a notebook, "I'm living a life transparent." That's it.

Your idea can literally grow from anything. They're everywhere, if you're willing to look. If a writer is ever lacking ideas, that writer isn't looking hard enough. Ideas are so abundant, so common, that as you gain experience telling stories, you'll soon learn to recognize which ideas to pursue and which ideas to discard. Not all seeds will sprout, and not all those that do will bear fruit.

Let's go back to the cave for a moment. There's a seed in this mound of earth at our feet. It needs to be nurtured. We need to give it time to sprout. Some ideas only take a few hours or days; some may take years. How long is up to you and how much you're willing to feed the idea.

Yes. I said "feed."

Remember when I said we'd need a knife? Hold out your hand and don't flinch. This is going to sting.

II.
The Feeding

That wasn't so bad, was it? Make a fist and sprinkle your blood over the mound of earth. If you're thinking this metaphoric act of self-harm bears a ritualistic quality, you aren't too far off the mark. What you're feeding this idea is a little bit of your own pathos. Your fears, your nightmares, your vulnerabilities—the things that make you who you are will be the substance for this horror story.

If we step back from the metaphor, you'll see the act for what it is: Mining your psyche for content. You have to cut yourself to feed the demon seed because you're looking into the things that scare you, the events that have scarred you, and searching for the right terrible combination that will give your story a life of its own. As before, this could literally be anything, but for starters, let me suggest you choose something with which you are intimately familiar. What are you most afraid of?

For the sake of example, I'll use one of my own fears. When I was a kid, my granny would send me outside to check her mailbox every day. And one day, when I stuck my hand inside the box, a white-hot pain shot through me so fast that it took my breath away. I yanked my hand from the box and screamed when I saw wasps crawling over my fingers. The makings of a small paper nest sat at the far end of the mailbox, and I'd stuck my hand right into the middle of it. To this day, I can't check my mailbox without looking inside it first.

You could take this fear literally, a fear of wasps in a mailbox, or you could condense it down to its base nature: fear of the unseen or unknown. Rooted at the heart of this fear is the agonizing memory of past trauma. I've drawn from this trauma whenever I've needed to convey a sense of dread, and I'm drawing from that trauma now to show you an example of one author spilling his blood. If I've done my job correctly, the reader will be on the edge of their seat, biting their nails, terrified along with the character of what may be waiting just across the threshold of the unknown.

But this is just one example. Dread is one way of nurturing your story. Maybe you're afraid of the dark, of blood, or of clowns. Whatever you choose, it's important that you be honest. The reader will know when you're lying.

III.
Dark Meditations

Now that you've fed the demon seed, it's time to sit back and watch it grow. Depending on the seed and what it's been fed, this could take a while, so get comfortable. Fold your legs and sit upright in a lotus pose. Focus all your creative energy on the seed's growth. There's a kind of primordial soup of creativity working its way into the soil of your imagination right now, and it could use some positive vibes. With some luck, this is where that seed takes root, soaks up all the darkly rich nutrients in your blood, and begins to sprout into a misshapen sapling of an otherworldly nature.

I like to take my time with this step, and for good reason: this is where the idea grows into an actual premise. Some of my stories took years to incubate and grow. Whenever I went back to them, thinking they might be ready, I found they needed more time to develop. Sometimes it's a matter of the story not being ready, and sometimes, *most* times, it's a matter of the writer not being ready for the story. Either way, I think it's important for a writer to wait until the premise has developed before beginning the actual writing itself.

Your premise is the sprouting of your idea into reality. When it first breaks the surface, that sapling is going to be green and weak. It will need time to mature and grow, forming a nice layer of bark along the outer ring so that it can stand upright. The entire story is going to revolve around this premise, so it's important that it be given enough time to develop. Start too soon and the story will fall flat beneath the weight of your brilliance. You'll break the stalk, possibly kill the story entirely, and you'll have to start over from the beginning. Maybe the seed can be salvaged, but certainly not the sapling of your tale.

Now, while we're meditating on the premise, let's consider the questions it should ask: What if? Why? Why Not? Since we're talking horror here, a question of, "What if?" is probably the most common in our genre. For example:

What if a scientist creates a man from stolen body parts?

What if an ancient evil lurks beneath the sewers of a small city in Maine?

What if the residents of a rural New England fishing village mated with the fish-gods living beyond the reef?

"What if?" is a speculative question found at the heart of horror as a concept. I would argue that it must be asked of the reader in a horror story. What if those slimy things in our imagination are real? What if there really is a monster in your closet? Or what if there's a nest of wasps in your mailbox? The nature of "What if?" is an invitation to suspend disbelief. It's the Ouija board of fiction writing, enticing the reader to open a door they can't close.

"Why" and "Why not" are altogether different beasts, antithetical to the speculative nature of "What if" but no less important, and furthermore, entirely contextual for the story you're writing. While I believe a good premise must always ask "What if," I also believe that it should only ask, "Why?" or "Why Not?" when necessary, and only if the story calls for it. Maybe we *need* to know why the scientist made a man from stolen parts so that we can understand who the real monster is? Maybe it's necessary that we *not* know exactly what's lurking beneath the reef off the coast of Innsmouth?

What if? Why? Why Not? These are the questions on which we must meditate if we are to formulate a solid premise. When used to full effect, they will further enhance the tale you're telling and engage the reader in ways that will leave them thinking on your story for days afterward. A strong premise is the backbone, the absolute point of your story. Without it, that sapling you're growing is going to break.

Speaking of which, our sapling has sprouted and is starting to grow at an alarming rate. Are you ready? I hope so. This is the hard part.

IV.
The Incantation

This probably goes without saying, but in case you haven't noticed, we're doing more here than simply growing a plant. We're conjuring something from the soil of imagination, and like any good ritual, there's an incantation involved. So far, we have our demon seed (the idea), it's been fed (the pathos), and now it's sprouted (the premise). The next step is an incantation to encourage growth.

I liken this to an incantation because the act is like a magic spell. The right words, in the right sequence, will summon something incredible—or something terrible. Here in this dark place, you have everything you need to make this happen. An idea steeped in your fears and experience has taken root and sprouted with a premise. It's time you sing to it and make it grow. Speaking without metaphor, this is the part where you write.

Yeah. The hard part.

Before you begin, let's take a step back and look at the premise. You'll notice it has little limbs and buds and leaves sprouting every which way. These are your characters and plot, and as you write, you'll find them growing in ways you didn't expect. Occasionally, you may have the urge to trim them back, and it's vitally important that you resist. I can't stress this enough. Do not stop your incantation to trim the plant. That part comes later. Right now, you need to let this creepy plant, this horror story of yours, grow however it wants.

The only way to do this is to write and write often. Don't disengage from the story. I've tried different methods of habit—writing every day, writing at a certain time, writing with the door open or the window closed, and the one thing I can say with certainty that works without fail is the act of remaining consistent. Don't want to write every day? That's cool—maybe you're an every-other-day sort of writer. Maybe you're the type who wants to treat writing like a job, writing on the weeknights and taking weekends off. That's fine too. The trick is to remain consistent.

So how do you remain engaged with the story if you're allowing yourself a day off? Let's be honest here: if you're reading this, you are most likely a writer of some degree. Have you ever been able to not think about a story you're working on? No, I didn't think so. Non-writers have a tough time understanding that a writer's mind never shuts off. We're always thinking of our stories, our characters, our plots and the like. The gears are always turning in our heads. We are always writing even when we're not committing a single word to paper. The incantation is always given voice.

Finding the right habit requires experimentation. Figure out what works for you. Maybe you need a solid hour of writing time, or maybe you write best in quick fifteen-minute sprints. The important part is committing to the act, no matter how you choose to do so.

You'll know you've found your groove because the words will come easily, and time will cease to exist. The plant you've nurtured from a sapling will grow and mature. Flowers will bloom, and leaves will sprout from its many branches, because it's no longer just a small plant. With perseverance, the incantation will work, and your story will become a massive tree in the center of this imaginary cavern. It will grow so wild that we'll barely have room to walk around, its limbs so gnarled and scattered that they scrape the rock walls, seeking sustenance from the shadows.

And when you're done, when this awful thing you've conjured from your imagination resembles the sort of story you wanted to tell, you'll know the incantation worked.

V.
The Shape

Now your story is complete, but it's far from finished. Open your eyes and gaze upon the thing you've conjured from the void. It's a wild, awful thing, with errant branches and tentacled limbs seeking all directions, poisonous flowers and barbs and ivy wrapping the trunk. This atrocious thing is only sort of what you imagined, but it's riddled with a festering mass of unresolved plot threads and flat characters. It's so horrible that you can't bear to look at it.

And that's perfectly okay. Furthermore, it's perfectly normal. You've completed a first draft. It's bloated, needlessly complex, and isn't at all what you wanted it to be. But the heart of the tale, the body of the tree itself, is still there, shrouded by all that growth, and when you're ready, you're going to take that knife and start hacking away.

First, I have a confession: I overwrite pretty much everything (and my editor certainly agrees). If you're like me, most of those saplings down in your imagination often want to grow into massive redwoods. I've abandoned far too many stories because of their tenacity and a lack of time on my part. If I'm being honest, I'd say that every completed story came at the expense of four or five others that were abandoned. Because everything wants to be a tree, and if you aren't careful, one will become two. Before too long, you'll have a whole forest, and you'll lose sight of where you began. This tendency for stories to grow unchecked is why second drafts are necessary. Sometimes a third or fourth, maybe even a tenth draft is necessary, but always a second draft at minimum.

Right now, you aren't quite ready for that second draft just yet. You need to leave your story alone for a while. Could be a few days, could be a few months. How long is up to you, and something you'll develop a sense for with each completed story. The important part is that you step back to replenish the creative well and remove yourself from the project. When you return, you need objectivity to do what's necessary: trimming this thing into shape, one slice at a time. Return too early and you'll be hesitant to make the proper cuts. They'll be jagged, unclean, and might cause more harm than good.

So, I want you to step away. Go wander the other chambers of this cavern. Wander until you've forgotten this place and this awful thing you've birthed into existence. Wander until you can't think of this abomination of words and story without feeling revulsion and disdain. When you can't stand the sight of this awful thing anymore, when its existence offends you, and when you've reached this point, you're ready to do what needs to be done. You're going to take the knife and cut away the overgrowth.

Maybe you're thinking, "Shouldn't I have an axe for this?" Yeah, you probably should, but all you have is a knife. An axe would take off too much, too fast. A knife is slow and intimate. And this knife is special. You've stained it with your blood. What's a ritual without a ceremonial blade?

I point this out because it's necessary that you go into the second draft with your pathos in mind. Whatever you instilled in the premise to give it that special blend of horror should remain, and if you find that it isn't, the second draft is your opportunity to rectify the absence. Furthermore, the second draft is an opportunity to enhance the horror. Maybe it's a different scene, or maybe it's more direct language—whatever your choice, you must go into the second draft with your pathos in mind.

Second drafts are intimate surgical affairs, allowing the writer to step back, examine the story, and see what can be cut away to improve the shape. Maybe your story is bloated, or maybe it's too thin; maybe the story has an awful character growth that's cancerous, or maybe the story is lacking in character and needs a transfusion. Whatever the malady, the second draft is your way of taming the story into something that's not only terrifying, but also readable and enjoyable. There is one caution, though: Do not trim so much that you cut into the roots of your story. If you cut the roots, you risk undoing the progress you've made. The story may die (or transform into something else at the very least), and you will have to start this entire process from the beginning.

When you're finished trimming and shaping, step back and observe the horrific thing you've created. Does it look like you wanted it to? Are the limbs growing in the right direction? Should those flowers be there? What about the ivy around the trunk? All good? Wonderful! Your story is ready for feedback from your peers, and if necessary, another draft. Repeat this process until every sentence sings, every character is defined, and every page is dripping with blood.

VI.
Germination of the Seed

I have a personal philosophy about art as a concept. Art begets thought. *Good* art begets more good art. Naturally, the definition of "good" art is entirely subjective and ripe for a debate among people far more intelligent than myself. I only mention this philosophy here because if you've done your job well, the art you've created will inspire someone else.

Don't get me wrong—what you've created is probably something horrible and revolting that will turn stomachs and make readers question your sanity, but that's not the point. The point is that if you've fully committed yourself to this venture, spilled your blood, performed the sacred rites, and conjured a monstrosity purely from the power of your mind, your passion in the telling of your story will bleed through and speak to others. That's the true magic of storytelling, friend.

In keeping with the metaphor, your gnarled and shapely tree of beautiful terror is going to bear poisonous fruit. It's going to fall to the earth, rot, and with luck, take root in someone else's mind. You will inspire them to do the same, and so on. In fact, this seed we've planted and nurtured together was born from other things: Stephen King's *On Writing,* Anne Lamott's *Bird by Bird,* Neil Gaiman's *Make Good Art* speech, personal chats with authors far more talented than myself, thousands of words and dozens of failed stories, countless hours of writing experience, and a lifetime of reading fiction.

If your intentions are pure, you will inspire with your words. That's the incredible power we writers possess. Stephen King says to never go lightly to the page, and I'll add to that edict: Always go with your heart and eyes open. Let your passion bleed into everything you put to the page. The reader will appreciate it; furthermore, so will the other writers reading your work.

Let the demon seeds take root. Let them possess you. Grow something fantastically horrible from them. Scare the hell out of your readers by telling the most terrifying story you can. That's your job now. That's why I'm leaving you to find your way out of this cave.

I forgot to mention that, didn't I?

You can't leave until you've created something yourself. Those are the rules. You'd better get to work, though. All those demon seeds in the fertile earth are hungry. It's time to feed them.

Artwork by Luke Spooner

LEARNING THE BASICS

THE CULT OF CONSTRAINT (OR TO OUTLINE OR NOT)

YVONNE NAVARRO

THIS IS THE magical document that will tell you, yes, you personally, whether or not you should make an outline for your project, be it a short story, novella, novelette, or the next GAM (Great American Novel).

Uh . . . right?

All kidding aside, this is a question I've heard many times, both in person from other writers (new and not so new) and on convention panels. I'm not the expert on this. I can't even point you to the person who is. There is no expert.

Outlining, or not, is one of those annoying chores of a writer's life that falls under the "You Have to Figure it Out for Yourself" column. Every serious writer ends up in a situation where outlining either helps or hinders. The best I can do here is tell you how both of those situations affected me.

Fast forward in my past and go beyond the first couple of novel attempts that crashed and burned because of blatant inexperience, and the half a hundred or more short stories that followed, and pick up this tale where I got down and dirty on my real first novel. I had an idea, and of course, I thought it was a damned glorious one. I had done my homework and knew that the best course of action was to find an agent, and to do that I needed to submit a synopsis, full outline, and the first three chapters of my book. I also knew that because I was a new novelist, my book had to be finished.

I was excited to get to it. I had done all the location research. Little did I know that during the writing of my GAM I would research until I bled from my eyes and my fingers had undergone the Chinese torture of Death by a Thousand [Paper] Cuts, and I knew the beginning and the end. So I would know what the city of Chicago looked like devoid of people, I had even gone downtown to take photographs so early that nothing but pterodactyls soared over the city streets.

Everything went, as they say, swimmingly . . . until I got a little over halfway done. I still knew how I wanted it to end, down to the precise words my character would say, but by then I had a lot of characters doing a lot of things. They were all good, making great decisions and doing even greater things.

Now was the time I decided I needed to pause and work on that outline. It needed to be done, and to my mind it would be easier to do it as I went along rather than all at the end. So I went back and did my one paragraph per chapter until I caught up, and then I pretty much kept going. What I didn't notice was that I'd switched what I was doing—from writing then outlining to outlining then writing. I finished, I edited, I perfected. It took a while but I finally scored an agent and he sold the novel in three weeks, as part of a three book deal. Voila!

And she lived happily ever after.

Er . . . no.

Now I had not only an agent, but a publisher, and the publisher, per the contract I'd signed, would get a synopsis and a full outline for each of the next two novels, and those two things would be the basis for whether I could go ahead and write the proposed book. See, having a contract didn't give me a full speed ahead, but a good synopsis and a well-written outline based on a solid and exciting idea would.

So I learned to outline, and honestly? It's no big deal. It's one small paragraph for each chapter. That's it. In my humble opinion The Big Scare for writers usually boils down to this claim: they don't want to outline because they don't have any idea how the story they want to tell is going to unfold, they only know they want to tell it. "It just needs to happen naturally," they insist. Or to use a word being flung around these days: "It needs to happen *organically.*"

Folks, organic is a word that doesn't have a place in the writer's brain. Everything we eat and drink affects our writing, especially drinking. Aspirin, blood pressure meds, wine, shots of tequila. What outlining critics are really saying is, "I don't want to be constrained," and many seasoned writers will point out, that's just bullshit.

Yes, there are plenty of longtime famous and not-so famous writers who don't outline, and it works for them. But for those with not so much experience? In the great and grand tradition of that old commercial, "Give it to Mikey. He hates everything." And then . . . "He likes it. Hey, Mikey."

Don't think of it so much as an outline, but a

lifeline. There you are, floundering in a sea of words (OMG, the bad puns!), and someone throws you the lifeline. Yeah, maybe you can get pulled straight to the boat, and if so, lucky you. Or maybe all those words and ideas are the wreckage floating around you.

The character who really doesn't have a reason to be in the book to begin with.

The door to the basement. Yeah, that—you left it open in Chapter 7.

The foreshadowing you did in Chapter 16 would help you get the hero from Point A to Point C without having to do Point B. What? Oh, you forgot about that, too.

That sense of actually *knowing how to get to the end of your book.*

Story Number Two: Six years have passed, other novels have been written and published, and now I'm working on my fourth book. In this one, I've decided to destroy most of the planet. Tap-tap-tap, typing right along, and now I'm somewhere in the final third or final quarter of the manuscript. I've just killed a major bad guy and pretty much all the characters are standing around the body. It's a complicated personal situation, so they can't just sing, "Yay," and move on. So in their world, they look up at the sky, penetrate time, space, and dimension, and ask *me,* "Now what?"

I have no idea.

I remember a show, black and white, about the time that *The Twilight Zone* became popular. It wasn't a TZ episode, but something like it. In the show, a bunch of people at a diner kept reliving the same scene over and over. Nearing the end of the scene, they all got the same puzzled expression on their faces and started asking each other, "Haven't we done this before?" and "What's that sound? Don't you hear it?" Finally, the camera pulled back and all you saw was a view of the diner from above and its patrons looking up toward the camera, surrounded by blackness. And all you heard was the sound of typewriter keys.

I am not kidding. In that precise moment, that's exactly where I felt my characters were.

"Now what?"

You guessed it. I went right back to the basics of outlining. Starting from Chapter 1 and all the way to where my characters were [still] staring up at me. And then I kept going, pushing to the epilogue. And you know why that was a good thing? Because for this 190,000 word novel, I had no clue how I was going to end it. And the outline led me there, one step after the other.

And yeah, now I outline every book I write. *Beforehand*, not mid-book or afterward. It just makes it a whole lot easier.

Before I end this (no outline, no idea—ha), I do want to address the Cult of Constraint. Those who insist that following an outline won't let them do what they want in the story, please? Who's writing the story?

You, not your outline.

For that matter, who wrote the outline?

You. And if that's not enough to make you realize that an outline is a flexible thing, go back to that ocean of words. Your outline is your lifeline, and you follow it *around* the wreckage, avoiding crazy mistakes because you can see them coming, taking advantage of great opportunities that pop up along the way, fixing really stupid shit before it makes it into the final manuscript.

My advice?

Make an outline, then use it.

It's a road from here to home, and no one says you can't do a bit, or a bunch, of sightseeing along the way.

ZOMBIES, GHOSTS AND VAMPIRES—OH MY!

KELLI OWEN

I **HAVE WRITTEN** ghosts, zombies, vampires, monsters, myths, creatures, serial killers, and the psycho next door. I'm a horror writer, and these are my closest friends.

All horror writers hang out with a similar crowd. Monsters, creatures, and humans teetering over the abyss are all fodder to create conflict, exacerbate the situation, and push the protagonist forward, but not everything that goes bump in the night is the same, even if related. Or at least, they shouldn't be.

Patiently waiting in my to-do folder is a file with the opening line: *A ghost, a vampire and a zombie walk into a bar.* The entire storyline began with that sentence, as the beginning of a joke with no punch line, and quickly fleshed itself out in my mind. The muse demanded pen and paper, and notes were jotted. Now it's on my whiteboard, quietly smiling at me, *daring* me, from the fourth seat on the bench. I tell you this not to tease you regarding the storyline, but to point out the trio of characters introduced. Let's talk of those things, those antagonists, who go bump in the night, my closest friends, the good, the bad, the overused, and underappreciated.

Originally I was going to dive into a generalization of tropes, but as I started thinking about it, started jotting notes down, I realized no trope stands alone. They lean, heavily, on the characters, monsters, and stories themselves. While the definition of tropes has changed and become more fluid, it has been generally used to describe a theme, a device, or a metaphor, which can appear as a character, part of the plot, or the storyline itself.

A ghost is a character trope. A haunting is a story trope. A ghost who doesn't know it's dead is a plot trope. To go deeper, metaphorically, werewolves have been used to portray menstruation, while vampires are often used for anything on the seduction spectrum—whether it's lustful desire or taboo behavior—and the girl in high heels, running away from both of them, will eventually trip in the woods.

If some plot device is an abused and overused trope, you know it immediately by the groans you earn, whether it's from a live audience or the little voice in your head while you're typing. That girl falling in the woods? Don't.

It's cheap and easy, and you're better than that.

The haunted house?

Of course you can use it, just tell a different story.

The monsters?

That's where a horror writer shines.

Sometimes the story is actually about the monsters themselves, either their survival or ultimate demise, while other times they are only background noise for the struggling protagonists, usually humans, but before we dive into those well-loved and occasionally misunderstood monsters, we must first clarify, define, and separate. Because while tropes, clichés, and archetypes often drink at the same bar, they almost never order the same cocktail.

A cliché is the most overused of the three—he sits at the bar, as *expected*, and orders *his usual*. He is familiar and often used out of comfort, which makes him easy but predictable. A cliché is the lumbering monster that walks, while its victims run. These are tired and worn out, and at this point brings audible sighs to audiences when it happens. Unless there's an explained reason for the cliché, the term essentially means audiences and readers are tired of this and it shouldn't be used.

Archetypes are necessary at the very core of character, but they can often *become* cliché, especially if left in two-dimensional form. You need the hero, but not necessarily in shining armor. You need the shadow, but is he only-and-always evil, or does he blur the lines?

The mentor, the ally, the herald, and the rest of them have become recognizable sidekicks, passing characters, or plot pushers. They're part of the reality of fiction, and they do need to be included, but they needn't be standard, or become clichés in their obviousness, or worse, tip over into tropes.

Speaking of tropes, character tropes are nothing more than archetype clichés. Beautifully defined as fluid examples in the movie *Cabin in the Woods* are: the jock, the brain, the joker, etc. Story tropes were also cleverly pointed out in the basement of said cabin, as the standard fair present and waiting to be chosen for this particular group of characters, but let's talk more specifically about *monster* tropes. Because if we are to be honest, the genre has been divided, separated, segregated, and sub-genred to death by the likes of tags, keywords, and marketing departments who can then turn around and say, "Number One Best Seller in urban paranormal reincarnation voodoo horror."

No matter what type of horror you write, no matter how you tell the same story time and again, no matter if you are using tropes or avoiding them, you have a *monster* of sorts—be it human, supernatural, or other. There are many monsters to choose from, not just those I listed back at the beginning, and let's not forget those you create on your own, such as the creatures in my *Live Specimens*. Actually, let's take that and run with it, reducing all of them to *creatures*, because calling them monsters insinuates they're the evil, the bad guy if you will, and even though they are playing the role of adversary, they're not always the enemy. It's a muddy puddle of characters and motives and metaphors, and we need to wipe our feet in the grass and focus on a single aspect of it: creature tropes.

These tropes are often overused, abused, and become not only cliché but confused as being the cliché in and of itself. Say "vampire" or "zombie" and watch your audience either slump in tired resignation, or perk up with an affection for said creature, before they even know the storyline. That negative reaction, that "oh god, not another one," comment, is not necessary and can be avoided, even if you're using something familiar, something overused. It's all in how you present it—both within the story itself, as well as how you market the finished product.

They say there are only thirty-six plots, or rather, *situations* from which to create and travel your storyline. Some claim there are only six. Either way, there are far more stories out there than six, or thirty-six, so the differences must be in the way we tell it. Stephen King's *IT* is a far different story than Mary Shelley's *Frankenstein*, even though they both fall under the basic plot of "overcoming the monster." The same can be said of creature tropes.

Let's look at a couple of the more popular, standardized creatures for a moment. Vampires, while they did exist in campfire whispers, lore and superstition long before they were written about, the version we all know was birthed from *Dracula*. Bram gave them rules, guidelines, and certain truths: fangs, aversion to sunlight, immortality. These have been mostly adhered to for over a century.

Werewolves, also based on legends and myths, are really only the finite expression of any monster with an occasional human form (full moon, notwithstanding). Ghosts were once living people. Zombies were the same, but still maintain a human shell. And then there's Frankenstein's monster, far too often incorrectly referred to as Frankenstein itself. This is a unique creature. Sure it's had several incarnations, many movie versions, a couple of modernizations, but the story is the same—a doctor creates life where there was none, and then we question who the monster truly is.

This type of creature, the unknown, the shiny and new, can relay horror in a whole new way because the audience doesn't know its rules, its behavior. The monster in Dean Koontz's *Phantoms* falls under this category, as does the mythical creature in my own *Floaters*, and of course, the aforementioned, *IT,* by Stephen King definitely falls under this umbrella, as the monster hiding behind the body and makeup of a clown is truly unique and horrifying.

How do you kill it? Where did it come from?

Everything about it is up to you and has the ability to dig deeper into the psyche of your reader.

But what about those old standards we love so much? What about the vampire, the werewolf, the zombie, and the ghost?

I'm not saying don't use them. I'd never suggest such a thing. They are the royalty of the horror genre monsters. You simply need to deliver them with a new twist.

The difference between Anne Rice's vampires (Lestat, et al.) and Stephen King's (*Salem's Lot*) is exactly what makes us keep coming back for a creature we already know. Sure, you know how to beat it—stake, sunlight, or a little holy water—but what about the people fighting it? What about the creature's feelings or its turmoil? What about the location?

It's more than just the familiar monster. It's the setting, the storyline, the plot, the characters, and the universe holding it all together. If we all know how vampires act, we can concentrate solely on telling the story of either running toward or away from those bloodsucking fiends. If we change what our audience knows, we can breathe new life into old creatures. We can shake up what the reader *thinks* they know, and quite possibly surprise them. Maybe even scare them.

My newest release, *Teeth*, includes vampires. You'll note I didn't say it was *about* vampires. They are there, but not like you're used to. In a broad sense, you could say it's about vampirism, but that's still not quite right. You see, I changed the rules on vampires. Or rather, I changed vampires themselves. Completely. I stripped them down to the base idea of "different than us, sharp teeth, need blood," and rebuilt their entire truth.

Truth, not mythos, because they're not a myth in my universe. They are real—as real as you and I. I didn't treat them as creatures, just *different* than humans, and made them the newest minority in our global society, giving them the same problems any other minority has faced.

It was a complete rebuild of a known monster, and more daunting than anything I'd done before it. Would the vampire lovers hate it? Would the vampire haters give it a chance? I had a story to tell and vampires were the perfect vehicle to tell it.

It wasn't about the vampires; it was about the people, who occasionally happened to *be* vampires. Thankfully, the reviews and readers are all pleased with it so far.

So how do you change a known creature? How do you breathe life into something that has a hundred years of short stories, novels, movies, plays, even video games?

Very carefully.

For, *Teeth*, I built a fully three-dimensional creature separate and different from what readers are used to defining as a vampire. I gave them a new name ("vampire" is derogatory after all), developed their entire history, and had a list of the usually referenced weaknesses or traits and how each of them was explained with science or society. I had copious notes regarding things that never made it into the book, but I was aware of them and how they would shape a character's actions, behavior or beliefs.

In the case of, *Teeth*, vampirism was genetic, a recessive gene that awakens with puberty. It was never intended as a metaphor for menstruating. Instead, it was a lot of research on the adult onset of genetic diseases, which was then all twisted around to create my version of our favorite fanged creature. Some people get blue eyes from their parents, others get new teeth and dietary needs.

I was recently asked if I read a lot of other vampire novels while creating my own.

No, I did not, but you do *occasionally* need to read what's come before when working on something with theme or situational similarities. For instance, I'm currently reading Ronald Malfi's *December Park* because it's a coming-of-age tale set in the early 90s, and I'm working on a novel in the 80s. Our age, and therefore era of childhood, is close enough that I don't want to have any crossovers or unintentional nods to the same memories.

Likewise, a couple of years back, F. Paul Wilson read my *Waiting Out Winter* when he and Sarah Pinborough were writing, *A Necessary End,* so our "fly apocalypse" wasn't the same. So yes, sometimes you do read things to avoid specifics, but in general, if what you're doing is attempting to change the known, the overused, and the standard, well, it's known and overused and standard. You are well aware of what it entails. So there is no need to reread the classics that created it, or the modern selections still building on the same mythos.

I knew what had been done before and I changed it all. Then I plotted out the story and used these lovely new creatures in a number of ways—as a metaphor, as both protagonists and antagonists, and even as a thematic commentary on our current social climate. All while including enough blood for the horror crowd and eliciting unease and discomfort for the thriller circles. Never once did a vampire wear a cape, rest in a coffin, or fear sunlight. Nor did it sparkle.

In the end, not every vampire is a bloodsucker. Not every ghost haunts. Not every monster growls, bites, or attacks. Not every story with a creature trope in its pages is even about the monster.

Most tend to not be. Still, sometimes a particular trope is purposely chosen as the threat because it's not about *what* the threat is, but rather that there *is* a threat. In those cases, choosing a known creature, a common trope with a set of standard or recognized rules and behavior, frees the writer to tell the story of everything except the creature. So when using a trope, the question becomes: will a trope deliver the necessary evil, or is the evil beyond tropes and requires a bit more attention.

How many horror novels do you suppose come out in one year? What's going to make yours different?

It's not just what the story is, but how you tell it, how you populate it, and what is threatening the balance in your universe. Maybe the next time you need a creature, you can think *outside* the box. Create a new monster, or give a new spin to an old standard. Tell the story in a way that makes both the creature and its part in this tale unique, but never ever be afraid to use a trope. They're standard because they're loved.

Sometimes they're perfect just as they are, and sometimes they need a facelift.

It depends on the writer and the story they are trying to tell. My newest release includes vampires.

Sort of.

Not really.

Because they were a creature trope, an overdone one, and one I decided to reinvent. I dare you to do the same.

THE MANY FACES OF HORROR: CRAFT TECHNIQUES

RICHARD THOMAS

THE LAST TIME we spoke, I talked about the many faces of horror, as far as storytelling techniques. This time around, I'd like to address specific craft aspects, and how those can help you to create horror, terror, and tension in your dark fiction.

Showing vs. Telling

This is a big one for me. When you show something, you take the time to unpack it and really give us details, layers, and emotion. When you tell us something, you're only doing that—telling us, and it doesn't work well, especially in horror. The best way I can illustrate it is to walk you through a little exercise.

So, I'm going to give you a place and then a word to describe it. Read the words, and then I want you to close your eyes and picture what I've described. Are you ready? Here we go.

HOUSE.

SCARY.

Okay, close your eyes, and picture that house. It's a scary house. Are you scared?

No, of course you aren't.

That's telling: "The house was scary. It was big. And it was dark out. The woods were also dark. And there were noises. Sounds I couldn't describe. Oh, the horror."

Yuck. Right?

Let me try to do this justice. Read this, and then close your eyes, and see if you can picture it.

"At the top of the desolate hill, at the end of a dirt road, surrounded by dying oak trees, sat the Billbap Sanitarium. For many years it had been abandoned, and as the moon rose over the dark landscape, the cracked windows, busted shutters, and wild grass showed the state of neglect. A single owl hooted in the forest, a cold breeze pushed over the land, something rotten in the wind—sour mixed with sweet."

So, not the best thing ever, but can you *see it*? Can you feel any sort of emotion? Hopefully. I didn't get all of the senses in there, but at least I'm working toward scary.

When you say a woman is beautiful, or a man is dangerous, those are empty descriptions. They don't mean anything, really, you're being too vague. You need to fill in the details, and then let us judge, let us define that moment. This is one of the defining aspects of horror, whether you write minimalist horror or maximalist (it's a thing, honest), whether you write classic or contemporary horror. You must create atmosphere, mood, and dynamic settings, and one of the best ways you can do that it is by showing us the darkness, the insanity, and horror in great detail.

Do you do this all of the time? No. Think of it like saffron, or hot sauce—just a little bit here and there, when it's important. If you are too dense, if you slow down and unpack all of your story, all of the time, then nothing will shine. Unless you're Cormac McCarthy, but you aren't. Nobody is.

When you do that, when you slow down and unpack, you are showing us that this is important, and we pay attention.

Passive vs. Active Voice

The way that I think about this is when you're passive, you're a victim—the world does things to you, and you react. When you're active, you're calling the shots, you're in charge.

So why does this matter?

We want to feel something strong for your characters. They are the protagonist or the antagonist, the hero or the villain, but either way, we need strong emotions, love or hate. How does this come into play for voice?

Let's explore this a bit.

Here is a quick example:

Active—The man shot the alien.

Passive—The alien was shot by the man.

That's really basic, but at least we see the man taking action here, in the active sentence.

I also like to see characters creating their own story, not reacting, and being a bystander in their own narrative. If you want us to see your protagonist as strong, on a mission, with a cause to fight for, a plan, and heart he has to be active, doing things, addressing external conflicts, as he deals with his emotions.

What if you want your character to be passive?

Well, there you go. In that case, you might want to lean *into* the passive voice. Show that the protagonist is weak, a victim, always responding, never taking the first step, suffering, and alone, failing. That can be powerful too, especially when you finally do flip the story, when you change that person. Every story has to build to a climax, and have change, and then a *denouement*, or understanding of what just happened, that epiphany. It can be powerful to take a passive character and make them the hero (reluctantly or not), just like it can be equally powerful to take a strong character and have them fail. You get to see what both are really made of, right?

Gillian Flynn wrote a book called, *Gone Girl*, and in that thriller, the two main characters, Nick and Amy, hand off sympathy back and forth. We like Nick, then we hate Nick. We root for Amy, then we root against her. By the end of the book, we see they are both monsters, and they deserve each other.

Similarly, look at, *Come Closer*, by Sara Gran, an excellent novel about possession. We go back and forth between things happening *to* her, which creates tension, and a sense of chaos, being out of control, and her investigating, and trying to solve her problems, which only get worse.

Can you imagine Batman being passive? No, you can't.

The Grip of It, by Jac Jemc is another great novel about a haunted house, and how the main characters react, and then plot their own course.

Most of the time you're going to want to write in an active voice, your protagonist the hero of your story, working their way from inciting incident through conflicts to a satisfying climax, but along the way there may be passive moments, and voice, as well. It's important to know how to use *both* voices in your writing, so that you can manipulate your reader, and get them to feel what you want them to feel. If your protagonist is sweating, tense, and unhinged at what's happening in their house, your reader will be too (hopefully).

Backstory

This is a tough one, but it's essential. I often hear from my students that they struggle with the opening of their story. Why? Because I ask them to do quite a few things—narrative hook, inciting incident (that moment in time after which things will never be the same), setting, character, internal and external conflicts, etc.

Wow, how do you pack that all in there?

When do I give you the backstory?

It's tricky. Because you want to start your story where the story actually begins, that's the inciting incident. Not at their birth, not at some random point in time, but when the story actually takes that epic turn.

So, the backstory. How do we get to it?

There are a few ways.

If you're starting your story in a place, say when the protagonist is a child, and he sees his parents gunned down in an alley (yes, this is Batman, dammit, shut up) then what came before it might not be so important. I mean, beyond showing us the happy family life, but when you think of the origin story of Batman does it start in the alley?

No, it does not.

We actually get this backstory much later. Whether it's the comic, a film, or television show, where we start is probably with THAT specific story, that villain, that chapter.

But we all know his backstory, right?

As we see Batman, or Clarice Starling (*Silence of the Lambs*), or Carrie White (*Carrie*), take the stage, and dive into the plot of their narrative, we don't start with their backstory. No, Bruce Wayne tells his backstory in a powerful moment, revealing the truth, not only tying his identity to Batman, but showing us why he does all of this, why he fights crime.

With Carrie, it's told over time. We see her and her desire for a normal life, but her mother is religious, she has rules, and there are stakes. We start with the shower scene, and Carrie getting her period, we start with the news of a rainstorm made of stones, we start with the news that she has telekinesis. We'll get to her home life later, when it makes sense. We'll see her home life when she goes home embarrassed, seeking support from her mother, understanding, and she gets none.

It really depends on the story, but it should feel organic; in other words, natural. We need to get that backstory so we can care, so we can feel empathy and sympathy, so we can understand what came before (good and bad).

When I tell my students that, "All things serve the beam," I'm quoting Stephen King, and his Dark Tower series. It means all things serve the plot, the story. So, however you work in your backstory, be sure that it serves the story. When you share it, how much, and what you choose to show is up to you, but make sure it reveals character, and advances the plot.

Foreshadowing

When it comes to horror, there are several elements: the tension and set up, and then the reveal, the horror. I think of it as the terror, and then the horror— anticipation, and then fulfillment of that promise. Foreshadowing is key to making this all work.

Think of your favorite horror movies, television shows, short stories, and novels—pretty much all of the set-up, anywhere from one page to one chapter to most of the book, is foreshadowing. It's the hints, the clues, and symbolism you sprinkle through your story, sometimes in subtle ways, leading to an "a-ha moment" or epiphany, other times, more in your face. That's up to you, your style.

There are many different ways to foreshadow, let's talk about a few.

The way you show your protagonist, your character, and their behavior, should hint at what's coming. Do they have a repetitive habit? Maybe they are slowly coming unglued, leading to their meltdown? Or transformation.

It doesn't have to be as obvious as a vampire or werewolf—blood on the sheets, dirt under their nails, aversion to garlic vs. torn clothes, waking up naked in a field, loss of memory when there is a full moon, but those are hints, clues, at what is coming. I find a lot of slow burns are fascinating, and a pattern of behavior should clue you in.

I also love to see symbolism in foreshadowing. Do

we see birds everywhere (crashing into windows, sitting on wires, lining a park bench) or perhaps a slowly growing suspicion that is supported by certain items—cold weather, shadows, mirrors, crosses, tiny sculptures, etc? It can be the use of color: black for death, red for blood, blue for water. It can be a phrase, or word, something that becomes a trigger, or hint. It can also be an accumulation of things, items that don't necessarily mean anything on their own, but when put together, they add up to something nefarious, unsettling, and frightening.

Think of the books, stories, and films that surprised you—the way Stephen King's *The Mist* hinted at something in the fog, only to shock us with something else entirely; think of the slowly growing tension of *The Amityville Horror* or *The Conjuring*, leading us toward a haunted house or possession; think of, *Angel Heart*, and the hints that accumulate, adding up to a truth that the protagonist, and the audience, don't want to believe.

Who is the true killer? What is really going on? And what can we do about it? That's tension. I mean, when it comes to *The Witch*, and the way that film ends, didn't we see it coming? The Puritanical life, the doubt of character, the promise from the dark forces manipulating Thomasin? Wouldst thou like to live deliciously? Oh yes, we would.

However you decide to foreshadow the unveiling of the creature, the event, or the tragedy, make sure you are leading us down the right path. Avoid red herrings, and tangents, those places and clues that don't serve the beam, don't reveal character, and don't support the plot.

Broad vs. Specific

I think it's also essential in horror to show us both the broad and the specific. Let me explain.

When you speak of horror, there are broad ideas, huge concepts, massive threats that linger, that grow, and eventually engulf. One way to really get under the skin of your audience is to speak to a larger concept, which is why we see so many post-apocalyptic settings. A virus, a flood, aliens, whatever, the big concept, the one main idea, that needs to hang over the entire story, and pose a serious threat. We're talking major stakes here, not whether or not the girl at the grocery store will go out with us, whether or not our dog is going to die, we don't care about your sleepless night, or your old Chevy that needs new tires.

Let's look at *The Stand* by Stephen King. These are epic stakes, right? This is good vs. evil, the LAST STAND, this is a looming apocalypse, a virus that will take out most of the world's population, and that's just the start.

We can look at several ways that this book is broad, in size and depth, as well as consequence, and emotion—the page count, the characters, the depth of humanity in the large cast, the presence of evil, and the way that good rises up to fight it, there are so many ways this is a big story. But it's also specific as well.

If you can pair with the broad narrative details that sell your story, that give us authority, that show us up close and personal how this is going to play out, then you have depth. This is everything from the clothes a character wears, to a catchphrase "M-O-O-N, that spells Tom Cullen," to the way the disease manifests.

These are the moments when you slow down and unpack, showing us everything that is important—all five senses, pointing out the horror, showing us the grotesquery, or a bit of magic hidden in the woods. That's a nice balance.

I can still picture the opening scene to, *The Stand*, can you? The father getting his family, waking them up in the middle of the night to flee a looming disaster. What he sees in the lab, it scares him, he runs, but unfortunately, he takes the plague with him, his wife sick first.

"By dawn they were running east across Nevada and Charlie was coughing steadily."

Those characters aren't even in the novel, they die. It's when they crash into the gas station, Bill Hapscomb's Texaco, outside of Houston that things really get going. This is showing us the specific, when Bill finds them, and sees how sick they are. Stu Redman is in this opening, too. There is a grand thread at hand, this virus, we know that, and we also have the specifics of how it's going down. There is foreshadowing as well. It's an intense opening to one of my favorite books ever.

Broad and specific—go back and forth—weaving them together like a basket, or a rug.

Body, Mind, & Soul

I talk a lot about mechanics in my classes: Freytag's Triangle, for example, giving us the basis for problem/resolution, the advice that Vonnegut gives us, with every sentence either revealing character, or advancing the plot, as well as the other things I've mentioned so far. I want to go a bit deeper. This is more complicated, so buckle up.

Another craft element that I think is essential in storytelling, and definitely something that is needed in horror (I'm seeing more and more of it every day, less reliant on gore and shock) is the balance between body, mind, and soul.

What do I mean? In order to have a deep narrative, in addition to all of the things I've mentioned in this article, as well as last year's entry, I think you need to get your story to work on three levels: body, mind, and soul. You could also call this the physical plane, the mental plane, and the spiritual plane. Or you could think of it as tactile, intellectual, and emotional.

Let's start with body, which is probably the easiest. This is what I mean when I talk about using all five senses. Sight is the most obvious, as well as sound, smell, taste, and touch. To have a truly immersive experience, and to really feel the tension and horror, we need to be in the moment physically. Not just showing us what's going on—the woods, the weather, the setting, the people, the world, the technology, but the sounds that fill those environments, the smells and scents (good and bad), the tastes that add history and character (not just food, but in sexual moments, or fear), and touch as well (pain, as well as pleasure).

I hate reading a story (or novel) where the narrative is flowing along and I have no idea if my protagonist is male or female, young or old, buff or deformed, beautiful or plain. I need to see them, and get to know them ASAP, so I can go on this journey with them (and you). When I say body, and tactile, that definitely includes setting, too. Build that world, show me, insert me into that moment, and then go deep—give your woods trees and bushes, with sensation and sound, water running, and the chirp of birds, something sweet yet musty under the bed of wet leaves; give me the haunted house, with the damaged shutters, the weather vane of some odd animal, the shimmer in the glass, and the inside with its moldy wallpaper, the cold wooden floors, and the tapping in the walls that just won't stop. I need all of that, for your protagonist, and your narrative.

Mind is more difficult. Often when a story fails, or struggles, the external conflict is done well (avoid the werewolves, destroy the asteroid, exorcise the demon) but the internal is lacking. What does your protagonist want? What do they need?

This will exist in the mind, as well as the soul, but let's focus on the mind right now. This is your concept, your story, your plot. What does your protagonist think, and how can you transfer those thoughts—fears, planning, education, work, analytics, etc.—to the page? This is how you get your authority.

You may need to do research. I spent weeks studying a concept called, "The 100th Monkey," for a novelette I just wrote called: "Ring of Fire," out late in 2018. I've spent time Googling hotels, so I could show a believable lobby, and a fancy one at that. I've had to research plants and animals that exist in tropical settings, the Arctic, or the desert.

Mentally, your character has to have thoughts, but they also have to be consistent—show us how they are, and what they think, so we can try to decipher and understand what they are going through. You may get there first, but that's okay, maybe the ending will still surprise you. So, when I talk about mind, I mean not only insight into the thoughts of your protagonist, but also the intellectual level of your story, how original are you being, how much research did you do in order to get that level of authority, and can you get us to buy into this all?

It's not easy.

When I talk about the soul of your narrative I mean emotion, what we feel when reading your story. This is also hard to do well. You can get us to care, and you must, ASAP, through empathy and sympathy, yes, do that. You need to go deep. Tap into all of your personal experiences: every time your heart was broken, and how that made you feel, every time you broke somebody else's heart, and how that might have felt different, every sexual experience you've ever had, every moment of glory and failure.

Use it all. Then, find a way to ratchet it up.

I think the best emotions also tap into something I mentioned earlier, the broad vs. the specific. You want to tell the unique story of your protagonist, but if you can wrap that in a universal truth, even better. We all love, we all hate. This also taps into the intellectual plane I just mentioned—the concept and idea. When that really hits a note, when it really pushes a button, your story will work so much better. I'm talking about everything from love and friendship, to loyalty and betrayal, to fear and longing, and so much more.

At the heart of just about every story ever told there is one idea, one central concept: your protagonist (and your villain) just wants to be loved for who they are, appreciated, accepted, and needed. Batman wants to be understood and respected, but so does the Joker.

Interesting side note: rarely does the villain consider himself the bad guy. They're just doing what they think is right, what works for them, what they believe, whether they are Hannibal Lecter, Dexter, or Thanos.

If you can balance body, mind, and heart in your story, establishing each plane, your story will have a lot more depth.

Driving Force & Emotion

This is almost the exact opposite of what I just wrote about, but I want you to consider this idea. If your character gets lost, if you aren't sure what to do next, if you are having trouble figuring out your story or novel, consider this, what is the singular driving force, or emotion behind your narrative?

Quite often when working with my students, they'll get confused, uncertain of what should be driving the story. I ask them the usual questions about internal vs. external conflicts, the inciting incident, the genre, what the plot is about, etc. But try this trick—focus on that one event, that one moment, that one force or emotion.

What do I mean?

It's usually pretty simple. What is your story about? What is the one thing that your protagonist has to do? What is the inciting incident—that moment in time after which things will never be the same? What are they feeling? Not sure? Try this.

Your protagonist wakes up (don't start your story there, please, for the love of God, don't start your story there)—what are they thinking? What are they feeling?

Well, what just happened?

We're not starting with their birth.

We're not starting at some random moment in their life.

Whether this is the first line, or the opening to a new scene, or a new chapter, what is the first thing they think about?

If their child was just kidnapped, I can guarantee you they aren't thinking about what's on sale at Target. If there is an asteroid plummeting toward Earth, they are not thinking about playing a game of Wiffleball. If their child was just killed in a horrible car accident, yes, they may be dealing with the funeral home, yes, they may try to comfort the surviving brother, yes, they may have to take out the trash, but I guarantee you that the threat, the enemy, the horror—it is always front and present, always hovering over everything that is going on—lurking, influencing, undoing everything that has been a part of their peace, structure, and normal daily life.

With horror, think of opposites, what your protagonist wants is a quiet, safe house and what they have is a home filled with bleeding walls, cracked mirrors, and doors slamming in the middle of the night; what they want is a loving relationship, and a supportive spouse, and what they are getting is a cheating husband, a conspiracy that goes deep, gaslighting friends, and a world where nothing makes sense any longer; what your hero wants is to right a wrong, to keep the city safe, and what they are fighting is an enemy that is hell-bent on destruction.

Keep on Track

When it comes to horror, every decision you make is calculated. That's the same for any genre, really, but think about the specifics of what makes a horror story a horror story, and then do that, but you can't be bleak all the time. It's a balance.

If you just hit that one note, that one flavor, it quickly deadens the ear, the taste, we become desensitized. We want the exact opposite. We want you sensitive, on the edge of your seat, as tight as a piano wire. There are so many different styles of horror: classic, contemporary, psychological, gothic, Lovecraftian, slasher, splatterpunk, etc. Just pick your lane, or flavor, and run with it, but along the way here are some questions to ask yourself:

Are my narrative hooks broad and specific, with high enough stakes?

How does this setting add to the atmosphere of my horror story?

How does this plot choice elevate (or release) the tension?

What did I just do—and should I now do more of that, or the opposite?

What am I doing to escalate the narrative, the tension, the horror?

Did I just have a violent scene? Should it continue, or should I let the audience breathe?

When was the last time I sprinkled in this symbol, or contributed to my theme?

Did I just have a major reveal? If so, what comes next? What changes?

Am I balancing the external threat with the internal desire?

Is this cliché horror that we've seen done a million times? How can I innovate?

Have I scared myself yet? If not, why not? What would it take? Go there.

Have I used all five senses yet? If not, where are my opportunities?

My setting—is it expected, a trope, or can I be more unique?

If there is a monster in my story, what am I doing to make it MY monster, and not cliché or expected?

How is the balance between tension and release?

When I show the gore, the violence, the horror—does it work? Is it too much?

Have I put any of my personal fears in this story? If not, why not?

When I end a scene (or chapter) is there a hint, a cliffhanger, or a reveal?

Do we care about the main characters? If not, why not? Go back, and put in emotion, backstory, and tragedy.

Do we believe what's going on here? Give us authority with your darkness.

Are you being too subtle? Are you not being subtle enough? Tough call.

Did you surprise the reader in any way, at any point?

When it's all over, does your story linger, does it resonate?

Just keep coming back to the heart of what this genre is all about, and really look at every aspect of your story to see if you're staying focused.

In Conclusion

There are a lot of moving parts in any story, but when it comes to horror, there are specific elements that are essential. Look at how you show us your horror vs. telling us what is happening, to see if there are opportunities to slow down, unpack, and paint a vivid picture. Keep an ear on your voice, and use both active and passive voice to your benefit. Work in a detailed backstory to give your character depth, and to solicit emotion—usually empathy and/or sympathy in horror, since your story will certainly be tragic. Remember to foreshadow. Give us hints of what's coming, build up layers of clues and symbolism, and lead us down the path toward enlightenment. Use both the broad and specific to scare your readers, large, epic, sprawling concepts and ideas paired with personal moments of tragedy, violence, and terror.

Work top down, or from the bottom up to give us layers and depth in the form of body, mind, and soul, using all of your tools to create fear that is not just on the surface, through the use of intellect, emotion, and tactile sensation. Then keep asking yourself questions along the way, in regards to horror specifically, so you can keep your audience entertained while you build up a dense story that scares on a number of levels.

I've said it before and I'll say it again, the hardest things to do as an author are scare us, make us laugh, and turn us on. It's all so subjective. Your story won't work for everyone, but if you put in the effort, and utilize some of the tips I've given you in this essay, I think you stand a better chance of finding success; with the story, with editors, and your audience. Good luck!

GIVING MEANING TO THE MACABRE

RACHEL AUTUMN DEERING

"SHOW, DON'T TELL."

You've heard it more times than you can count and you'll hear it again, I promise. It's a fantastic bit of advice, but few sage lips will follow up the phrase with a deeper explanation. It's one of those things that seem out of time, like it's always existed. No one knows from whence it came, it simply *is*.

You're expected to know how to apply it to your writing. The next time an editor marks up your manuscript with their red-inked rod of wisdom and you see that esoteric scrawl–*show, don't tell*–remind yourself of the difference between plot and theme.

Plot concerns the details and events which make up the narrative structure of the story itself. This is not to be confused with plotting, the act of planning out the details of your story before you begin writing it. A talented writer can easily plot without the need *to plot*. Here is an example:

Introduction: Steve is on his morning run with his best friend Jake, a shaggy old golden retriever. He's been by Steve through his recent divorce and his resolution to retake control of his own life. He's promised Jake he would find a sense of purpose and give them the life they both deserve. They're running to get back in shape, see? Jake wags his tail and pants and drools. Cute.

Inciting Incident: A school bus driver is busy screaming at the children and doesn't notice when the bus hops the curb and nails good old faithful Jake on the sidewalk. Steve falls over Jake and begins to cry. When the bus driver attempts to lay all blame on everyone but herself, Steve shoots her a look that freezes the blood in her veins.

When she suggests maybe Jake shouldn't have been running so close to the road, Steve regains his composure and surprises everyone by agreeing with her. He collects Jake up in his arms, tells the bus driver to have a good day, and walks away.

Rising Action: Steve is haunted by the sound of the bus wheels chirping on the curb. By the sound of Jake's last yelp. By the cacophony of the kids, some of them actually laughing at his tears. By the bus driver's denial of culpability.

He's losing sleep. He's losing all the progress he'd made in taking back control of his life. He's breaking his promise to Jake. Steve is on the verge of suicide, but he drops the gun and walks out the door, into the night. He walks to the school bus lot and waits until morning when he sees the bus driver pull up in her personal vehicle. He makes a mental note of her license plate number.

He uses this information to find out where she lives. He begins to stalk her, to learn everything about her. He devises methods of chipping away at her sanity and revels in watching it all unfold. The bus driver loses her job. She begins to drink and take drugs and in her paranoia she accidentally stabs herself while defending against something that isn't even there. She asks her daughter Jill to come stay with her.

Steve watches from the shadows. Jill is blind and has a beautiful black lab guide dog she calls Pepper. Steve fights the feeling, but he's developing a thing for Jill. And Pepper. The more he watches them, the harder he falls. Soon enough, Steve is spending more time simply watching Jill and less time terrorizing her mother. The bus driver kicks the bad habits and returns to work.

Climax: Steve drugs Pepper's food and puts him to sleep. He breaks into the home, careful to leave no fingerprints, and confronts the bus driver. Before she can give away his identity, he slits her throat and watches her bleed to death on the floor. He turns to leave and sees her beautiful daughter standing in the doorway. She's heard the murder but has no idea who Steve is. Jill sniffs at the air and her head follows Steve as he leaves through the window.

Falling Action: Steve hangs out at the back of the bus driver's funeral. When it's over, he puts himself in the path of Jill and Pepper. Steve is friendly and asks if he can pet the dog. Of course Jill warms up to Steve and so does the dog! How great. How icky. Steve helps Jill through her grief and the two develop a relationship. Steve has moments where he almost confesses to Jill. It is really eating at him, but ultimately he convinces himself that the bus driver deserved what she got.

Resolution: Steve arrives home from his morning run. He finds Jill on the sofa, petting Pepper. Steve is sweaty and announces he's going to take a shower. He kisses Jill and heads for the bedroom. Jill enters the bedroom moments later and sniffs the air. She's holding a knife. She walks to the hamper and fishes out Steve's sweaty, smelly running clothes. She smells them, inhaling deeply through her nose. She drops the clothes and walks into the bathroom.

It's a fine enough plot. It presents a series of events in a logical fashion, but there's more to it than that. I've shown a lot here, yet I never told you a thing. I didn't have to beat you over the head with themes because, hopefully, it's apparent to you on a subconscious level.

Plot has a structure you can generally follow throughout a story, but theme doesn't need structure, it is not explicit. Like the mysterious origins of "show, don't tell," theme simply is and always has been and always will be. What are some of the themes of this story?

Love, loss, grief, revenge, fulfilled promises, and probably a handful of others you could easily pick out if you spent enough time thinking about it.

Steve loves Jake. Steve feels grief after his divorce. Steve is devastated at losing Jake. Steve is angry at the bus driver. The bus driver is a terrible person. Steve deals with grief in very strange ways. Steve finds his sense of purpose and fulfills his promise to Jake, but in doing so forces Jill to experience loss and grief and eventually, we are left to assume, she get her own revenge.

The themes repeat, but I didn't come right out and tell you any of that. I presented a series of events and the characters' reactions to them, and through reading the story, the lizard part of your brain told you the story was about love and loss and grief and revenge and everything else. The plot justified the themes.

It is possible to have a plot without themes, but I wouldn't recommend it. A guy walks out his front door and stabs three girls. Okay, you have a series of events there, which is technically a plot, but there are no reactions, emotions, or consequences and so there are no themes. A bad writer will give you a lot of plot and very little theme. They might tell you what's going on in painstaking detail, and that's fine if their goal is to be an uninformed gossip, but if they never lay out the feelings that elicit the responses that drive the action, you'll have a hell of a time caring about what's going on, no matter how many people get stabbed, what they're wearing, or what their names might be.

THE HORROR WRITER'S ULTIMATE TOOLBOX

TIM WAGGONER

ONE OF THE interview questions I get a lot is, "What advice would you give beginning horror writers?" I always struggle to answer this. There's no way to distill my thirty years of writing experience into a few glib responses, and how can I select just two or three things that writers need to know?

So when it came time to write an article for this book, I wondered if I could finally settle on a few bits of advice that I think are vital for any horror writer— beginning or otherwise—to know. And thus "The Horror Writer's Ultimate Toolbox" was born. Following are three principles/techniques to help you write kick-ass horror.

Down to the Bone

One of the secrets to writing good horror is understanding that, like all good fiction, horror stories are about people. Too many beginning horror writers make the mistake of thinking their fiction should be focused on a single image which they present at the end: *And then she opened the door and saw . . . the severed head of her dead husband floating in the air like a grisly balloon!* Or their stories are little more than video game walkthroughs with underdeveloped characters who exist only to get mowed down by the story's Big Bad. But if you want your fiction to truly affect readers, if you want your stories to matter to them, you have to go much deeper.

Horror is internal more than external.

Writers who've spent more of their lives watching horror movies instead of reading horror fiction often make the mistake of writing their stories from the outside. In their mind's eye, they view a scene with detachment, as if they're merely watching a character dealing with some horrific threat. That's an external view, but horror comes from *within* a character. It's an emotional response. Writers should imagine themselves in the character's position, and try to understand what sort of thoughts, feelings, and physical responses the character would have. The character's *experience* is the story, not simply the events that happen to him or her.

Horror stories are reaction stories.

Characters in horror fiction are living their lives, with everything going relatively smoothly, when "Something Bad" happens. The story is about how they *react* to the "Something Bad," how it affects them. And not just how anyone might react but how that *one particular character* would.

Does your character deny the existence of the Bad Thing? Does he or she flee from it? Charge toward it? Try to get other people's help in dealing with it? Try to make a bargain with it? Try to feed other people to it to save their own life?

The more you understand how each of your characters react to threats, especially in a novel where you might have a large cast of characters, the more effectively you'll be able to shape your story because you know what your characters will and won't do.

Horror stories aren't about monsters.

They're about how characters react to monsters (or to becoming monsters). I'm using *monster* as a generic term here. The monster could be human, inhuman, natural, supernatural, a disaster such as an earthquake, etc. Imagine a werewolf story where the lycanthrope is standing in the middle of a field at night beneath a brightly glowing full moon . . . all alone. Nothing happens.

The werewolf stands around for a while, growing increasingly bored, and finally goes off to catch a rabbit. The werewolf only becomes interesting when there's a person to interact with it. Focus on the people who are confronted by whatever horror dwells in your story and show us how they deal with it.

Horror stories work best with a deep point of view.

Write with a close point of view to show your characters' emotional reactions to events. If readers empathize with your characters, then the threats these characters face will be meaningful. Give readers a window into your character's thoughts and emotions so they can experience the story alongside the character. Imagine that not only is there a camera mounted on your character's shoulder to let readers know what they see and hear, but there's a cable running from the back of the camera into their head, allowing readers to know what goes on inside the character's mind: thoughts, feelings, memories, mental comparisons (*That tree looks like a giant skeletal arm!*) Let your readers know in real time what's happening inside your character as outside events occur, and your fiction will have more depth and narrative energy.

The Horror Writer's Palette

Painters select from the colors on their palette to create their masterpieces, and horror writers are no different, but our palette contains emotional reactions instead of colors, and knowing when and how to use these reactions is what makes the difference between ho-hum horror and horror that deeply affects readers. If your fiction doesn't hit readers where they live, what's the point of writing it? Following are five emotional reactions, the horror writer's "colors," to use in your stories, from highest and most sophisticated to lowest and simplest.

Dread

Dread is the mounting anticipation of a threat drawing

ever closer. This is what's meant by the term *slow-burn horror*. It depends entirely on the character's (and the audience's) realization that "Something Bad" is happening bit by bit, step by step, and this "Something Bad" gets worse with each occurrence until the suspense becomes absolutely unbearable.

Good examples of this: Shirley Jackson's novel, *The Haunting of Hill House,* and the movie, *Hereditary*. Dread is considered the highest emotional response in the horror writer's palette because it requires a deft hand to create an atmosphere of suspense and to develop the story's threat with increasing intensity. Dread is extended, masterful foreplay, and the story's climax is all the more satisfying for it.

Terror

Terror is a deep emotional and intellectual reaction to a threat. Lovecraft's characters experience terror when they finally understand what the story's Cosmic Horror truly means: *Humanity is insignificant, reality is meaningless, all is madness and chaos*. The characters in John Carpenter's, *The Thing*, experience terror when they realize that any one of them could be replaced by the alien entity, and if the entity manages to escape Antarctica, it will replace every human on Earth. In *Salem's Lot*, characters experience terror when they realize their friends and relatives haven't only become vampires, they've become creatures of pure evil, and there isn't anything remotely human about them anymore. Terror may not require the same careful crafting that dread does, and its emotional response is more immediate, but it still deals with deeper emotions on the part of your characters.

Horror

Horror is an immediate reaction to a threat—disbelief, denial, a turning away. The concern is entirely self-focused on the part of a character. No worrying about the fate of the world or the implications of what the threat might mean. Characters who experience horror are worried about what's going to happen to them, or to people they care about, in the immediate future.

They also may seek to deny what their senses are telling them. *Such things cannot be!* If a monster approaches a victim and that victim shakes his or her head in disbelief, screams and attempts to flee, that's horror. This is film's stock in trade. Audiences might lose patience with mounting dread, and the deeper implications of terror might be lost on them, but a character screaming as a killer or monster approaches?

That works just fine for them. Horror is the meat and potatoes of dark fiction. Effective but common.

Shock

Shock is a surprise, an adrenaline rush. It's a technique that works much better in film than in prose. A movie can show the sudden appearance of a threat on screen, often accompanied by scary sound effects and music. This is the equivalent of a walking through a carnival spookhouse and having someone dressed as a monster jump out in front of you and yell, "Boo!"

You're startled for a moment, but the moment passes. I'd argue that the closest prose fiction can get to shock is when a plot twist is presented to readers, whether during the course of the story or at the end. But just as you can get used to having people yell, "Boo," at you in the spookhouse, readers can become used to plot twists if you employ too many of them, and they'll lose their impact. Shock is the fast food of horror fiction, tasty but ultimately empty, and bad for you if you eat too much.

Disgust

Disgust is a queasy visceral reaction. It's the equivalent of a young child waving a dead lizard in their sibling's face to make them go "Eew." You can get a strong reaction out of readers by using disgust, but if it's too simplistic, or used too much, you might drive readers away.

Edward Lee is the unrivaled king of disgust in horror fiction, but he uses it to create a distorted, nightmarish reality that readers can't escape from until they've turned the last page—and even then the images will remain in their minds, perhaps for the rest of their lives. In the film, *Rawhead Rex*, the pagan monster god urinates on one of its kneeling worshippers to mark him as its servant. It's disgusting, but the action tells us something about Rawhead Rex's primitive animal nature, and it shows us how the worshipper is willing to debase himself for his god.

Considering the existential nature of that debasement, you could argue disgust overlaps terror in this story, but most writers and filmmakers aren't so skilled at handling disgust, and they use it simply to gross out readers and viewers. Simplistic, unskilled use of disgust can make this technique horror's equivalent of cheap porn: a story designed only to stimulate a basic response without any regard to artistry or meaning. But used well, it can be just as effective a tool as any of our other "colors."

Dread and Terror are arguably the most effective hues on our palette, but they all have their place, and when used right, they can work together to create a deeply effective work of horror. The movie, *Martyrs* (the original, not the remake), is one of the best examples of this. It's the story of a group of people who believe that if they subject someone to enough torture, this person will achieve a higher state of being allowing them profound insight into the nature of reality in the few moments before they die. The story has mounting dread, existential terror, horror, shock, and disgust, all combined to create a brutal, harrowing, and strangely beautiful work of art.

Experiment with the different colors on your palette. Maybe you're more naturally drawn to one than the others, but try them all and see what sort of effects they create in your fiction. Who knows? You may end up becoming the horror equivalent of Rembrandt.

The Horror Hero's Journey

Let's get this out of the way first: you do *not* need to use any kind of formula to plot your fiction. You don't have to plot it at all. You can just write and see where the story goes and keep reworking it until you end up with something you like, but if you're looking for a technique to give you some structure when you write—especially if you find yourself writing the same kind of stories over and over—the Horror Hero's Journey might be for you.

You're probably familiar with the Hero's Journey archetype. It's a story structure as old as humanity itself. At its simplest, the Hero's Journey has three stages: the hero leaves his/her familiar world, the hero learns to deal with an unfamiliar and dangerous world, and the hero returns to his/her familiar world stronger in mind and spirit. The Hero's Journey is effective because it's hardwired into our DNA, probably because it mirrors in microcosm the pattern of human existence from birth to death.

The way most writers interpret the hero's journey is thus: 1.) hero has a goal; 2.) hero takes steps to reach that goal; 3.) hero encounters obstacles on way to achieving goal; 4.) hero succeeds or fails, in whole or in part. But characters in horror stories don't choose to go on an adventure to solve a problem or obtain an important object. They're reacting to a threat that's entered *their* world. Horror characters have their own story archetype, which I call *Some Poor Bastard's Descent Into Hell.*

I'm using *bastard* as a gender-neutral term here. The phrase *poor bastard* implies an empathetic reaction from an audience, and it also indicates that the character is a normal person, not a hero with special skills or powers. *Descent Into Hell* means the character's situation steadily and nightmarishly worsens throughout the course of a story.

Hell can be physical, spiritual, mental, emotional,

internal, external, or any combination. For example, in the movie, *The Grey*, the characters survive a plane crash in Alaska and struggle to overcome the threats of weather and terrain, as well as a pack of wolves that's stalking them. Their Hell is physical—the land, the weather, their injuries, the wolves. It's also mental and emotional—they must deal with each other and with their frustrations, doubts, and fears. It's also spiritual, especially for Liam Neeson's character, who was on the verge of suicide before the plane crash and must find a reason to fight for survival. Combining types of Hell like this can help you expand a story idea into a novel, while focusing on only one or two allows you to write a nicely focused and contained short story.

The Poor Bastard's Descent into Hell has a number of different story outcomes.

The Poor Bastard Escapes Hell. The Poor Bastard doesn't have to be just one character. In the movie *Poltergeist*, an entire family is plunged into Hell, and they come out the other side, relatively unscathed. In *Jaws*, the shark is blown to chunks of bloody meat and the hero cheers. This outcome is horror's version of Happily Ever After.

The Poor Bastard is Eternally Damned. The movies *Seven, Angel Heart,* and *Krampus* are excellent examples of this outcome, as are many of Lovecraft's stories and numerous episodes of *The Twilight Zone*. No matter what the Poor Bastard does—or *because* of what he/she does—they are damned, symbolically or literally, in the end. The character doesn't die in this outcome. Death would be a relief, and that relief is denied our Poor Bastard here.

The Poor Bastard Escapes with Severe Wounds

and Scars: These don't have to be—and often aren't—physical wounds. Mental and spiritual damage are equally as likely as injuries to the flesh. Many of Stephen King's protagonists survive their ordeals, but they don't do so unscathed. We learn in *Doctor Sleep* that *The Shining*'s Danny Torrance became an alcoholic as he grew up because of the emotional scars left by his experience at the haunted Overlook Hotel. The first *Purge* movie ends this way, with the survivors having lost a family member, having to become ruthlessly violent to survive, and having had their view of themselves and their neighbors altered forever.

The Poor Bastard is Transformed by Hell. In this outcome, the Poor Bastard is tainted to the core by his/her experience. *The Exorcist* is a good example, as is *Psycho*. In the case of *Psycho*, the Poor Bastard is also the Devil (if unknowingly so), but only the Devil remains in the end.

The Poor Bastard Carries Hell with Him. In this outcome, the Poor Bastard might escape Hell, but it's still there with him/her in the end, like a chronic disease that cannot be cured, only managed. *The Babadook* is a good example of this outcome. And while the most recent iteration of *The Mummy* was more of an adventure film than horror, in the end Tom Cruise's character carries Hell with him.

The Poor Bastard Drags Other to Hell or Brings Hell to Them. The Ring and *It Follows* are excellent examples of this outcome. In both films, characters must choose to bring Hell down on others in order to escape Hell themselves.

The Poor Bastard Becomes the Devil. In the end, the Poor Bastard becomes the thing that he/she was fighting. *Friday the 13ᵗʰ Part IV*, where in the end it appears Tommy is going to take up where Jason left off, is a great example of this, and it becomes a story element in *Part V*, when Tommy is suspected of being the new Jason. The novel *Hannibal* ends this way, too, with Clarice Starling becoming the very thing she's fought against.

There's a lot more to writing great horror fiction than the three techniques I've discussed (which is why there are other chapters in this book, of course), but if you master the techniques in the Horror Writer's Ultimate Toolbox, your stories and novels will have a much greater chance of making it out of the slush pile and into the hands of eager horror readers who'll devour your work and beg for more.

SARAH PINBOROUGH INTERVIEW

MARIE O'REGAN

SARAH **PINBOROUGH IS** the *Sunday Times* #1, *New York Times* and Internationally best-selling author of 25 novels. Published in over 30 territories her work spans a variety of genres, from YA thrillers, to dystopian/sci-fi crime and historical cross-genre horror. Her recent psychological thriller, *Behind Her Eyes*, was an international hit and is greenlit for a six part series, filming in 2019 with Left Bank and Netflix. *Behind Her Eyes,* was also shortlisted for the Crime and Thriller book of the year at the British Book Awards. Her YA thriller, *13 Minutes*, is also in development with Netflix and Michael De Luca.

Her most recent novel, *Cross Her Heart*, was sold in the US for a healthy seven figure deal, and is already in development with World Productions. Her Dog-Faced Gods trilogy is in development with Lionsgate and Festival. She is also a screenwriter who had written for the BBC and has several original projects in development. She lives in Stony Stratford with her Romanian rescue dog Ted. She's taken time out of her busy schedule to talk all things writing-related with Marie O'Regan.

MOR: How did you get into writing? Was it something you always wanted to do?

SP: I think all professional writers have written or told stories since they were very young, so it was always part of my life. As I grew up I wrote stories and plays but I was also very into drama and really wanted to go to Drama School, but that didn't pan out and I was just too lazy for it. But I did keep writing as all writers do, and then slowly started to take it more seriously in my late twenties and started to focus on making it a career.

MOR: At what point did you decide you could go full time?

SP: I didn't is the honest answer. My first 6 novels were published during 6 years of full-time teaching. I knew something needed to give if I was going to step up to the next level. After being offered the chance to write a Torchwood novel and saving some money up, I decided to take six months out from teaching to write a crime-crossover novel, which would become: *A Matter of Blood*, the first of the Dog-Faced Gods trilogy. Thankfully, I sold them to Gollancz on pitch and then I never went back to teaching. That was ten years ago, so fingers crossed my time in the classroom is done for a while.

MOR: Your first novels were horror—you've also written historical fantasy, fairy tales, as well as crime novels and thrillers. What drew you to each of these?

SP: The fairy tales I wrote because my editor at the

time, Gillian Redfearn, asked me if I'd be interested in writing some fun, sexy re-tellings after we'd both become obsessed with the first series of, *Once Upon a Time*. I wasn't sure at first if it was right for me, but once I had started thinking about the story of Snow White I wondered what kind of man fell in love with a pretty much dead woman in a box, and then I had my way in. *Mayhem,* and, *Murder,* were inspired by reading, *The Terror*, after which I wanted to find an unsolved crime with a cast of interesting real life characters that I could weave some supernatural elements into. It's very much a crime-crossover duology rather than historical fantasy.

I also write YA, but I don't actually consider this a separate genre—I've written psychological thriller YA and dystopian and even a YA fantasy trilogy, but they're as complex as any of my adults' books. My recent novels have been straight thrillers, but I still dabble in the weird. I've got a European supernatural crime TV series well into development at the moment and I tend to put my more 'out there' ideas into TV or film. However, all of my stories tend to have a mystery at the core, and they're all, even the fun fairy tales, pretty dark in places, so that's what draws me really. Dark mysteries.

MOR: You've also written for TV—was that a difficult discipline to learn, compared to prose?

SP: Yeah, it's a very strict discipline compared to prose. Structure is everything and any mistakes are glaring because there are fewer pages. I really enjoy it, though. Less is always more in screenplays and novelists tend to make the mistake of trying to do the director and DOP's job in the screenplay by describing everything! The difference for me between the two is that I tend to hand my first draft of a novel in and then there's just the edit, but a screenplay first draft is just invariably to show you what is wrong with everything in it and then you scrap it and start again.

MOR: Do you find it easier to work alone, or as part of a team, as you would for screenwriting? Which do you prefer?

SP: Well, in screenwriting you work alone for much of the time—obviously once things get more serious and lots of producers are involved there are more meetings and notes but the actual work is done alone. I enjoy the meetings a lot of the time, and hammering out series arcs in a room full of people is way more fun than doing it at home alone. But for actual writing, I don't think I could have a writing partner. I'm too much of a control freak.

MOR: How much research do you do for your novels? Or do you take Stephen King's approach—'enough to make the story work', often done after the first draft, but no more than that.

SP: With, *Mayhem,* I researched a lot to get the crimes and the timelines right, but the rest was research as and when I needed it. So if they were having a dinner, I'd research when writing that scene what time people ate in 1898 and what they ate. if you research too much too soon then you forget it when you need it, and sometimes never need it at all. If you're setting a book in a particular place then it's good to go and walk around it and get the atmosphere of it, but that's not research so much.

MOR: Describe an average working day, for you.

SP: God, it varies so there's no real routine. I used to aim for 2000 words a day or whatever, but now the thinking time is as, if not more, important to me. Plus it all has to fit in around Ted's walks and whatever Netflix has released. I'm not one of these 'Oh, I go to a shed and work for ten hours straight' people, I'm pretty sure they're all lying. ;-) I am better at doing actual writing in the early mornings though.

MOR: How important do you think it is to attend things like conventions and literary festivals, if you're just starting out?

SP: I think they're a good way of learning some basics and meeting other writers and editors etc. and making friends. I don't think they're vital though, not in this world of Twitter etc. where you can engage with other professionals on a daily basis. However, Twitter isn't quite the same as chatting face-to-face in a bar. I really loved going to cons when I started out for the fun element as well as the work. I do quite a lot now, so my enthusiasm for them has worn a bit thin, but I'm lucky to have great groups of friends in all the various genres I work in, so even if I'm not really in the mood, they always pull me out of my anti-social grump.

MOR: What comes first, plot or character?

SP: A vague plot or set-up and then character very quickly behind, and then the plot solidifies around them. Occasionally—as in *Cross Her Heart*—I had the lead character and her back story fixed in my head before I had the book's plot, but the two were almost intertwined.

MOR: How integral is setting in a story?

SP: Ha, that really depends on the story. In some, it's not relevant at all. But in others it can say an awful lot about the story and the characters because it can show us how privileged etc. they are and the challenges they face. Sometimes, like in Jane Harper's *The Dry*, which is set in the Australian outback, setting is almost a character of its own as with the aforementioned *The Terror*. I quite like setting to have some relevance, but I don't think it's vital to a good story. If you're relying on your setting over your plot you need to rethink your story.

MOR: How do you develop an idea from that initial spark to a fleshed-out plan for a novel?

SP: I don't have a fleshed-out plan ever, really—I have notebooks and I have my ending and my opening and then I brainstorm sections as I go, and may try and get a skeleton of key events down somewhere, the structure lesson I learned in screenwriting, but it all changes as it goes. The only thing that doesn't change is the ending, and I can't even start writing until I'm sure I've got the ending I want locked down.

MOR: Are there any subjects you wouldn't write about?

SP: I probably wouldn't write a rape scene. I can't think of a story I would tell where that would be necessary, plus it's been done to death. Although that doesn't mean I will never do it.

MOR: Are there any books on writing you'd recommend?

SP: I don't read a lot of books about writing—I've always been quite solitary about the process and I'm pretty sure that most of them are written by people you've never heard of, however, I would always recommend Stephen King's, *On Writing,* and for screenwriting, *Save The Cat,* which a lot of people can sneer at, but I know loads of professional screenwriters who run their stories through the *Save the Cat* beats to check it works.

MOR: Is there an area of writing you haven't tried yet that you'd like to? Say, comics/graphic novels?

SP: I have got a graphic novels company wanting me to do something for them and I'd love to try it, but I'm also aware that I'm capable of overloading myself, and at the moment the novels have to come first. But yeah, I'd love to do a graphic novel. I'd feel like one of the cool kids.

MOR: Finally, what one piece of advice would you give to writers starting out?

SP: Ignore pretty much all writing advice because so much of it is bullshit, especially lists of it on Twitter. Just remember—the worst that can happen is that you write a bad story. It's not brain surgery. Always be charming at events, don't take it all too seriously, and remember, one day your writing hero may read your story and like it—happened to me with Stephen King—and then all the bad times will be worthwhile!

Artwork by Luke Spooner

CHARACTERIZATION

CONVEYING CHARACTER

F. PAUL WILSON

AT THIS POINT in the development of your craft, you've all read essays and/or taken classes on character. Along the way you might have noticed that most of them focus on *creating* engaging characters—an indispensable process of such obvious importance that it can't be emphasized enough. I'm going to deal with some of that, but I'm going to focus on *conveying* characters to the reader. Because you can create the most dynamic, engaging, lovable, admirable characters, but if they don't *connect* with the reader, if they don't become real people in the readers' heads, then all that work in the character design shop was for naught.

The key is not simply creating a relatable character, but *conveying* that character to the reader—making the reader *connect*. Because the next step after connecting is *caring*.

The Rules—not

There are Rules for writing a good story. Unfortunately no one knows what they are. Mainly because the process is different for everyone—we can all find different means to the same end. So I'm not going to give you rules, but I will point out some signposts and what works for me.

A caveat, however: In the search for your own rules, don't look too hard, don't over think. Go with your gut. Too much analyzing what makes a story work can be like dissecting a frog—when you're done you may or may not have learned a lot about frogs, but one thing's certain: that frog's not jumping anymore.

The importance of character

It's a truism that we humans love a well-plotted story, and we love it even more when we get hooked on the characters populating that story. Advocates of mimetic fiction turn up their noses at plot (and at all genre fiction in general), but horror readers thrive on it. The more suspense and dread the plot generates, the better. That's what keeps them turning the pages, but if you can entwine living, breathing, relatable characters in that harrowing plot, then you've got a winner.

Because *plot happens to people*. So if readers care about those people, then they have two reasons for turning the pages: 1.) watching where the story goes; and, 2.) seeing what mayhem happens to the characters. When you achieve that, you've got a work of fiction that readers will remember and talk about . . . and recommend to their friends.

Memorable characters make memorable authors. If an author is going to have a legacy, it's not going to arise from plot or setting—it's going to be characters. Homer had Odysseus, Verne had Nemo, Dickens had

Scrooge, Austin had Lizzy, Hugo had Quasimodo, Twain had Huck, Doyle had Sherlock, Hammett had Spade, Chandler had Marlowe, Mitchell had Scarlett and Rhett, Tolkien had Bilbo, and so on. Modern authors are still writing about many of these characters.

Worry about your legacy later. The immediate importance of your characters is that you're asking a reader to sit down and spend hours with these people. Remember that: *Your characters should be people readers want to spend time with*, so make them interesting. That doesn't mean they all need to be lovable. Take Hannibal the Cannibal Lecter. Not exactly a teddy bear, but Harris's novels come alive whenever he steps on-stage.

The first question every writer should ask when starting a new work of fiction is: *Whose story is it?*

Once you answer that question, you know who's going to carry the story, and thus you know where to concentrate your character skills. Because if you can't entice your readers to spend time with this pivotal character, then you're going to have tough sledding making them stay with the story.

Character traits

So let's start with a character sketch.

Assigning personal characteristics over which a character has no control is the easy part: race, birthplace/nationality, large/small family, physique, economic status, work experience, straight, gay, voluptuary, aesthete, prejudiced, non-judgmental, interests, morality, relationships to other people in general (garrulous, friendly, gregarious, or a sardonic loner) and to fellow characters in specific.

What Works for Me

I often refer to a table of traits (you can find them online), skimming through them in the spitballing stage of character development. Often a word will trigger something in my head. Like, say, "thrifty." I'll think, *I've never written about a thrifty character before. Let's see . . .*

Or "nitpicky." Perfect for an annoying character—make him or her a pettifogger.

Yeah, I know, it sounds like the antithesis of "organic," but don't knock it till you've tried it

Now the parts over which characters can assert some control: Level of education, job, married, single, divorced, hobbies, good/bad relationship with parents and sibs, taste in clothes, music, books, drink of choice (or not), popular or loner as a kid, etc.

This sounds somewhat mechanical and, to some extent, it is. But what you're doing at this point is creating a skeleton (which has a mechanical function), a framework on which to hang various layers of flesh.

Galley slaves . . .

"My characters are galley slaves," says Vladimir Nabokov.

Caution: Do not get too detailed with your character sketch—keep it a *sketch*. Why? As the author, you determine the flow of the story; *you* decide where it twists, where it turns, *not* the characters. If you create too detailed a vision of your protagonist, you may start thinking of him or her as a real person, a separate entity. Allow that and you risk arriving at a spot in the story where you'll say, "Wait, Harry wouldn't do that. I'll have to change the story."

What I'm about to say is sacrilege in some quarters, but here goes: You can't allow a character to dictate a horror story. You created Harry. You're his god. He does what you want him to do. You don't change your story to accommodate Harry; you change Harry to make him a better fit for the story. That's why you keep him a *sketch* with blank areas you can fill in as you go along.

Before the villagers arrive with their torches (and I cry "Nabokov said it!" in my defense) let me add that, with a more literary, peripatetic, character-driven novel, you can let the characters run the show. And in any fiction, you should listen to your characters; sometimes they'll nudge you to reappraise your thought line and you'll have a *Eureka!* moment that prompts you to change course in a direction better than you were originally headed, but be wary. Writing a horror story is like juggling: keeping those tumbling daggers in the air depends on precise timing—of events, reveals, twists, turns, reversals. You can't let your characters throw off your timing or everything will fall apart. Look at Blatty's balancing act in *The Exorcist.* He's in complete control of his characters.

The Exception: Of course, all of the above goes out the window if we're discussing a series character. After a couple of books into a series, your main character's personality and traits are established and the plots have to be written around him or her.

What Works for Me

Try the contrarian approach: Take what's become a genre cliché and turn it on its head.

I've done this throughout my career. Horror fiction has always been my first love, and by 1979 there was finally a market for it. So I left the SF I'd been writing and looked around. What I saw was everyone doing riffs on *Carrie* and *Salem's Lot*—all small-town horror. I decided to go widescreen and make what happens in an out-of-the-way pocket fortress in the Transylvania Alps *matter*—not just to the characters on the scene but to the whole freakin' world. I'd been reading a lot of Ludlum and you can spot the influence of his paranoia/trust-no-one motifs in *The Keep*. The result was a horror-thriller the likes of which no one had ever seen. It made my career.

I took the same approach with Repairman Jack. I needed a tough protagonist to survive what I was planning to throw at him in *The Tomb*, but I didn't want the typical steroidal ex-Special Forces guy. Back in the early 80s, Jason Bourne and James Bond types were proliferating. I decided to turn them upside down and create an anti-Jason Bourne: no black-ops training, no SEAL or Special Forces chops, no CIA or police background, no connection to officialdom. In other words, no safety net. No one in the government he could call on. He has to rely on his own wits and his own network. I made him wiry rather than muscular, not suave or good looking; in fact, he expends a lot of effort on looking so ordinary that he barely registers with passersby. I pushed it even further and took him off the grid—totally under the radar with no Social

Security number, no legit identity, a guy who's never even seen a 1040.

Nobody had ever encountered a protagonist like that before. *The Tomb* was supposed to be a one shot, but it hit the bestseller lists and never went out of print. The fan base grew until, after 14 years of pleading letters and emails, I gave in and wrote a second Repairman Jack novel. And then a third, and on and on. I finally put him out to pasture after #23.

Maybe the contrarian approach can work for you.

Digging Down

After we've dealt with the mechanics of character development, we come to the art of making that character come alive.

For that we need to delve deeper. Each character, whether protagonist or antagonist, should have a *Life Outside the Plot*, maybe a dream, something they're striving for beyond surviving the writer's plot—or, in some cases, surviving the writer's prose. This gives characters an extra dimension, allowing them to exist for a purpose other than simply serving the plot.

The extracurricular life doesn't have to be elaborate—in fact, you should avoid making it *too* elaborate because you don't want to distract from your main story. Simply imagine what your character would be doing if he or she weren't busy saving the world.

He played soccer in college and manages a kids' soccer team in his spare time. He has to keep rearranging schedules because of your damn plot.

She sells commercial real estate and has a pending deal with a huge commission that will cure her financial woes, but your plot keeps interfering with the closing.

He's a Tangerine Dream fan and is on the lookout for an almost mythical soundtrack they created.

You get the picture.

The same holds true for the villains. An excellent example of a bad guy with a life outside the plot is Stringer Bell from *The Wire*. He's second in command to West Baltimore's drug lord, Barksdale, and he's doing all the drug-thug things: selling dope, intimidating witnesses, torturing and murdering rivals, but in spite of all that, you find yourself rooting for him. Because he's smart. He knows this drug thing can't last forever. He takes business courses at the local community college, he's using the drug money to buy politicians and real estate for the future. He conducts meetings with his street pushers according to Robert's Rules of Order! A fascinating bad guy.

Physical appearance

Writers disagree on the degree of physical description necessary. Some prefer to give (and some readers need) an almost photographic description of a character. Others provide a handful of details and let the reader fill in the rest.

I tend to side with the latter. Gender and race, sure, but go much beyond that and it's just packaging. I'm more interested in what's going on *inside* the package.

Unless of course the packaging has had an effect on the character. If a deformity, morbid obesity, or even stunning beauty has caused the world to treat that person differently and affect them inside, then I want to know about it. Do I care if the eyes are blue or brown? Not particularly—unless we're talking about a Mayan with pale blue eyes. Do I care if the hair is red? Only if the serial killer stalking the area has a thing for redheads.

It's up to you how much description you use. Whatever floats your boat.

The Character Arc

The arc is a progression of mental and emotional changes (the inner journey) wrought upon a character by the events of the story (the outer journey).

Johnny Cash's song "A Boy Named Sue" by Shel Silverstein is a succinct example. The narrator spends most of the song hating his dad for naming him Sue before abandoning him. He finally catches up to his old man and is ready to kill him when his dad explains why he named him Sue. The narrator has a change of heart and embraces his dad (but he still hates the name).

That's a paradigmatic character arc: from hate to love. Arcs abound in fiction: the drunk gets sober, the racist comes to appreciate people of color, the brother comes to accept his challenged sister, and so on.

How many arcs happen in real life? Who can say? Not so many, I think.

People tend to resist change, but fiction isn't about real life. The promise of fiction is that it's *not* real life (which is why we call it fiction), that it's *better* (or worse) than real life. That's why people love a good story—it imposes symmetry on the chaos of quotidian existence.

No matter what you think of character arcs, readers tend to like them. An arc means the character didn't go through all this *tsuris* for nothing, without learning something, without it affecting him, without being changed somehow.

Shading your Heroes and Villains

Few characters are less interesting than a Dudley Do-Right protagonist or a mustache-twirling villain. No one is perfectly good, and even the vilest villain isn't evil all the time, but you'll probably find it harder to add warts to your hero than to add some shine to a villain.

It's a truism that most evildoers don't think of themselves as evil. They're often the hero of their own story. Look at Hitler: Do you think he suffered a moment's regret over the death camps?

He epitomizes the banality of evil. But then look at the parody videos from *Downfall* where he flies into rages over Susan Boyle not winning *Britain's Got Talent* or the shortcomings of the new iPad. Suddenly he's human, he's a person.

Conflicted villains tend to be more interesting. The reader is more willing to spend time with them, and they give the writer more to work with.

In *The Tomb*, the antagonist, Kusum, is an honorable man who vowed (for good reasons) to scour the Westphalen family from the face of the Earth. It finally comes to a point where the last Westphalen is a seven-year-old girl. He's repulsed by the idea of harming a child, but he made a vow to his goddess . . .

Conflict is the heart of drama, and Kusum must put aside his humane impulses to honor his vow.

Consider: Which Hamas terrorist gives you more to work with, more hooks to grab your reader? The one who gleefully covers his wall with hatch marks representing the Israeli deaths he's caused—women, children, no matter: no Israeli is innocent. Or the one who lies awake at night, sickened by the innocents he's had to kill—and will have to go on killing—to throw off what he sees as the yoke of Israeli oppression.

Then again, why choose? Use them both. Two terrorists butting heads adds another layer of conflict to your story.

Villainy comes in all shades. At the extremes: Pristine evil, almost a force of nature, like the aforementioned Hannibal Lecter. He's virtually an alien presence. He views the rest of humanity as a lesser species, suitable only for his larder, and shows his contempt by preparing gourmet meals of our carcasses.

At the other end of the spectrum is the regular guy next door—a good guy, a non-violent man who wishes no one harm, but who makes one ill-considered decision that sucks him into an accelerating downward spiral wherein he learns the depths to which he can sink. A great example is Hank in *A Simple Plan*. He and his brother and a friend find a gym bag containing over a million bucks and, rather than turn it in, decide to keep it. Events spin out of control and by the end Hank has murdered four people and is complicit in the death of a fifth.

The ground between these two extremes leaves space for innumerable variations.

Don't be afraid to make your villain vulnerable— sociopaths and even psychopaths have been known to care more for their pets than people, but this is a two-edged sword, so be very careful. Too vulnerable and your villain stops being a threat. Portraying the villain as the victim of childhood abuse has been overdone. We don't always have to provide an experiential reason for why he's a bad guy—we know that some people are simply born bad.

Don't be afraid to have him or her perform an act of kindness or experience justifiable moral outrage. His mother or a neighbor gets scammed and he deals harshly with the scammer. Maybe his sense of fair play is offended and he takes revenge on behalf of an injured party who once showed him kindness.

Your villain can be an honorable person, can even have a strict (though skewed) moral or ethical code. Fu Manchu, the archetypal Yellow Peril, would devise the most fiendish ways to dispose of people who stood in the way of his plans, but he would never break his word. If you reached a stalemate with him and he said you were free to go, you could turn and walk away without fearing a knife in your back, but your reprieve would last only so long as you stayed out of his way.

Or a mobster with a code: members of rival gangs are fair game, but their wives and children are off limits. He deals harshly with one of his own henchmen who steps over that line.

Heroes too should have a code, even anti-heroes. I think Sam Spade epitomized it best in *The Maltese Falcon*: "When a man's partner is killed, he's supposed to do something about it. It doesn't make any difference what you thought of him, he was your partner and you're supposed to do something about it."

Of course you can play with codes too. Consider two cops in *The Wire:* Bunk Williams has no code for his personal life where he's a drunk philanderer, but has a strict code for the Job. Jimmy McNulty, on the other hand, has no code for either the Job or his personal life—the end justifies the means for him.

Tarnishing the shine: Ideally your protagonist's defects should impinge on the plot, but they don't have to. It can be a phobia (snakes, spiders, wasps) or an addiction (lots of protagonists have gone through 12-step programs) or a medical problem (an ulcer, an allergy) or personality disorder (bipolar, depression, panic, hubris, anger issues). Anything that adds an extra dimension and, even better, a possible plot complication. (See the first season of *Homeland*.)

What Works for Me

I start out with *very* sketchy characters. I barely know them when I type page one. I blast through the vomit draft with rare looks back, and only when I need to check for consistency. (This helps me maintain narrative momentum.) As I spew, I get to know the characters; and as I learn about what kind of people they are, their inner conflicts, their relationships with each other, and what kind of people the story needs them to be, I start filling in their blank spots. By the end of the vomit draft I know them pretty well. I let the manuscript sit for a couple of weeks, and then I start the tidying and back-filling process where I prune and tune the prose, and add layers of flesh and personality to these people who are going to make my story work.

For me, story is king, and so I let the story design the cast that will best serve it.

Your mileage may vary.

Now that you've assembled your cast, it's time to put them to work, time to introduce them to your story, and thereby to your readers.

But how best to do that?

The perfection of art is to conceal art

"Show don't tell." How many times have you heard that? Ad nauseam, right? Well, keep saying it. Make it a mantra. Because that's the way to make your characters come alive for the reader.

Series aside, in a stand-alone novel every character starts off as a *tabula rasa* for the reader. Your job is to paint portraits of those characters on your reader's consciousness. To do that, you have to use every narrative device at your disposal. You are the conduit from the character's thoughts, feelings, and motivations to the reader. How do you fix that character in the reader's mind?

PARTICIPATION

Remember that word. By showing rather than telling, you can nudge readers into participating in defining the character, which is the key to success, and the best thing is, readers won't be aware that they're participating.

A simple example: I spend a paragraph or two telling you that Elwood is a well-known skinflint and you can take my word for it. Or I can show you Elwood grabbing all the coins from the penny tray at the 7-Eleven counter and slipping them into his pocket. In the latter scenario I haven't *told* you a thing, but you're thinking, *The cheap SOB . . .*

See what happened there? *You* stuck the tag on Elwood. *You* characterized Elwood. You're *participating* in fleshing out Elwood for my story. Reader and writer have just become partners.

This is because you've started up what I call the reader's *Inference Engine*

When you turn the ignition on that, the reader becomes a participant in your story. You're showing them different facets of your characters, and they're unconsciously putting it all together. Here are some routes you can take . . .

What a character finds funny says a lot. Show him cracking up when he sees an old lady trip and fall on her butt and your reader will think he's a creep, and in reacting to what you've shown and making that decision, the reader has participated with you in defining that character.

What Character A thinks about Character B says a lot.

You can convey bits of character by showing the simplest things. Like what section of the paper he turns to first. Does he skip the headlines and go straight to the funnies? Or the sports pages?

Every little thing you show adds a bit more flesh to the character.

Using Voice to convey character

Voice is the persona of the narrative—its personality, if you will, but *whose* personality? The author's or the character's?

Ideally, the character's. Some writers, however, can't keep themselves out of their fiction, and every character is a thinly disguised version of themselves, but the more versatile author will have POV characters who are *fictional people* with values, interests, viewpoints, and levels of education that differ from his own.

Again: The voice should reflect the personality of the point-of-view character, not the writer's. And speaking of POV . . .

Using Point of View to convey character

To get the most out of POV, you have to adopt the Stella Adler form of method acting: You get inside the character's skin and tap into all his or her senses and emotions. This allows the reader to get to know the character from the inside, to experience what the character experiences, to perceive the world as the character perceives it, to share in his or her prejudices and frames of reference.

To do this right, you must adopt the POV character's attitudes and prejudices. You have to react to situations the way he or she would, even if you find that reaction repellent. Remember, this is not *you* the reader is perceiving—you're a ghost in the machine. If you're doing this right, the reader is seeing only the character.

In POV you must *become* the character.

For instance, if the POV character of the moment is a truck driver who dropped out of school on the day he got his driver's license, hardly read when he was in school, and hasn't picked up a book since he left, can you have allusions to Absolom's kiss in *The Miller's Tale* wafting through his mind as he hurtles down the open road? (That's the writer making sure you don't forget he has an MFA in English.) Hell, you can't even have the word *waft* waft through his mind. You've got to cut him open, step into his skin, and zip it up so you can filter everything through his senses and his sensibilities. In this case that means thinking like a high school dropout; it might even mean using bad grammar and throwing out a few hoary clichés now and again.

Even the length and construction of the sentences you use in a given character's POV sends a subliminal message to the reader.

Using Frames of Reference to communicate character.

A character's frames of reference—the work she does, the books he's read, films she's seen, places she's traveled, sports he likes—*must be consistent with their life experiences*. This intersects with POV.

Using Dialogue

You can develop character through dialog just as with narrative voice and POV. The way a person speaks tells a lot about them: sentence structure and vocabulary and attitude (the voice of their voice) are telling.

The master of character-driven dialog was Gregory McDonald. Pick up a copy of *FLETCH*, the first of his Fletch mysteries. He has pages of pure dialog with no attribution because you're never in doubt as to who's speaking.

Sometimes what characters *don't* say is more important than what they do.

Again, the goal is **participation**. Get the reader's *inference engine* going.

Here are 2 divergent approaches:

(A)

"This isn't going to be another Montauk, is it?"

"No way. Everything's gonna be fine."

The average writer will now insert narration explaining what happened in Montauk, making the reader a *recipient*.

Don't be the average writer: start up the reader's inference engine, get the reader to *participate*.

(B)

"This isn't going to be another Montauk, is it?"

"No way. Everything's gonna be fine."

"That's what you said before Montauk."

"Well, this is different. We will *not* have another Montauk."

And leave it at that. *Don't* tell us what happened at Montauk . . . at least not now. Maybe never. Make the reader wonder what happened at Montauk.

Even without the explanation, we can infer that these guys have a history.

Right away we can infer that they're not perfect—something went wrong in Montauk . . . and that means *something can go wrong again.*

We perceive a comradery but also a certain wariness.

Guess what? We haven't been passive recipients—we've been deducing and inferring—i.e., being *participants.*

Let's take two characters and see how each might explain his involvement with a loan shark:

"The operation in whose debt I find myself consists of a rather unsavory fellow who runs his usurious enterprise out of an antique auction house just south of town."

"I'm in hock to this southside shy; uses some kinda antique place as a front."

I've overdone it a bit to make a point, but do you have a problem inferring the relative education and social standing of these blokes?

Putting it all together:

Combining voice, POV, dialogue, and frame of reference.

Consider two very different characters entering the richly appointed office of a bigshot CEO. Same place, same name, different guys:

(Tommy)
"Have a seat. Mister Drexler will be with you shortly."

"Okay. Thanks."

Cute gal, Tommy thought as he wandered toward one of the ornate chairs. Wonder if she's attached.

He stopped and looked around. Pretty damn big office. The building might be brand new but Drexler's space was totally crammed with all sorts of old stuff. *Old*-old stuff from the look of it; not new-old fake antiques—the real deal. The desk alone probably cost more than Tommy's net worth—on a good day, and lately the good days hadn't been all that good.

But what was with the wallpaper? Busy as all shit. Like one of those optical illusions where if you stare at it long enough it looks like something else.

His gaze wandered toward the ceiling. Christ, who did the trim here? An Orc? Probably uses a framing square for a hammer. Ever hear of a level? Or a bevel gauge? And look at the corners.

Jesus, if the trimmer used a miter box even once Tommy'd rename himself Jesus and go for a stroll on the bay, and *damn* if that load-bearing wall didn't look like it was plumbed by a blind man.

Glad I don't work here.

He dropped into one of the antique chairs. Look at all the gingerbread on this thing. Nice to see furniture that looked like a human being had had a hand in it, and someone had had his hands *all over* this baby—someone who really knew his way around a wood chisel. Must have taken him a looong time to get this right.

(Thomas)

"Have a seat. Mister Drexler will be with you shortly."

"Thank you, Anne," Thomas said, making a point of using her name.

Always remember the names of the little people. They appreciate it and you never know when one of them will come in handy.

Love the William Morris, he thought, admiring the wallpaper as he crossed the room.

But it clashed with the rug, which he was sure was Iranian. Without stooping to feel it, he gauged the thread count at about 300— ostentatious for sure, but nothing compared to the furniture. Good God, Louis XV? For Christ sake, couldn't Drexler have chosen the next Louis? *Quinze* to *Seize*. Only one more Louis up the line, but a world of difference. *Seize* might be over gilded, but had much cleaner lines and was *so* much more tasteful than this Rococo shit. Look at that desk. Ready to collapse under the weight of all that crap carving.

Obviously Drexler had money, and flaunting it was fine with Thomas, but if you're going to flaunt, flaunt with a little style, a little elán.

Okay . . . what can we infer about these two guys?

Tommy: You might have decided he's a skilled carpenter in the lower end of the middle class who might have graduated high school but certainly didn't go higher; you might have decided he's a regular guy who takes pride in his work and you wouldn't mind having a beer with him.

Thomas: You might have decided he's a cultured man, acquainted with the finer things in life. A scion or perhaps an antiques dealer catering to the one-percenters. Either way he's a snob and you can't see yourself having a beer with him. In fact, you kind of doubt he drinks beer.

Look at all the appraisals you've made about these two men without being *told* anything. All you did was experience a richly furnished room through their senses and frames of reference. Look at how you've participated in fleshing out their characters.

That's what you want your readers to do. Because then they've taken your characters and made them their own.

Well, that's it. The key take-away from all this blather is that the best way to make your characters live for your readers is to make those readers participate in realizing them. I've suggested ways to do that. I hope you find them useful.

F. Paul Wilson
The Jersey Shore

SYMPATHETIC CHARACTERS TASTE BETTER: CREATING EMPATHY IN HORROR FICTION

BRIAN KIRK

"I try to create sympathy for my characters, then turn the monsters loose."
—Stephen King

PLEASE INDULGE ME with a simple exercise. Think of your favorite book.

Quick, no one's judging you.

What pops into your mind first? Hold that thought. That lovely book that shines brightest in your heart.

What earned it the top seat on a teetering tower of well-worn novels? Was it the setting? Probably not.

Most people don't cherish books based on ambience or geography. The style? For as much as authors labor over voice and word choice, readers rarely buy books for prose alone. The action scenes? The plot twists? The story arc?

This is horror . . . so, the body count?

While all of the above aspects are vitally important to the enjoyment of a story, they are rarely the single most important factor. That would be the characters. Even more specifically, the reader's emotional attachment to the characters, those both good and evil, human or otherwise.

The reason millions of readers wanted to attend Hogwarts School of Witchcraft and Wizardry wasn't because they thought Quidditch was cool. Rather, they fell in love with Harry Potter, Ron, and Hermione (and loved to hate Draco Malfoy), and could relate to their adolescent conflicts and desires. The reason horror fans still rave about Jack Ketchum's, *The Girl Next Door,* isn't because they're into sadism or torture. It's because they bled along with that poor girl tied up in her neighbor's basement. They felt her terror and pain.

Connecting with a character on an emotional level—revulsion counts here, too—is perhaps the single most important criteria for a successful story, one that readers will remember and talk about for years to follow. Like most things, however, it's easier said than done. Let's learn how.

Pull From Experience

Write what you know. This applies to the landscape of human emotion as well. As a writer, you are likely more sensitive than the average person. Maybe even painfully so. Writers are notorious for being both empathetic and observant. Not only do you see details that others miss, you often feel the joy and heartache of others more keenly as well. Laughter is contagious around you. You cry listening to old blues tunes. And, unfortunately, you have probably experienced some form of trauma in your formative years.

It's rare to meet a creative person who lacks a painful, or at least *interesting*, past. It's why most of us prefer to work alone. It drives our need to share from a safe distance.

Not all writers have to suffer for their creativity, mind you. But many do, if not most.

People are good at hiding how they feel. We keep things *bottled up*. Why do you think psychological therapy is a billion dollar industry? Because there's a big demand for help in healing our mental and emotional wellbeing. Because so many people don't know how to handle their pain.

All of us have experienced broken hearts. We've all desperately longed for something out of reach. We've been hurt physically and emotionally. We have the scars to prove it. No one gets through this world unscathed.

On the flipside, however, we have all smiled at something both simple and profound. We all experienced a tender and loving touch that made our skin prickle, tickled a baby's chubby cheeks, smelled puppy breath. We've all experienced a moment of such pure enjoyment it made time disappear, watching an engrossing movie or while surfing a wave. Despite our struggles, most of us would choose life over death if faced with the option. Because the potential for pleasure outweighs the reality of pain. We all want our shot at happiness.

It's important that writers spend time with their emotions. Observe them. Don't push them away. Consider what you're like when you're happy.

Say you just got a promotion at work. How does that feel? What do you do? Some people will treat themselves to a nice present, such as a new television, or an expensive dinner, or even a car. They've been working hard for this moment and appreciate the recognition. It motivates them to try even harder.

Others, however, will head in a more self-destructive direction. They'll go to the bar and pound drinks until they're blacked-out drunk. Maybe wind up in a fight. Maybe wind up in a stranger's bed with a worried wife at home. Because that blip of pleasure is too fleeting for their tastes, simply masking over a deeper level of dissatisfaction. Emotions are complex.

What does it feel like to fall in love? To stay in love? For the fires of passion to mellow into radiant embers? To fall out of love? To be betrayed by your lover in the most obscene way?

Go into that place, no matter how much it hurts. That's where authentic connections with readers are made.

As writers, we must be open to the full spectrum of emotions. Not everyone is happy all the time; therefore, our characters cannot be either. Nor is anyone always angry and vengeful. Even the most sadistic killers enjoyed their first spoonful of ice cream, or taking a warm bath after coming in from the freezing cold. They have all had friends, even if they'd kill them without hesitation if it came to that. Someone loved them, if only their mother, and if only for a little while.

Catalogue your emotional states along with the thoughts and behaviors they induce. Sadness, mania, anger, boredom, silliness, frustration; this is your color palette. It should be vibrant and varied. Paint with your heart, not your mind.

Applying Emotion to Your Characters

There are various methods writers use in order to conceive a fully developed character. Character sketches. Mock interviews. Some will attempt a form of method acting, where they take on the persona of their character in real life (I've tried that one, and don't recommend it, ha!). Use whatever method allows you to fully visualize the extent of your character's appearance, personality, and temperament. A character's nuanced emotional state—or his emotional response to a situation—can be a bit trickier, though.

First, attempt to identify each character's overall purpose in life, and desire within the present moment. What fuels his or her heart and soul? Is she living her ideal life? If not, what is preventing her from doing so? What does he or she want or need to be happy, or free from suffering, and to what lengths is he willing to go to achieve it?

Each character should be driven by some fundamental desire or need within the overarching context of the story, and within each individual scene. This is what propels the story forward. It doesn't need to be something overly complex. It can be as simple as getting to work on time. Because today is the day of the big presentation to the firm's largest client, and Barbara's nervous—because that asshole Jon is gunning for her job—and she sweats when she's nervous, and drinks too much coffee, which only makes her sweat more, creating those unsightly armpit stains on her blouse. She knows she'll be lifting her arms to point at the presentation screen, so she takes the blouse off in her office in order to dry it off. That's when Jon barges in—that asshole who wants her job—and there she is, naked behind her bra.

Barbara's emotional disposition will inform how she reacts in this situation, not only driving her immediate physical actions, but coloring her internal state of mind as well. Does she allow the imposition to rattle her and sabotage the presentation? Does she shrug it off and rise to the occasion, nailing the presentation in Jon's smug face? Or is she more spiteful? Does she use this intrusion as an opportunity to frame Jon in an act of impropriety, eliminating her rival at the firm?

Oooh, I like that one.

Here's a prompt that can help uncover a person's emotional framework. Think of a character and consider the following: *This character is the type of person who would . . .*

What pops into your head first? Go with it. Follow it.

Roger is the type of guy who thinks he would run into a burning house to save a life, but when he's confronted with this very situation—alone in the wee hours of night on an empty street—what does he do when he hears a young girl's frantic screams and feels the searing heat of the flames. Does he think about his own little girl at home who would grow up without a father if the fire took him? How hard is his heart pounding as he stands there, watching the windows shatter and the support beams crack? Is he afraid, horrified, or bolstered by the courage he always knew was in him? How will he feel if he doesn't run in there and rescue her? How will he feel if he does, but not in time? What kind of scars, both physical and emotional, will the fire leave either way?

See how that one prompt helps uncover a character's emotional state, and establishes a premise for a story. Follow that trail and it might lead all the way to a novel.

Convey Emotion Through Observation and Action

1. Observations

Continuous descriptions of setting and action become tedious, weather, physical description, forward motion, yawn. Readers want to become immersed in the scene in which they're reading, and experience the fictionalized world from inside the character's skin. Many writers focus too much on what someone is doing, and ignore what they're thinking, how they're feeling, and how these internal conditions influence a character's outlook and behavior.

It's easier to show action than it is emotion. But the old adage, "show don't tell," applies to emotions as well. No one wants to hear about how someone is feeling. *Johnny woke up feeling sad* (and . . . we're skimming). They want to experience the sadness themselves. This requires immersing the reader in the mind and body of the character so that the reader sees and feels the world through the character's eyes and heart.

Let's say Johnny indeed wakes up feeling sad. How can we show that instead of say it? First, why is he sad? Maybe he had to put his canine buddy Roscoe down the day before. You can write something like:

Johnny awoke to a gloomy day without the

comforting weight of his old pal Roscoe pressing against his side.

Sure, that gets the point across. You can probably tell Johnny is sad and know why, but do you really *feel it*? Not so much. Let's try another approach that conveys Johnny's emotional state through his waking observations.

Johnny awoke and his cheek was dry for the first time in twelve years. Nothing was tugging at the covers, trying to wake him up at sunrise on a Saturday morning. Nuzzling his neck and making that chuffing sound that grew into a bark the longer his owner made him wait. Johnny opened his eyes and realized he could sleep all day if he wanted. But the bed now felt cold and inhospitable. The loft quiet.

A strand of Roscoe's dark fur was caught in his mouth, so at least that hadn't changed. He knew he'd have to take a lint roller to the covers at some point, and vacuum the lingering hairballs from the floor, but wasn't quite ready for that. Then there would be nothing left of Roscoe but memories, and memories fade with time.

Okay, perhaps that wouldn't make the final cut, but at least it's beginning to impart some feeling, some heart. That's because we're experiencing Johnny's emotional state through the lens of his wounded perspective. The absence of Roscoe is like a black hole that has invaded his home, sapping it of hospitality and warmth. He's clinging to the past, trying to hold onto something that's already gone. We don't have to say he's sad, you can sense it through his thoughts and observations.

When you're in a good mood you are more apt to

focus on the positive. You're happy when the phone rings. More willing to chat with the barista taking your coffee order. More inclined to see the sun through the clouds or smile at a stranger on the street. You're also more apt to be in the present moment, focusing on the things right in front of you. Maybe even things you never noticed before.

Susan thought she'd heard music on this street before, but never realized it was coming from a three-piece jazz band playing under the bridge until today. The sound had always been muted in the background as she hurried by, her eyes tracking the shadow stretched forward at her feet. Like it was leading her. But today the sun was on her face—the shadow stretched behind—and Alex was just now coming into sight up ahead. Oh, God. Was he holding a bouquet of roses? Her cheeks burned with embarrassment, but her smile gleamed.

One rule of thumb is this, if you're not feeling the emotion you're trying to apply to a character during a particular scene, your reader probably won't either. If it's a joyous scene, you should work to infuse your character with such joy you're smiling yourself. Just reading it makes you feel happy. Same if they're angry or sad. You'll know you're doing it right if your heart is pounding or you feel like crying.

2. Actions

What comes first, action or emotion? Who cares, just make sure one informs the other. Would you punch someone in the face if you weren't uncontrollably upset?

I hope not.

Slit someone's throat?

I *seriously* hope not.

Actions are more believable, and more compelling, when they come from a well-established emotional conflict. We want to see what drives someone to murder. Insanity is insufficient. Even the most psychopathic serial killers experience emotional distress as they wrestle with the decision to fulfill their dark urge. Most of them were abused as a child, or experienced major trauma early in life.

There are no robotic humans. No evil monsters devoid of any emotion at all. If you want your character to act in extreme ways, it should be accompanied by an equal measure of internal conflict. Doing so not only helps your readers form a stronger connection to your character, it helps to suspend disbelief as well.

Readers are more likely to accept a supernatural monster if they can relate to the real world in which the character exists. If you want to go even further, find a way to form an emotional connection to the supernatural monster.

What emotions motivate it? Hunger? Okay, yeah, but what else? Give us more.

Trey Parker and Matt Stone, the creators of the animated series, *South Park*, presented a story formula that I feel applies to the interplay between emotion and action. Imagine you have a sequence of scenes. If you can put the words "And then" between those scenes, you're screwed. What you would rather have is, "*Therefore* and *but then*."

The first example goes as follows: This happens

and then this happens *and then* this happens. See, pretty boring.

Here's the better method: This happens *and therefore* this happens *but then* this happens *and therefore* this happens.

People often act to change how they feel. They're sad, so they do something to make themselves feel better, like book a vacation. Or they're sad so they do something to make someone else feel worse, like have sex with a friend's significant other. Emotions trigger actions that change emotions, and so on and so on.

For example: Gary hears a strange noise in his house *and therefore* he's scared *but then* he remembers the gun he bought last year to protect his home from invaders *and therefore* he is now armed and ready to confront the intruder *but then* the lights go out, turning the intruder into an indistinguishable dark shape *and therefore* he's even more frightened now in the dark, so he shoots without warning, striking the intruder *but then* he hears his daughter's voice cry out. He wasn't expecting her home from her trip for another several days. And now she's dead; he's killed her *and therefore* he turns the gun on himself.

Don't think you have to constantly show a character's ever-changing emotional state like one of those Tragedy and Comedy masks. Just be mindful of how a character should be feeling throughout the story and how that might change over time or by circumstance. Stay inside the character as much as you can. Step too far outside and readers will begin to feel distant. Like they're watching a puppet show.

Summary

You want your reader to care about your characters, even if you plan to put them in horrible situations, especially if you plan to put them in horrible situations. The best way to get them to care is by creating sympathy through an emotional connection. Don't be afraid to go where it hurts. What's horror without pain?

VIRTUE & VILLAINY: THE IMPORTANCE OF CHARACTER

KEALAN PATRICK BURKE

SHORTLY AFTER THE publication of my novel, *Kin*, a story about heinous people doing heinous things in the backwoods of Alabama, I started getting a disproportionate amount of email from readers expressing sadness that one character hadn't ended up with another specific character at the end. Nothing unusual there, you might say. Except in this case, it's very strange indeed. Luke Merrill, the character to whom these readers referred, starts the book off as one of the antagonists. He's a hunter, defiler, eater of human flesh.

When we meet him, he's stalking the lone survivor, Claire, tracking her path as she tries to get away. He does this because he has been raised this way, bound by the warped doctrine instilled in him by his parents that marks everyone but the family as a threat, a "sinner", interlopers who must be killed and devoured for the sake of the clan. Claire escapes, and Luke returns to his family emptyhanded, and with burgeoning doubt about the principles he had been instructed to follow for so long. This is the point at which Luke begins his path to (a kind of) redemption.

I won't say much more about the plot here, but what I can tell you is that Luke has done some horrendous things. For years he has butchered those whose misfortune led them across his path. He was implicit in Claire's horror show before she manages to escape. These characters never come face-to-face again in the book, and yet a veritable legion of readers all said the same thing, "I wish Luke and Claire had somehow found each other."

On some level, I can kind of understand this need. Wouldn't it have been nice if those who suffered most found solace in each other? And make no mistake, by the time the story is done, Luke suffers plenty, but it doesn't change the fact that he was also instrumental in Claire's suffering as well as in the suffering of countless others.

Why then, does he get a pass? What was it about him that made readers willing to reward him with love and forgive his monstrous transgressions?

The simplest answer is of course, his character. Luke is not just some mindless killing machine hell-bent on causing misery wherever he goes. In fact, we get the sense that his family's methods have never sat well with him, but his fear of them kept him loyal. On the one occasion in which natural pubescent longing moved him to violate their tenets, they mutilated him. Thus, he was governed by his terror of them ever after.

The letters I received suggested the reader would have liked to have seen some Stockholm syndrome action here, the victim and her tormentor reunited in love, and the idea of such a thing never occurred to me.

That, for me, would have pushed this book into the realm of the exploitative and even further down the path of tastelessness. Plus, it just made no sense to me in the context of the story. But it seemed to make sense to the reader. So again: why?

As a writer, you live for these kinds of reactions, even—and sometimes, *especially*—if they're not the reactions you expected. Despite being baffled by this yearning for bad guy and good girl to ride off into the sunset together at the end, the main takeaway for me from this correspondence is that I succeeded in my overarching goal when writing the novel in the first place, which was to make every character, both good and bad, complex and three-dimensional. I didn't want everything to be cut and dried. I wanted you to be horrified to find yourself empathizing with monsters.

How, then, do you accomplish this? It's not hard. You must stop thinking of the villain as *the villain*, prone to sneering, long-winded monologues, and mustache-twirling, and look at them as normal, like what they're doing makes absolute sense, even if it's appalling. Because it makes sense to *them*. They must be human, even if they're monsters, because I don't believe anyone truly ever *sets out* to be evil. (One imagines a bad guy at the breakfast table, staring off into space as he eats his bowl of Raisin Bran, thinking of all the ways in which he's going to fuck up the world today.)

Luke certainly didn't.

Very early he found himself in love, surely the most innocent (and most complicated) emotion. Then it was taken away from him in punishment, and he was introduced early to the kind of darkness so prevalent in the world. His choice then became kill or be killed, and who among us, when faced with such a choice, would volunteer our throats to the knife as a moral protest?

He goes along with it because he must. He becomes numb to the horror, knowing that if he resists, it will result in his undoing. He is terrified of his family. They will kill him if he strays, but when the opportunity to rebel finally presents itself, he takes it, because there has been good in him all along. A *warped* kind of good (he's not doing this for anyone but himself), but good nonetheless.

Luke simply doesn't want to be trapped by his family, or trapped by himself, anymore. The weight of his soul, ultimately, goes unmeasured. He lives in a grey area, where he will stay no matter where he finds himself, or with whom.

Readers felt sympathy for Luke, and that's what I wanted, and I believe they did so, despite what he'd done, because he, as the best villains do, reminds us of ourselves. Sure, most of us are lucky enough not to have been raised by religious zealots who hunt and murder passersby, but who among us has not been afraid of our parents? Who hasn't rebelled? Who hasn't felt confused by our feelings? Who hasn't lost someone, or had their heart shattered into a million pieces by someone we loved? Who hasn't been raised by parents who want you to live a certain way and express dismay when you resist? Who hasn't either embraced religion or abandoned it and felt their life change as a result? And who among us, if the day ever came, wouldn't do horrible things if it meant the difference between life or death?

So yes, Luke is a villain. There's no question about this. Any shreds of decency do not outweigh his sins. But he's also *us*. He's human. And being human means being imperfect, troubled, perhaps doomed by your own poor choices.

He wants to be better, wants to stop, and this creates a conflict both within his family and in himself. He was bred to be a killer. Even if he escapes, can he ever really claim he isn't one after everything he's done? It's a complicated situation, which makes for an interesting character. If we can see ourselves in him, it humanizes him. We are appalled to find ourselves relating in any way to such a monster, but we do so because we know how easy it can be for good people to go bad.

The basic premise of *Kin* is a question: What becomes of the survivor of *The Texas Chainsaw Massacre* after she drives away from the horror? What's waiting at home after what she's been through? As an audience, we're relieved, happy for her. She escaped, yay!

Who doesn't like a happy ending?

Except, if you think about it, *really* think beyond the endings of stories such as these (*Chainsaw*, *Wrong Turn*, *Deliverance*), what would life be like for such a survivor when they get back to the world? We have breathed a sigh of relief for someone who watched her close friends die in unspeakable ways. She may even have been chased by a mumbling lunatic wearing the flesh from her dead lover's face. This poor soul is not going to be back at work on Monday morning, quirkily discussing with her fellow employees her narrow brush with death.

No, she'll likely be in the hospital for a long time. Once she recovers physically, she will likely need therapy, at best medication, at worst, institutionalization. She will not sleep for the foreseeable future, and when she does, she will replay the events of that awful encounter over and over again, only this time she won't survive it. She will see the faces of her dead friends in the grief in their parents' eyes. She will be a reminder to them of all they've lost, and so she won't be welcome around them anymore. Those grief-stricken people will be glad for her survival, eventually, but for a long time there will be the unspoken accusation in their faces that asks why *she* survived and not their child?

In terms of creating character, it's important to ask yourself these questions. What would *you* do if you were in Luke's situation? Realistically, what would life be like *for you* if you survived an atrocity like the one that kickstarts *Kin*, or that you've seen in the aforementioned movies? The escape is important, but so too is the aftermath. So too is *who* such events make you become, the transformation, how your experiences alter who you are, and how they change you.

It's not enough to have a character faced with a conflict and to document how they do or do not achieve their goals. The reader must care about the character, must know who they are if there's to be any investment in the outcome. And sure, you can get away with having your badass take down a legion of malcontents while cracking wise and flying their jet aircraft into the Namibian sunset and it could still be a good book. There's certainly a need for those kinds of no-muss, no-fuss what-you-see-is-what-you-get type potboilers. I enjoy them myself on occasion! But we're here to talk about character, and a *memorable* character needs to be more than what they can do with a katana and a sex swing.

We need to know *who* they are, and *why* they are that way. If you've ever found yourself asking yourself that question: who am I and why am I this way? you already know what it takes to create a realistic character.

Perhaps my proclivity for dark themes explains why I have focused a lot here on villains and villainy, but the very same rules apply no matter whether the character in question is good or evil. Your character's response, the feelings and emotions which dictate their reactions, require just as much of you to make it believable. Take this scenario, for example:

You are walking down the street one day when a car mounts the curb, cutting you off. The door flies open and a gunman in a ski mask steps out. He points his gun in your face. I think it's safe to say we would all experience great terror in that moment.

You might raise your hands and beg for your life. I know I would. I would tell them to take my money, or to please not hurt me. I would think I was probably going to die, and would already be wondering if I would feel any pain. Then worse, I would wonder if the gunman was not going to shoot me, but instead take me as a hostage and bring me somewhere to do even worse things to me. I would hope someone was seeing this and might intervene, but the one woman I saw seeing this, ran. I might think of my mother or my girlfriend or my dog and begin to grieve the life I was going to lose and maybe had never fully appreciated.

Now let's move to the gunman.

We look at him and notice two things that completely alter his character and the tone of the scene, while raising all manner of delicious questions: 1.) his hand is shaking; and, 2.) there are tears in his eyes.

This introduces an element of hope and tragedy to the scene but also makes us ask what brought the gunman, and you, to this moment where the paths converged. It makes the scene interesting in ways that make you and the reader find out how we got where we are.

And that's the crux of it.

We are all walking puzzle boxes, a composite of our experiences to date: the joy, the heartbreak, the love, the hate, the light and the dark. We each have questions, always the questions that dog our every choice, every decision, every action.

You should ask the same questions of your characters.

Who are they?

And why?

Because you can build a good book on the answers.

ELEMENTS OF STORY:
THE HORROR EDITION

MERCEDES M. YARDLEY

So YOU WANT to write a story. Not just any story, but a horror story. Something wrenching and gutting and wonderful and perhaps whimsical and full of emotion and demons and rot. Or however you choose your horror story to be.

The beautiful thing about horror is that it's subjective. We're not all scared by the same things. Gross body horror most likely wouldn't faze a nurse or paramedic, for example. They see blood and guts on a daily basis, and to them, it's a story about just another Tuesday at work. Ghost stories might not scare those who don't entertain the idea of ghosts. A story about demons wouldn't frighten a person who doesn't believe in gods or demons or anything paranormal. To them, it might be a tale of undiagnosed mental illness.

If there aren't any universal scares, how do you write a story that will touch your readers? It isn't as easy as "insert clowns/crows/serial killers/cruel mothers/scary ghosts/ here and watch the screams roll." But there are so many things that we, as readers and human beings, all identify with. We all know what it's like to be scared. We all understand being alone when we don't want to be. Perhaps we aren't specifically afraid of the dark, per se, but we have all, at one time or another, been lost, or couldn't find our way, or were nervous about a situation or a future that we couldn't predict. The way to create a story that instills tension and dread in your readers is to focus on the similarities that we all experience as humans, and to do our best to strengthen the story itself.

As a writer, you're most likely familiar with the five elements of story. Perhaps you've faithfully filled out a diagram in English class. Perhaps you're rolling your eyes and tuning out simply because I mentioned it.

"Elements of story sounds like work!" you cry. "I'm not reading this book in order to get a class lecture. I'm here to make this pertain to me and my lust for filthy, filthy horror. Mwa ha ha ha ha!"

Perfect. If you are deeply sighing as you read this, then you are the perfect reader for this essay. Because I deeply sigh when I hear about story elements. I don't want to write to a certain format. I want to write deeply from the soul! I want things to be as fresh and exhilarating for me as they are for the reader! Writing is supposed to be joy, yes? Don't weigh us down with homework.

You will find, as you write, that you're most likely hitting all of these markers naturally. But let's go over them, especially as they apply to a horror story, since this is what we're aiming for. Your bloodlust is beautiful, by the way.

Characters. For me, personally, this is where my story begins. Some authors are analytical and start with a carefully constructed plot. I admire that to the moon and back, but that isn't how my brain works. This is okay. Whether you are a plotter or a pantster, you are doing it exactly right. Whatever works for you is the best thing. It doesn't matter how you do it as long as you make your characters real. Who exactly is taking the journey? What do they want? Because, oh, they *want*.

They want love, or they want revenge. They want to bring their child safely home, or go after their little girl's murderer. They want to be part of a family. They want to be alone. They want to atone for your sins or sup directly from the roaring vein in your throat. The entire story is based on their ferocious want.

Describe them so the reader can see them. You can be as detailed or as vague as you want. "She was a tall, muscled woman with red hair and golden eyes that burned with hellfire." "He was a man without a face." The reader will conjure up their own vision of your characters, not to worry. However you choose to guide them is completely up to you.

These characters need to do something. They can't simply stand around in the ether looking pretty or hideous, as they case may be. What are they doing? In fact, where are they? That leads us to . . .

Setting. Where does the story take place? Is it on earth? Is it in Hell? Is it in an old house, on a different planet, in a storm drain, inside somebody's head? What does that look like? What does that smell like? Your lovingly-crafted characters need a frontier to interact with and move around on. Do they clamber over rocks? Are they floating around in space? Does the entire thing take place under the sea? The setting is important because that changes the flavor of your entire story. Think of Romeo and Juliet. We're all familiar with this tale. How would it be different if it didn't take place in Italy, but rather in Dracula's castle? In a sterile laboratory? What if Romeo was a patient in a cold, dark asylum and Juliet was the daughter of the head doctor? What if they met up in a post-apocalyptic world where the forests were made of meat? Same story, but distinctly different flavors. The change of setting doesn't alter the fundamental story of two star-crossed lovers, but it certainly changes everything else.

Plot. Plot is the actual story being told. We agonize over plot. Plot makes us bash our heads against the wall. It's easy to become hung up on the intricacies of what we want to do. However, when you boil it down, plot tends to be quite simple. For example: "A girl is taken by otherworldly beings." That is the plot to Poltergeist, one of my favorite films. Oh, there's more that goes on than that. There are terrifying trees that try to eat kids and static-filled televisions and ancient burial grounds and a family that calls in the cavalry to fight something they don't understand. There's nuance and memorable characters and terror. But the basic plot is simple. Discover your plot. What are the basic bones of your story? You will add the bells and whistles when you add in details. Your characters and their fun little quirks will add layers and nuance. Setting will make your story lush and full. And don't forget what really makes your story sing! (Or howl horrifically, as the case may be.) That would be . . .

Conflict. Oh, conflict is what makes your heart hurt. As an author, you need to do things to your characters to break them in any way possible. This pertains to stores written in the romance and thriller genre as well, but especially in horror. Horror is created to make us *feel*. Whether it's fear, dread, relief, anger, or any other emotion, horror is particularly good at wringing it out of us. Have you ever walked out of a movie with your heart tight, hands trembling, and your adrenaline running? Have you ever closed a book, put it on your bedside table, and then listened for every single creaky noise made in the dark? Your characters have the things that they want. Conflict is whatever tries to keep them away from those things. You can have large conflicts, like the monster that stalks the character and tries to eat their souls, or small conflicts that build up over time, like the car that never starts so the character misses that important meeting. You definitely want one huge main conflict, like the shark in Jaws who gets in the way of people having a great swim. Then pepper in the other smaller conflicts. The stupid, greedy mayor, the need for a bigger boat, the people who won't believe there is really a problem. Conflict is exciting. Right before the end of the story, during the climax, there needs to be an ultimate showdown where the main conflict is faced head-on. Then you will hit the . . .

Resolution. Oh, glory be, the resolution. This is where the conflict is solved and your heart rate can slowly go back down to a sustainable level. Resolution doesn't mean that things have to be wrapped up 100% neatly, and it certainly doesn't mean that the problem has to be solved in a pert, coming-up-daisies manner. Sometimes the favorite character dies. Sometimes in stories, just like life, the bad guys win. Sometimes monsters are real and no matter how you fight, you can't stand against them.

But that is a different essay for a different time.

Romeo and Juliet both die. The shark-infested waters are safe, at least for now. While things never completely return back to normal in the story, and you don't want them to, because that would invalidate all of the character's growth, there is a period where everyone can sit on the grass and take a deep breath.

At least for a while, because if horror has taught us everything, it's that monsters always return. Make way for the sequel, because horrors never die.

I'd delighted you're writing in this genre. There's a dignity to horror that isn't often explored, and we can always use more authors littering bones across this wondrous backdrop. Best of luck to you, my friend. Make us scream.

"DON'T LOOK NOW, THERE'S A HEAD IN THAT BOX!" SHE EJACULATED LOUDLY

Creating Effective Dialogue in Horror Fiction

ELIZABETH MASSIE

I'VE HAD THE pleasure of presenting creative writing workshops over the last 25 years, working with writers as young as ten and those as old as, well, people who have been retired a good fifteen years or more. During my programs, we get down to the nitty-gritty of fiction, the barebones of story creation. And one primary focus during these sessions is the development of characters.

In its simplest terms, a story can be defined as a problem and a solution or attempted solution. Fiction depends on the presence of a problem or issue that needs to be addressed, be the problem or issue huge or minor. Every short story, every novel, every play or movie or television drama is built around a problem or problems, both large and small. In Joan Aiken's chilling short story, *Marmalade Wine*, Roger Blacker—a man "given to exaggeration"—lets bragging and strong drink snare him in an inescapable trap. In

Gaston Leroux's dark novel, *Phantom of the Opera*, Christine Daae is abducted by Erik, the Phantom, and held in his gloomy underground chamber. The Broadway musical, *Little Shop of Horrors* (as well as the non-musical film on which the play is based), has our hero Seymour making a big boo-boo by bringing a flesh-eating, alien plant into his uncle's flower shop. Cleopatra, the trapeze artist of Tod Browning's film *Freaks*, decides to seduce, marry, and then poison Hans in order to inherit his wealth when he's dead. Walt White of *Breaking Bad* faces the specter of terminal cancer and decides to make money for his family by creating and distributing "quality meth" ('cause what could possibly go wrong?) Even the simplest children's story will feature at least one problem for the characters to tackle. Because if there is no problem or issue, you don't have a story. Rather, you have a vignette, scenario, or fictional "slice of life." And without characters, there is no problem.

A friend of mine who has a PhD in malacology, explained to me that, scientifically speaking, something is not a problem until someone experiences and/or defines it as a problem. For example, a tornado is not a problem; it just *is*. It only becomes a problem when defined as such by those who experience it. An earthquake is not a problem; it just *is*. It only becomes a problem when defined as such by those who experience it. A strange sound in an attic or a shambling zombie aren't problems; they just *are*. They only become problems when defined as such by those who experience them in one way or another.

And so, as writers of fiction, we must create characters who experience, define, and then deal with problems. As writers of horror fiction in particular, we create characters that are shoved headlong into terrifying, bizarre, or cringe-worthy situations jam-packed with problems or issues they then must solve, attempt to solve, or try their best to avoid altogether. Sometimes our characters are successful. Sometimes they fail miserably.

As many of us know, horror fiction is sometimes thought of as less than literary. Without checking to see if they are right, there are those who assume horror is all human centipedes and buckets of bloody intestines, with poorly imagined plots and no genuine character development. While we'll never convince some people, it should still be our goal to write the best fiction we can write.

What has this got to do with creating dialogue? So glad you asked.

In order to write fiction that rises above the schlock, our characters must be realistically imagined and realistically drawn. It doesn't matter if the character is a sweet young thing, a streetwise thug, a self-confident trucker-gal, a smooth and seductive vampire, a sociopathic serial killer, a mild-mannered waiter, or a plague-infected granny. We must get into their skins, get to know them, and then share who they are with readers.

Basically there are four ways a reader gets to know a character. It's done through:

1. What the character says
2. What the character thinks
3. What the character does
4. How others respond to the character

Which leads us to dialogue.

There are two kinds of dialogue—external and internal. External dialogue is the spoken word. It can be someone talking aloud to herself or himself or speaking with someone else. Internal dialogue is thought, which is another topic for another time.

Well-written external dialogue (which I'll just call dialogue from here on) serves very important purposes. It should help define the problem or issues characters will face. It should reveal a character's personality as well as how a character wants to be perceived. It should show us how a character relates to other characters. Dialogue should serve to advance the plot as a character muses or discusses what's going on with others involved. Well-crafted dialogue brings your characters to life and can endear them to your readers or make your readers hate their living guts. Both of which are great goals!

Poorly written dialogue, however, can throw a reader right out of the story and in search of something else to spend their time on. And horror fiction can be a breeding ground for some of the worst dialogue around.

Here are some things to keep in mind when deciding what your characters are going to say.

1. Dialogue shouldn't serve as unnecessary exposition.

In the remake of the film *The Wicker Man*, the hapless Edward Malus (played by Nicholas Cage) is tortured by having his head stuck in a small cage (cage for a Cage?) that is filled with angry bees. He screams:

"Oh, no! Not the bees! Not the bees! Aaaaaahhh! Oh, they're in my eyes! My eyes! Aaahhh!" Seriously, we see the bees. We see that they're all over his eyes. Edward doesn't need to tell us that. In fact, it makes the scene a bit ridiculous. If it were me with a bee cage on my head—or just about any other normal person with a bee cage on her or his head—there would probably be screams and not much more. The last thing I would do would be to speak or yell coherent sentences that explained what is happening to me. It's like writing, "Oh, no, the shark is eating me alive!" In cases like the bees and the shark, dialogue is not necessary. Just let 'em shriek.

Another example involves a novella I read a while back. I found instances in which the characters spoke as if they were detached narrators rather than taking an active role in the story. They weren't in the immediate peril that our hero Nick/Edward was, but they were certainly facing danger. Here's one bit of the dialogue:

"There's the zombie! Oh, my God, he's coming for us really fast!" says one character. Now, if a zombie was heading my way, I wouldn't take the time to explain what was happening, I'd get the hell out of Dodge. As a writer, I should describe the zombie's fast approach rather than making a character point it out verbally. My character would react instead of explain, such as shouting, "Shit! Run!" Or the character might not say anything at all but would be rendered speechless in his or her terror.

What can also be effective in a scene when characters are facing danger is a rambling, panicked commentary. He or she isn't narrating the situation but is realistically reacting. Imagine a terrorist has exploded a bomb in an apartment complex, a fire is raging, and there is the chance another bomb will be going off any moment. A character might say, "Jane, we've got to leave! Stop standing there! Move! Now! I swear, I'll kill you if you don't hurry!" If this was Jane's father speaking, he probably didn't mean what he said about killing her (unless you made him that kind of character.) But terrified people sometimes say things they wouldn't ordinarily say. And the brief, choppy exclamations are effective in revealing that character's terror. They mimic the shortness of breath that comes with fear.

2. Dialogue should move forward and not linger on the benign.

If you were writing a gentle love story, you might let your characters chat a bit more about how they spent their day, what they were looking forward to in the next week, how delicious the food is at the restaurant where they go on their date. But you're not writing romance, you're writing horror. Not only can dialogue about the day-to-day get tedious fast but it does nothing to advance your story. Say your story features a demon living amid the storage boxes in the garage of a family's new home. The family is in the kitchen, just prior to hearing the first snarling noises:

"How's your breakfast, Ricky?" asked Rachel.

Five-year-old Ricky shrugged. "It's okay, Mom."

"Pass the orange juice, please." Rachel reached out toward her husband, Richard.

"Sure, here," said Richard. He slid the container of juice across the table.

"I'm going to put the clothes in the dryer before I leave for work," said Rachel as she poured a cup of juice. "I don't like them staying damp all day long."

"Me either," said Richard.

Ricky looked under the table. "My shoe's untied. Someone tie it for me."

"Okay," said Richard. He leaned under the table to tie Ricky's shoe.

"Do you think it's going to rain today?" asked Rachel.

"I don't know," said Richard, sitting up again. "I can check my iPad and see."

"My neck itches," said Ricky.

Rachel speared a chunk of fried egg. "Then scratch it."

"Okay," said Ricky.

"I like your tie, Richard," said Rachel." Is that the one my mom gave you for your birthday?"

"Yes, it is. Nice colors, aren't they?"

"They sure are. The blue looks good on you."

"And I like your dress. Green compliments your eyes."

"Thanks, Richard."

"Do you like my shoes?" asked Ricky.

And on and on and on. A few bits of dialogue like this can certainly let a reader know that you have an ordinary family. But somewhere, in the midst of the above verbal exchange, the family should have heard something in the garage, even if it's a peculiar squeak or scratching sound. Otherwise, the conversation does little to enhance the story and is as exciting as the fact that the family has recently done their laundry.

3. Dialogue can offer foreshadowing.

Looking back at the scenario in #2, the mention of the dryer could be just that, a mention, written for no reason other than it was something for a character to say. However, it might also serve as foreshadowing for something that will happen later. Perhaps the demon in the garage decides to move into the house and at some point, hapless Ricky opens the dryer to discover horrible, reptile-like eyes peering at him from the tangle of sheets and socks.

As you work your way through your story, and you get to a place where something frightening happens, you might consider going back and giving a character something to say that would have seemed innocuous at the time but later on plays into the story. The reader might think, *Hey, I remember Rachel mentioning the dryer.*

Using dialogue in this way can be very tricky, however. You don't want to tip your hand. Make sure whatever bit of conversational foreshadowing you give a character, it blends smoothly and unobtrusively into the scene and doesn't stick out like the proverbial sore thumb.

4. Consider opening your story or novel with a bit of dialogue.

Story stories and novels, horror in particular, should start with a scene that takes hold of readers' hearts and/or minds and pulls them in. That doesn't mean we have to see blood and guts in the first paragraph or page, but it does mean that as writers we shouldn't waste what is one of the most important parts of any piece of fiction—the beginning. Forget extensive scene setting (unless you are James Michener; he is one of the rare authors who can get away with it and besides, he didn't write horror).

Dialogue can serve as a powerful opening tool:

"I can't look," Karen said as she turned away from the burning building and leaned heavily against her car. "Whatever is there, whoever is there, I don't want to see and I don't want to know."

Starting a story with the above gives the reader information as well as interesting questions right out of the gate. Not only is a building burning, but Karen is seriously affected by it. There might be friends or family in that building. Or maybe Karen is a sensitive person who can't stand the thought of anyone being hurt or killed. Or maybe Karen has, herself, dealt with fires before.

You could add another character, speaking to Karen:

"I don't blame you," said Mark. "I'll drive you home."

In this case, Mark and Karen seem to have a good relationship.

Or:

"You wanted to see what a burning building was like up close and personal," said Mark. "And now you're wimping out, after all I've done for you. I should have known."

In this case, Mark and Karen's relationship is edgy, a bit creepy. But in both cases, the story starts off with dialogue that intrigues the reader as well as offers some initial insight into the characters.

5. Keep dialogue tags out of the way of what's being said.

A dialogue tag is that little word that indicates a character is speaking. Dialogue tags should be as non-intrusive as possible. More often than not, that unobtrusive word is "said" or "asked." Such as "Let's cross to the other side of the street!" Marnie said as she grabbed Blake's arm. Or "Do you really want to open that thing?" asked the man with the tiny black eyes.

Other dialogue tags can get in the way of what is actually said. They can become crutches that try to prop up weak dialogue or circumstance:

"You have no idea what it's like to lose everything!" Angela wailed.

Yes, Angela might be wailing. But by now we should know that Angela is wailing or feels like wailing. We've been reading about her. We know she's stressed to the point of wailing. This can be improved by describing Angela on the verge of tears, or already weeping, before putting those words in her mouth. In addition, a bit more can be said in that particular sentence:

"You have no idea what it's like to lose everything!" said Angela as she collapsed onto the sofa. Collapsing on the sofa shows us that she is feeling weak and overwhelmed.

It's best to lay off the dialogue tags such as "keened," "yowled," "screeched," "hissed," "bemoaned," and my personal non-favorite favorite, "ejaculated." I've even read the dialogue tag, "hissed," used when nothing the character said even remotely sounds hissy:

"Wait until tonight!" the bloodstained killer hissed.

Not a single "s" anywhere in that sentence. You just can't hiss without an "s" as my mama used to say. Well, she didn't say that, but you get the gist.

What's even more distracting is when dialogue tags are saddled with what I call "frilly" adverbs:

"Hurry up and lock the damn door!" she screeched forcefully.

"I'll never see Carol again," he whined pathetically.

"Do you have any idea what that thing was?" she inquired curiously.

"Leave me alone," he shrieked distraughtly.

Reading the above makes me think the writer was desperate or just overly in love with adverbs. He or she wanted to make *sure* the reader knows how the character is feeling. But if the writer had already captured the character in that desperate moment, had done a good job showing what was going on, the distracting excess wouldn't be necessary.

Yes, there are authors of great renown who say we should *never ever* use a dialogue tag other than said. I won't go quite that far. And yes, I'll confess to using a rare "whispered" or "shouted." But I do understand their reasoning, and 95% of the time I stick with "said" and "asked."

"The writer should strive to show, not tell, how a character is feeling, speaking, or behaving," Massie reminded herself as she wrote #5 of her article on horror dialogue.

6. Expanding a bit on dialogue tags, it's unnecessary to use a dialogue tag for each character if there are only two in a conversation.

This is a pretty basic idea. Check out this conversation:

"If we hide there, we'll probably be safe," said Kate, glancing up at the attic door.

"I can't climb," said Pete. "My leg's really screwed up."

"I'll help you," said Kate.

"I'm too heavy," said Pete.

"Can you lean on me?" asked Kate.

"No," said Pete. "You go up. I'll hide in the closet."

"Over my dead body!" said Kate.

"It might well be," said Pete.

We've been reading the saga of Kate and Pete. We know the two characters in the scene. We also know the problem they are facing: floodwaters infested with vicious, human flesh-eating fish has begun to fill the house. So once the speaking order has been established with just two lines, it doesn't take many brain cells to keep up with what Kate says and what Pete says.

7. Avoid over-used terms or phrases that have become cliché in horror fiction as well as in film.

Use such terms and phrases very, very sparingly, if at all. Sure, people often talk in clichés or over-used terms. And all you have to do is spend a half hour with teenagers to know that the word "like" is spoken nearly as often as they take breaths. Yet, if you peppered your fiction with a teenager saying "like" every fifth or sixth word, it would be annoying beyond measure. A tiny bit goes a long way.

In horror fiction, the following are considered cliché and overused. And while your characters might say any of the following . . .

"There's something out there!"
"Don't look now!"
"Did you hear that?"
"Did you see that?"
"Don't go in there!"
"What the hell is that?"
"Let's get out of here!"
"I think it's haunted!"
"I'm scared!"

. . . put those words in their mouths infrequently if at all. While the above phrases are examples of brief, choppy exclamations recommended in #1, try to find more creative yet realistic phrases that basically mean the same thing.

8. You don't need to recreate the mumbling or shrieking sounds that your monsters, creatures, ghouls, or zombies make.

Sure, it's a fun exercise trying to imagine the sound and then putting that sound in quotation marks to indicate your creature is speaking (of sorts.) But such sounds don't necessarily translate to something that reads well on the page. The following examples are a bit too bizarre for the human brain to interpret:

"Orughm!"

"Mrrrmph!"

"Groooeark!"

"Auffteee!"

Rather than trying to decipher what a creature actually "says," try describing the sound instead:

"The monster's mouth creaked open and a garbled wail cut the air."

"The zombie's growl was low and threatening."

Yes, horror is a genre of fiction that wants to grab the readers by the short hairs and shake them for all it's worth. After all, horror, defined, means "intense fear," "revulsion," "terror." Because of this, we want to up the ante and scare the crap out of our readers. We want to blow them out of the human flesh-eating fish-infested water.

Yet we are also craft persons. Artists. Wordsmiths. We imagine the terror—the problem or problems—and the characters who will be forced to face the terror. Then we proceed to tell the tale. Effective dialogue reveals how characters interact with others, how they define, relate to, and struggle with the terror, and how they survive, try to survive, or succumb. What our characters say, how they say it, and when they say it will help readers get to know the people in our stories and will move the story along to its appointed conclusion. And who knows? Maybe our characters will be those who linger in the minds of our readers long after the book has been closed.

POINT OF VIEW: ~~OFF~~ *ON* WITH THEIR HEADS!

LISA MANNETTI

Point of View: A particular attitude or way of considering a matter.
"I'm trying to get Matthew to change his point of view."

(in fictional writing) *the narrator's position in relation to the story being told.*
"This story is told from a child's point of view."

the position from which something or someone is observed.
"Certain aspects are not visible from a single point of view."
—*Dictionary.com*

"My name is Alice, so please your Majesty,' said Alice very politely; but she added, to herself, 'Why, they're only a pack of cards, after all. I needn't be afraid of them!'"
—Lewis Carroll,
Alice's Adventures in Wonderland

WE **ALL KNOW** the Queen of Hearts keeps insisting that anyone who displeases her in the slightest way—or, in fact, for no reason at all, needs a damn good and immediate corrective: beheading. And as far as the Red Queen is concerned, that's a sight too good for most of them, thank you very much.

How do we know what her Red Majesty, and the characters around her (especially Alice) are thinking? Because Carroll drops into the little girl's inner voice, her thoughts, which essentially sums up point of view. It's what your characters are thinking and feeling about their situations, about themselves, about other characters, about memories, about the ongoing action in a book or a story.

Most frequently, point of view is told from the protagonist's perspective, but not always; sometimes another character (like a camera) has more to tell us. Sound confusing? It doesn't have to be.

Think of the shower scene in Hitchcock's *Psycho*. We all know the power the camera (and Bernard Herrmann's incredible score) assume and how they influence us as viewers. Think of them both not just as observers and commentators, but real characters for a moment. I'm going to let that sink in for a bit, no pun intended.

If you analyze that scene, you'll notice that with the exception of the very few seconds the translucent plastic curtain is thrown back; not one shot is from the main character, Marion Crane's, point of view. We really only see what Hitch wants us to see and the details he lingers on include the shower head cascading water, the cut to the swirling bloody water and the drain, the jump cut to Janet Leigh's unseeing, deathly still open eye and the slower pan to the disregarded daily newspaper we already know she's hidden the remainder of the cash inside of.

As a writer, you have to be like the director in a film, showing the most effective point of view at all times. When you work up a scene, you're simultaneously author, character and reader, right? As the author you control all the action, like the director, as the character you're inside that person's head. Ex: Janet Leigh seeing the dark, frightening and unexpected outline of a knife-wielding woman's figure), as the reader (the film audience) your viewing the terrifying action all the way through.

So how do you know which is the best approach to take? How do you decide whose head you should put on and get into? How do you choose among first, second or third person, and in third person, are you going to have multiple points of view or just one, or an omniscient perspective, more like a camera or the gods than a personal angle?

We're going to look at the various ways to handle point of view and some of the advantages and disadvantages for each. The main thing for you is going to be keeping in mind what will most help your readers turn pages because of their interest in your characters, their voices and their situations. Which characters, in other words, can tell your story best, which techniques can not only increase the nightmare factor, but assist you in writing the best possible work both commercially and artistically.

The first thing to keep in mind is that you're never going to appeal to every reader. Occasionally, you'll even hear readers (some of whom are writers) say, "I just can't get into first person narratives. I see that *I*, and I shudder and I turn away."

Fair enough. It's a personal preference. On the other hand, one of my earliest reading experiences was, *Jane Eyre,* when I was about eight. I fell madly in love with Jane and the 19th century. That gave me a clue to my own work and writing process.

I believe it was that novel that first made me aware of voice, specifically a character's individual voice. We all know that Jane, even if she is narrating, does not sound (or think) like Edward Rochester, Mrs. Fairfax, Bessie, her obnoxious aunt, Mr. Brocklehurst, the beautiful Blanche Ingram or her powdered-up money-grubbing dowager of a mother.

When I write first person I find it very easy to immediately get inside my protagonist's head and to let him or her find the right nuance and cadence in language, dialogue, description or whatever's needed to advance character and plot.

One of the secrets I discovered pretty early on was that writing historical horror, as I often do, using first person allowed contemporary readers to slip more easily into those long-gone (except for the verisimilitude reproduced in books, movies and TV shows) time periods. While some readers find first person off-putting, for others it can offer one big advantage: many readers will subconsciously identify with first person, because that is how we think inside our own heads much of the time.

"I have to go to the bank. I have to get my hair done. I've got to get that next chapter down; I'm going to binge watch Ripper Street this weekend."

Does this really work?

I can't say it's an absolute, though I will say that of the two Bram Stoker Awards I've won and the other five of I've been nominated for over the years, only two pieces, both short stories, have been in third person. Both those were also historical horror, but one was about Lizzie Borden (a fairly well-known historical figure) "1925: A Fall River Halloween"; and one, "The Hunger Artist," took place in part in a courtroom and was more naturally suited to third person. So, that's five first person fictional works that resonated with my peers in the HWA and garnered their respect.

First person can let you as writer speak about oddities and strange or long gone worlds with more authority and more ease which creates a natural entry that feels real and vivid for your readers. Here's the opening paragraph for my novella, "The Box Jumper," nominated in the long fiction category for both a Bram Stoker and for a Shirley Jackson Award and winner of "Novella of the Year" from This is Horror in the U.K.

It was the children who brought Houdini back. The ones who were dead or missing. He never had any of his own, but he loved children— made sure there were always free performances at hospitals and orphanages. Once, in Edinburgh, he saw so many kids running barefoot through the streets he even bought 300 pairs of shoes for them and fitted them up at his benefit show at the Lyceum. That's the kind of man he was. He was magical all right. I loved him before I ever met him, back when I was just a kid myself.

The narrator in this case, Leona Derwatt, is what's known as an unreliable narrator. It's up to the reader to decide and (you as author to portray) how much of what she says is truth or lies or some odd twilight zone in between. Some tellers of tales deceive themselves, some deceive others. The device can be a tremendous aid to the writer and used to deliver plot (sneakily) and deftly. Some famous examples include Humbert Humbert in Nabokov's, *Lolita,* Du Maurier's title character, *Rebecca,* and more recently, books like, *Fight Club,* by Chuck Palahniuk and, *Gone Girl,* by Gillian Flynn.

Just as in third person, some first person stories have a framing device, another character or series of events taking place as partial or outright prologue and ending, inside which the action is narrated. One powerful example that comes to mind is William Styron's *Sophie's Choice.* Stingo, young, naïve and trying to find his way both through life and as a writer, is the first person narrator.

The story he tells, and how it impacts not just him and his work, but the whole world, is the story of Sophie (and her lover, the brilliant but schizophrenic Nathan) and, most importantly Sophie's secrets and utter decimation as a prisoner in the Nazi death camp, Auschwitz. Frame stories (even in first person tales) can be extremely helpful. They can carry the action forward to the denouement (a device I used for *The Gentling Box* set in 19th Century Hungary and Romania) or allow the narrator to have the last word about the story he or she is telling to bring a satisfying resolution to the characters and the plot.

It's important to think about carrying your plot points all the way through, especially in first person, because when you use first person, your narrator is always going to be on stage. Information that he or she does not know or have the means to find out cannot appear or happen. While it's difficult to carry off, it can also be a fun and an inventive way to keep your character on his or her toes. Does he or she eavesdrop? Have a gossipy friend who tells all? Does she out and out spy on that husband she suspects of philandering? Maybe she finds a letter . . . maybe he reads her text messages. Maybe she takes out a huge insurance policy on Mr. Moneybags and he finds the policy . . .

When I wrote, *The Gentling Box,* I had Imre, the Romany protagonist, underneath a caravan looking up through the cracks in the wooden floorboards so that he could witness the secret ritual his wife performs in which she cuts off her own hand to make a charm she believes will save their child.

There are a lot of possibilities and as long as you're aware of what needs to be revealed and when (think of yourself as the C.I.A.: only reveal information to the reader on a need-to- know basis), you can get a lot of mileage out of your imagination and the situations you cook up. One of the most famous frame stories of more recent vintage is the device Anne Rice used in *Interview with the Vampire*. It's Louis's tale, but he tells it to the eager young reporter—and pretty much at the end, because it's so well told and she's created so much empathy, we all wind up feeling pretty much the same as he does when he declares, "Make *me* a vampire!"

Second person ("you") is pretty limited and to quote Styron it has "the effect of seizing the reader by the lapels." It can be very effective as in Robert Penn Warren's, *All the King's Men,* or more recently, Jay McInerney's, *Bright Lights, Big City.* Consistency of voice will be critical (get right into your character's head, pull on that mask and stay there) and be aware that you are addressing the reader directly and calling on him or her to closely follow every word and to agree on some level. Some readers may lose patience, others will follow your lead. Successfully carried out, it has as much of the crackling transformative power that characterizes the speech and stage presence of hypnotists, televangelists and cult leaders, so don't discount it.

Before we jump to third person, which is the point of view most often used by writers, there are a few other possibilities or special cases (and their genres) to consider, some of which can be applied no matter which perspective your book or story takes shape around.

The non-human point of view can also be powerful. Animals, aliens, shape-changing characters like werewolves or dybbuks, supernatural folk like wizards and fairies, those non-human creatures who may exist, those who've never existed and probably never will all play a part in literature. The key to carrying it off is going to be getting as deeply as possible into the voice of the character and giving him or her or it, in addition to their otherness, real human qualities that your reader can identify with. Think of the rabbits in, *Watership Down,* or the good-evil division that is inherent in each of us by nature and the experiment that Stevenson portrays in both plot and character in *Dr. Jekyll and Mr. Hyde.*

One of the most famous of all such creatures, Dracula, was limned by employing yet another literary device—the epistolary style—technically letters, but any type of written communication. Bram Stoker used letters, diaries, newspaper clippings, and even ship logs to great advantage to lend authenticity and a sense of reality in what otherwise could have been considered then too fantastic a story. As readers, we find ourselves suspending any sense of disbelief and falling under his sway. This book actually frightened me so much that when I read it as an adult in my late twenties I actually had to sleep with the lights on—not only that, I frequently imagined I heard bats flitting against my windows.

Wilkie Collins's mid-19th Century novels *The Woman in White* and *The Moonstone* are also written in epistolary form. Ditto the erotic *Fanny Hill* by John Cleland in 1748, and both the bestsellers *Pamela* and *Clarissa* by Samuel Richardson, also published in the 18th Century. As they say, "That was then."

So, is it a style that is too far out of fashion, too antiquated to appeal to the modern reader?

Not at all. Consider, *The Color Purple,* by Alice Walker (winner of both the Pulitzer Prize and the National Book Award), or Stephen King's supernatural, *Carrie* (structured with news clippings, letters and book excerpts), or, *World War Z: An Oral History of the Zombie War,* by Max Brooks which uses interviews with survivors to tell the story.

Certainly with modern technology it's possible now to write a contemporary epistolary novel or story that might contain email, text messages, IM chats, audio or video clips (or their descriptions), as well as author-conceived future forms of communication. In my opinion, if you as the writer have a horrific idea that will make readers shudder or wince or wring their hands in anxiety, and the time period or the plot cries out for an epistolary style, take the chance and go for it: you'll be in some very good company.

Some third person books have a single point of view. Since one of the chief goals of writing well is to communicate effectively and thoroughly, this can result in satisfying a reader and creating the illusion that he or she knows your character intimately. For example, a single point of view book like Stephen King's masterpiece, *Misery,* compels reader immersion and identification—at a very high level. We know the background history, circumstances and current situation (shit storm may be a more apt term) the protagonist, Paul Sheldon, is enmeshed in. We know his antagonist, Annie Wilkes, just as well as we know him through Paul's perspective, descriptions, the suffering he endures and the newspaper articles he finds about her checkered and criminal history. The single point of view was a brilliant choice for this particular book because Paul is literally trapped in Annie's house.

In this case, there was no need for King to write some chapters from Annie's perspective. Like Paul, we watch in horror and cringe as the tension ratchets up and Annie perpetrates more and more hideous, unbalanced, and tortuous acts.

There are times when you might want a few characters, or even many, to tell your story and this can be highly effective, too. Great examples include three of my favorite books by Peter Straub: *Ghost Story, The Hell Fire Club* and *Shadowland.* All of them are not only highly inventive in terms of plot and fraught with terror, they're populated by unique and fascinating characters.

On the very long book (i.e. epic or near-epic) side, let's take a look at King's, *The Stand,* and some of the reasons using multiple points of view in medium-sized and long books can be very advantageous. Although each of them faces the catastrophic and near-apocalyptic effects of the tube-neck flu, King is careful to immerse us into each character. We learn about their backgrounds, the circumstances they found themselves in preceding the epidemic's outbreak, during the disaster itself and, naturally, after most of the world's population is dead and gone.

As we follow the characters we're so engaged, just by switching to another character's point of view, King automatically creates tension for the reader. Directors do this all the time. Sometimes we're so caught up in the action, we may not even notice because at the same instant we feel slightly torn away from the character that has involved us so deeply, the story moves forward and we become equally mesmerized by what is happening to the new character and in the latest situation. You can easily see how that pulls readers and viewers along, especially if the author or director cuts away at a high point.

You'll be wondering just what happens to Larry as he leaves New York City and then find yourself pulled in by Franny's history with her boyfriend, her relationship with her father and her feelings when she has to bury him. Just as later on in the novel, King will integrate almost all the characters on the big stage out west in Colorado so that the strands come together, he also weaves in characters early on who will interact at the end of the book. So, for example, it never feels like a coincidence that Franny knows Harold.

As a general rule, the bigger and more complex the book, the more points of view the story can sustain.

What about the loftier omniscient narrator? Can that be effective for horror writing? Will it feel too distant, too artificial? Well, *The Haunting of Hill House,* by Shirley Jackson (a third person point of view book with an omniscient narrator) is not only considered by horror fans as one of the best literary haunted house tales of the 20th century, it was also a finalist for a National Book Award.

Laura Miller had this to say about Jackson's chilling novel: (*Literary Hub,* September 28, 2016).

What makes, *The Haunting of Hill House,* a great ghost story is that Jackson also sets a trap for her readers. Eleanor Vance, the young woman around whom the uncanny events of the novel constellate, is no mere snoop. She is drawn into this adventure, the narrator implies, by the house itself, and the terrible things that happen there emerge from and express her inner life. Eleanor is a genuine literary *character* rather than a device of the narrative. She is a complicated and distinctive individual, peculiar even, although not so peculiar that she fails to engage the reader's sympathy. We experience the novel from within Eleanor's consciousness, and however unreliable we know her to be, we are wedded to her.

Just what I've been advocating right along—character is crucial whether you use a single or multiple points of view and whatever person you're writing in. Without distinctive voices unique to your characters the reader will not be pulled in no matter how adventurous or exciting the action of your story or your book is. Character (and by extension, point of view) is not merely a tool, it's one of the most critical and important aspects of your fiction. Even as a horror writer, you still have to pace your work so you're going to want to make your readers cry or laugh at times; you're going to want them to feel deeply about the characters you've created and experience a full emotional range.

Anger toward nefarious villains, empathy for the vulnerable, terror over the situations the characters they care about are caught up in. Point of view, getting inside your characters' heads, is the most effective way to pull it off. Point of view can also help you flesh out characters so that, for example, the villain/antagonist also has redeeming and admirable qualities and your heroes display less than sterling behavior on occasion.

As you sit down to write or absently contemplate your next foray into the dark passages of fiction, you might come up with the idea or the situation first: perhaps one of those devilishly charming tiny persistently intruding thoughts like *what if there's this rabbit hole?* A rabbit hole, as we know, can really be *anything*: a haunted house; a virulent, deadly strain of the flu; an obsession with blood or scientific experiments; or a rabid number one fan. As soon as that intriguing thought pops into your head you're also bound to realize that a little girl like Alice falls down the rabbit hole, a mentally frail creature like Eleanor succumbs to the seductive allure of Hill House and poor Paul Sheldon is saved and imprisoned by his number one fan . . . in other words, your characters and their points of view will ultimately be the true engines of your tales.

Characters keep readers turning pages, characters

determine the success of your work. Try on their mindsets, plunge yourself straight into your characters' heads, and you'll find the quickest route to the best points of view for your particular piece.

Artwork by Luke Spooner

STRUCTURE OF
THE PLOT

WHAT CAME FIRST: THE MONSTER OR THE PLOT?

In Conversation with Stephen Graham Jones

VINCE A. LIAGUNO

STEPHEN GRAHAM JONES is one of the most distinct and consistent voices in horror to emerge in the 21st Century. With his 2000 debut, "The Fast Red Road: A Plainsong," (Fiction Collective 2)—a surreal deconstruction of the mythology and pop-culture image of the American Indian—it was clear that Jones had a unique way of viewing the world and an even more unique way of presenting it in words. After two more crime novels and, "Bleed into Me," (University of Nebraska Press, 2005)—an acclaimed book of short stories that offered an often-piercing insider look at the lives of Native peoples—Jones broke through to genre audiences with, "Demon Theory," (MacAdam/Cage) in 2006.

"Demon Theory," is a wildly ambitious experimental work of fiction—part novel, part screenplay—that used a cacophony of footnotes, film jargon, and pop culture references as the literary equivalents of pop-up videos. In my own 2007 review of the novel, I cautioned readers that, "Demon Theory," was a challenging anti-beach read:

Although Jones offers no easy mass-market thrill rides here, the payoffs are well worth the workout of little grey cells. The ingenuity of, "Demon Theory," is the true marvel at work here, presenting as the intellectual literary cousin of Wes Craven's, *Scream*, trilogy. This cerebral terror trip is made even more so by Jones's staunch refusal to lay his cards out on the table as to whether, "Demon Theory," is an application of intellectualism to the horror genre or tongue-in-cheek boyhood homage to a genre he clearly loves.

Since the critically-lauded, "Demon Theory," more novels and short story collections have followed, notably: "The Ones That Got Away," (Prime, 2010) "The Last Final Girl," (Lazy Fascist Press, 2012), "After the People Lights Have Gone Off" (Dark House Press, 2014), and "Mongrels," (HarperCollins Publishers, 2016). Jones has also become a master technician of the short form with chapbooks like, "The Elvis Room," (This Is Horror, 2014), novelettes like, "The Night Cyclist," (Tor Books, 2016), and novellas like, "Mapping the Interior," (Tor.com, 2017), which won the prestigious Bram Stoker Award for Superior Achievement in Long Fiction.

It's also unlikely that you'll pick up any quality genre anthology these days and *not* find something new from Stephen Graham Jones. He's become a mainstay in preeminent anthology editor Ellen Datlow's stable of reliable scribes, often appearing in her themed collections like "The Devil and the Deep: Horror Stories of the Deep," "Mad Hatters and March

Hares," "Black Feathers: Dark Avian Tales," "Nightmares: A New Decade of Modern Horror, Children of Lovecraft," "Monstrous," "The Doll Collection," and several editions of her esteemed, "The Best Horror of the Year." If such widespread inclusion in the Datlowverse isn't a sign of horror superstardom, I'm not quite sure what is.

I preface my conversation with Stephen Graham Jones with this detailed introduction to hammer home a point: Jones knows monsters. He's a pedigreed master of the genre and his relationship with monsters is intimate and intricate, both as fan and creator. When we sit down to chat, it's in a virtual space that I envision as the film set from some long-forgotten 80s slasher flick—think Garth Manor from, "Hell Night," or the unnamed Canadian manse in, "Curtains," since Jones and I share a longstanding affection for and encyclopedic knowledge of the subgenre. Both times we've worked together professionally, as editor and writer, were on slasher-themed or inspired projects. Jones contributed several essays to my 2011 non-fiction anthology, "Butcher Knives and Body Counts: Essays on the Formula, Frights, and Fun of the Slasher Film," (Dark Scribe Press, 2011) and created an original slasher villain named Kissyface for his contribution of the same name to, "Unspeakable Horror 2: Abominations of Desire," (Evil Jester Press, 2017).

We begin with the basics: Where do his ideas for a new short story or novel come from?

"Usually it's just something in my day-to-day that I . . . not so much stumble on as become aware of," he tells me.

He cited an example, a story called "Uncle" he wrote. He was selling his house and having a routine home inspection done. The home inspector had him tagging along, room to room. "So he could impart all this wisdom to me about how ovens worked and return-air stuff," Jones supposed.

It was neat, but it was neater just listening to him be superior about everything—I thought I was stealing a voice for a character, not a premise for a story, but then at one point in all that he pulled out this, *Star Trek*, phaser looking thing that shot an actual laser, and was, surprise, a thermometer. It was about the neatest thing I'd ever seen. He let me play with it a bit, and, playing with it, I wondered what it would mean if I stumbled onto a temperature variation that didn't make any sense, just in some random part of the room?

Next day I wrote, "Uncle," about a guy kind of gifted one of those thermometer guns, stumbling upon exactly the temperature variation I didn't want to find myself. Most stories I write that aren't solicited, that's how they happen. For the rest, editors call me up, give me the premise."

I asked Jones if he ever considers the fright-potential of a piece before sitting down to write, which he said he doesn't. "I just always assume that, once I get into this build, the dread and terror will be there, like always," he says. "Even when I try to write something not horror, things always still veer dark. I think some of us, that's just how we're wired."

For Jones, worrying that a story isn't scary enough is never an issue since he's a firm believer that the scariness of his work is rooted in character.

"If a piece isn't turning out as scary as I think it could be, I just interrogate the character. That's the first question I ask of a thing I'm writing: What is sacrosanct to this person? What matters more to them even more than living?

Then it's just my job to jeopardize that, to come up with some dramatic situation that puts them in a position where they must make a decision about what they really want, what they're willing to trade. But, too, I may finish all my horror stories for a more basic reason: self-preservation. Stopping a horror story partway through means a part of your mind will now forever be trapped there in that dark place. You won't get to process through to the daylight.

When I saw, "The Conjuring," in the theater, there was a mom and her daughter (I presume) and her daughter's friend in the row with me. The girls were maybe twelve. And I don't think the mom knew what she'd bought tickets for, so much. About two-thirds through the movie, when things are pretty dark and bloody and creepy, I was thinking maybe I didn't have the nerve for this, the mom finally decided that was enough and hustled those two girls out of there. I felt sorry for them, for that. They never came through to the other side and are forever locked in the bad place.

Which is to say, if I start a horror story and don't finish it, that's where I'd be as well, and I don't much want to be in the bad place."

That brings us to the meat and potatoes of our conversation. I asked Jones if he thought it was the monster or the plot that's more central to a story's overall success. I was curious to learn if Jones shapes a plot around the monster or a monster around the plot.

"The antagonist in any story kind of gives the story definition, for sure," he begins. "The story will be about the protagonist's arc and development and decisions, of course, but those are largely, at first, reactive. If not prompted by the monster, the hero just sits at home eating cereal, right? And why not. So . . . I think between the monster or the plot being the most central, I'd come down on the monster's side."

I raised my eyebrows, not because I think I've just heard Linda Blair screaming from beneath us in the catacombs running under Garth Manor but at Jones' decisiveness on this point. I asked him to elaborate.

"Because plot is always a chart you see after the fact, of the main character's decisions, and those decisions, they're precipitated by the monster," he says. "Plot is more a function of character—*characters*—than character is a function of plot, I'd say. Or, that's how it works in my head. Twenty years ago, though, I was plot, plot, plot . . . that was all that mattered. Until experience taught me otherwise."

Having established that the monster comes before the plot, we switched tacks a bit and discussed how suspension of disbelief in speculative fiction—horror especially—is key to eliciting reader buy-in. I asked Jones how conscious he is while in the act of writing of working around the more fantastical or surreal elements of a work to achieve the reader's willing suspension of disbelief and if he employed any tricks or tools of the trade or litmus tests to accomplish this.

"Yeah, if you want the reader to emotionally and intellectually invest in the drama of your story, they have to believe it's a real enough place that this is a safe investment, or, one that's going to pay them back for their attention, anyway. Which is to say, you must create and maintain a convincing reality. It can be a cartoon, of course, but it needs to be a convincing one. I am conscious of this while writing, definitely, and I think the way I usually try to leverage it is by locking the narration into one person's head. That character will be resisting all this, but there's a tip-over point at which it all finally becomes real and undeniable to them. If I've gotten the reader to engage enough with the character going through that, then that tip-over will happen for them—the reader—there as well."

I asked Jones to take off his writer's hat for a moment and share with me what qualities or elements he finds—as a reader—the most effective monsters share.

"I like indifferent monsters the most, I think," he began. "I mean, Cthulhu, sure, he's so vast and cosmic and we're grains of sand in comparison. But, big and mean sharks too, right? They get can tee'd off at a certain person or group or place, but, really, they're just doing what they do. Or, what movie and novel sharks do, anyway.

My favorite monster of ever is China Miéville's Slake Moth, though. Those things are brutal, but beautiful too. They trance you out with their kaleidoscope wings, and then they inhale you with their sarlacc mouths. As for what elements I think are important, I think the most important is that monsters have to be bulletproof in some fashion. If not, then the military can just come in, wipe them out, story over. And that's boring. Monsters are best when we have to use our smart-monkey brains to outwit them."

Looking back on his own ever-growing catalog of

work, I asked Jones if his more effective monsters are reality-based or more fantastical incarnations.

"Reality-based, I think. Which probably says more to my ability and inability, really. But, when I someway have 'license' to go way out from the familiar, I tend to go way out to the edge of the believable, and then I expend all my energies trying to tether this unrecognizable creature to . . . something, and things spiral out of control a bit. At least to me. But, reality-based, yeah. The best of those I've done might be . . . William Colton Hughes, from, "The Least of my Scars?" But maybe he's just monstrous, an aberration. There's no tentacles or sharp teeth, any of that. I know: the gargoyle-things/demons/angels from, "Demon Theory." They're kind of off-the-shelf monsters. Very fun to use. Had a ball with them."

What are the key considerations Jones felt a writer should be cognizant of when creating either type of monster?

"I think one thing that's good to keep mind when writing monsters is to be sure to lock down that this story only works with this or these monsters. If you can lift the zombies, say, out, and replace them with locusts, or tornadoes, then your zombies aren't really part of the story. They're just the backdrop. And if this is trying to be that monster build we all know and love, where's it some Beowulf against some Grendel, then it's needs to definitely and only be Grendel. Or, you know, his mom."

Jones and I stayed focused on his own catalog of work for another round of discussion. This time, I asked him which of his monster creations has been his favorite to date—either reality-based or of the fantastical variety—and what is it about this particular monstrous creation that resonated with him as creator?

"I really liked the zombies from, "Zombie Bake-Off." I mean, because they're wrestler zombies infected by maggoty donuts, sure, with names like Graceland Elvis and Jonah the Whale, but, really, what made those zombies work for me was they had their own life-cycle. Well, species-cycle? So, the first generation, they're just brain eaters. But the second-gen, they're smarter, are nimble and fast. Then the third generation, they're—they're like the plants in *The Ruins*: they can kind of imitate a person. These were zombies I could believe in. These zombies, they were— they're an organism that's looking to the future, that has somewhere to go, and is taking steps to get there. Really, I think those zombies were kind of my model for the werewolves in *Mongrels*. What I needed there were creatures with their own biology and culture, and the reason I was able to maybe do that was that I'd already tried it once, with, "Zombie Bake-Off."

I ask Jones how important he thinks it is for writers to consider a monster's backstory—or is an intentional lack of backstory (i.e. Michael Myers in Carpenter's original, *Halloween*) more effective because we don't know origins of the evil?

"I think getting Francis Dolarhyde's long backstory in, *Red Dragon*, (the novel) took away a lot of his monstrousness, kind of just made him be another victim, yeah. A dangerous victim locked in a bad cycle, sure, but still a victim," Jones said. "I think overstating the monster's backstory," he continued, "can and usually leads to that. But? I also think you, the writer, need to know that backstory at the same time, in order to make the actions of this monster make sense, be of a system, of a person, of a single intelligence. Just, we don't need the whole iceberg. Just that pointy dangerous tip.

We can infer the rest. The only time I can think of where this has really worked for me would be Doomsday's origin story. Doomsday who killed Superman. How he's the result of so many cycles of natural selection—these scientists on some other planet throwing baby after baby into that inhospitable environment. Knowing that made this Doomsday we were seeing even worse, I think."

As both a reader and a writer, what's the greatest literary monster ever created in Jones' opinion?

"Oh, man, I already said Slake Moths, but . . . I've probably got to come down with Frankenstein's monster, finally. And? We do get his whole backstory, pretty much, same as Dolarhyde, but he's still scary. Just, in a different way. It's not that he's going to choke the little girl in all of us—though, sure—it's more that he's this articulate, pitiful, shambling reminder of our own worst tendencies. I'm not so sure it's scientific progress being warned against in that novel so much as our tendency to walk away from responsibility. Which is to say, what with the environmental issues we're living with today, that two-hundred-year-old book is pretty vital."

Recognizing and respecting the pop culture enthusiast in Jones, I expanded the question to the realm of greatest film monsters—and he was ready for me.

"As for best movie monster . . . Godzilla's the knee-jerk response, I know. And Godzilla's cool, for sure. But, for my money: *Relic.* What's it called in the movie version? "Kothoga," maybe? I like how it needs our hypothalamus to survive, and how it's a different monster each time, taking into account what biological scaffolding it's built on—very xenomorph, yes—and how it's not 'evil' itself, but has been kind of weaponized, has been perverted into a weapon. Yeah, I really like that monster. And it moves great, too. Very like the monster in, "The Host."

One of the more enduring provocative remarks about stories has been attributed to everyone from Fyodor Dostoyevsky and Leo Tolstoy to John Gardner and others. Uncertain ascription aside, the concept is that there are really only two kinds of stories: Someone goes on a journey or a stranger comes to town. Even Christopher Booker's 2004 assertion of seven basic conventional plot structures would support this presumption, with all seven of his. Indeed horror—in general—seems predicated on the latter, with some disruption of order serving as the catalyst for the horror that ensues. When it comes to plotting a horror story or novel, I ask Jones which approach is more effective within the traditional boundaries of the genre—the terrifying journey or the terrifying stranger (monster).

"Maybe there's even only one story, right? Sometimes you're the stranger coming to town, sometimes you're the townsperson encountering that stranger. But, of the two, I agree that Stranger Comes to Town is the more conventional build. I mean, most horror, as transgressive as it dresses itself up, is still basically conservative—it's fighting for the status quo before whatever intrusion's going on. And the best way to foreground that is for the reader or audience to key into that pre-monster/stranger status quo: the bucolic little town, community, family, whatever. That stability is what horror fights tooth and nail to re-establish.

The Someone Goes on a Journey build can work, obviously, but it's a lot trickier, as those kinds of stories are constantly edging over into a dark fantasy build, just because they're having to do so much world-building and mapmaking and explaining how things got this way. Do enough of that, and pretty soon we know all the rules of this reality. Pull a lever here, that thing over there moves. And that's fantasy at its most basic level: living in a world that makes sense. Horror's different. To me, horror's kind of specifically about pulling that lever, waiting for what should happen to happen, but, instead, the rules don't hold, and your lever has just opened up a door you can see, let something through."

BUILDING SUSPENSE

DAVID WELLINGTON

SUSPENSE IS THE blood of fiction. It's what keeps your reader hooked to your story, what keeps them reading even when . . .

Hey. You. Psst—I've got a secret to tell you. Don't flip to the next essay, not quite yet. If you just hold on a second, I'll tell you an easy, sure-fire way to build suspense into your book or story. A way that's guaranteed to work every time.

Except I won't tell you yet.

As I was saying . . . suspense is what holds a reader's attention and keeps them from giving up and finding something better to do than reading. Something like doing their taxes or considering where their lives went wrong. You need suspense if you want your story to be compelling, to get attention. Of course, to build suspense, you'll need to manipulate your readers. You'll need to treat them like gullible marks at a county fair, desperate to know what's inside the tent.

Sort of. It doesn't have to be that evil. Though the evil path does get quick results.

I said I would give you a sure-fire formula to building suspense, and now we're going to get into that. Then I'll tell you why maybe it won't work for you.

Here's the trick, one I learned from reading far too many best-selling thrillers: write very short chapters (about 1000-1750 words). End every single chapter on a cliffhanger.

Yes. It's that easy. It's not fair, honestly, how well it works. Readers will not be able to put a book like that down. They may throw it across the room in disgust when they're done, but they'll finish the thing first. Admittedly, it only works for one kind of story—plot-driven, high-energy stories with lots of action and quick reversals. If that's the kind of story you want to tell, you're golden. Nor will I tell you there's anything wrong with that kind of story. My early career came out of figuring out that formula, and I still enjoy those kind of stories. Most people do—they're quick, easy reads, they can be really fun. They're like an IV bag full of Ritalin on a rainy afternoon.

Is that the kind of story you wanted to write? Or did you have something else in mind? Maybe you wanted something character driven. Or a story with a lot of detailed world building where plot is secondary. Maybe you wanted to write a lush, lyrical account of a young person learning what love and adulthood mean.

You can still build suspense in those kinds of stories, as well. Of course you can. It's just a lot harder. Here are some of the devices and tricks you'll be using, and then I'll finish this essay with a quick discussion of why writing is all about taking advantage of your foolish, foolish readers, gulling them like the worst kind of rubes.

Stick around for that bit, it'll be fun. I promise.

Plot Tetris

One of the best ways to build suspense is simply by withholding information. Rather than dumping plot information in big exposition scenes, parcel it out very slowly over the course of your story. Human beings, a group which presumably includes most of your readers, are naturally curious. We love a good mystery.

Neuropsychologists have found that this is because we enjoy "cognitive flow", a kind of gentle tickling of the smartest parts of our brains. It's the same basic drive that keeps people playing Tetris long past bedtime. If you tease your readers with tiny hints, but fail to fully explain what's going on, you activate a system of mental rewards that readers find irresistible.

There are a couple of things to keep in mind when playing hard to get with your central plot mystery, though. Remember this is a process—you want to build flow, which means giving your readers a continual drip of information. Too little information at a time and the reader gets frustrated that nothing is happening; too much and it starts feeling like things are moving too fast. Big plot reveals are dramatic, but they can stop flow just as quickly as hitting a dead end in a maze.

The work of solving a mystery is fun and keeps things moving; having the solution feels like a big reward, but it's also the end of a journey. You want your readers hanging on every word, not waiting for the second shoe to drop, because once it does, where else can you go? Though dropping a third shoe might engender some all new suspense . . . look, you will need to present the big solution to the mystery at some point—but the best place for this is often on the last page of your story, when you and the reader are ready to stop.

Similarly, be very careful with red herrings. Tetris is fun while the blocks are all fitting together. It gets very frustrating when a piece falls in the wrong spot, ruining the flow. Red herrings, i.e. intentional misdirections, can be very useful in keeping a mystery from being too easy to solve, but when they're revealed to be irrelevant to the plot, readers often feel like they've wasted their time.

The trick is to maintain the flow as evenly and gradually as possible. Readers need constant rewards in the form of new information or new connections, but every new revelation should ask a new question, as well. Give readers a steady progression of clues and exposition and they'll stick around right to the end.

The Hanging Shadow

Foreshadowing gets a bad rap, which is a shame. It's one of the oldest and most successful devices in the writer's toolbox and when handled deftly it can do wonderful things toward building suspense.

We all recognize bad foreshadowing, of course—even when sometimes we still fall for it. When the narrator says, "What they didn't realize was that all of them would be dead in five minutes," we all groan a little. Yet you know who does this all the time, and gets away with it? Stephen King. He'll often put these little barbs in his stories, just to wake his readers up and get their attention. For him, it works.

Be careful that if you use this kind of authorial direct address, however, that you're as good at it as

King. Note how he uses this trick: typically only once in a book, and typically very early on in the story. There are good reasons for this. Doing it multiple times would make the readers feel like they're being railroaded through the plot. Doing it too late in the narrative would feel like a sudden intrusion of the author into a narrative the rules of which had already been established, which is typically a no-no.

A slightly more subtle but also cringe worthy kind of foreshadowing shows up a lot in horror stories: the "palpable sense of dread", which deserves it's own acronym: the PSOD. This happens when a character is moving through a perfectly prosaic or even cheerful scene, yet "feels an odd oppressive gloom in the air", or can't help but notice "a lingering scent of death under the cloying smell of the cotton candy." Yeah, you probably recognize these moments. These are often signs of an author panicking because they need to warn the readers that something terrible is about to happen. Related cases of clichéd foreshadowing that deserve their own acronyms include:

The Cryptic Warning, from an Elderly Person with Dementia: the CW(EP/D);

The Cryptic Warning, from a Preverbal but Psychic Kid: CW(P/PK);

The Prophetic Dream Including Jump Scare: PD+JS;

. . . and the Unusual Weather for This Time of Year: UWfTTY.

Of course, the Palpable Sense of Dread can be used more subtly, and to great effect. Dissonant elements in a scene can put the reader's hackles up, and get them wondering what's going on. Just be careful not to throw in PSODs that don't pay off. Those shady carnies had better be up to something.

Foreshadowing can be as subtle as you want it to be, but be careful. You can't guarantee that your readers are paying close attention to every sentence, and foreshadowing really doesn't work at the subliminal level as much as we would like it to. If a reader fails to notice the odd shadow lurking under the surface of the pond, they may think your story is about a boring day spent lazing about in a rowboat. When you attack the boat with your bog creature two pages later, it may feel more jarring than you intended.

The Right Rhythm

A great writer can keep the reader's attention on every page, even while allowing a story room to breathe and grow. The key to this is pacing, and pacing is the key to really top-notch suspense.

Pacing is one of the hardest skills to learn as a writer, and in my opinion it's the most important. Narrative can feel rushed or slow, it can feel jumpy and discontinuous or it can feel like the story is stuck in amber, unable to change and therefore stale. Pacing—specifically the modulation of narrative elements—is what gets you out of these traps.

Modulation simply means breaking up your story by altering your techniques. This does not mean hitting the brakes every time you accelerate. Immediately after an action scene, give your readers a slow character moment. This lets them catch their breath. But make sure the character moment has some significant content, all the same. You don't want to let your readers get complacent. After a long, detailed exposition dump (and yes, almost every book has these, we just try to be subtle about them these days), you need a quick, lively scene to get the blood moving again. But make sure the quick scene advances the plot and throws all that exposition into question.

You can't just plunge full speed ahead in most stories. Any stimulus becomes irritating when it goes on too long. A drip of water on the back of your hand can turn into torture. Modulation breaks up that stimulus by replacing it with a different stimulus. This feels to the reader like relief, but stops them from entering a relaxation cycle.

Modulation is all about contrast. Switching up the speed of your narrative, the emotional weight of scenes, even switching from the viewpoint of one character to another can have the desired effect. Be careful though to not always use the same magnitude of contrast. Flashing back and forth between big explosive action and tiny intimate dialogue scenes can get exhausting. Worse, it can get predictable! If you set up the same alternating rhythm throughout a piece, it loses contrast altogether. Sometimes you need to switch up even the type of contrast you spread across your scenes—think complementary colors rather than stark oppositions.

It takes a lot of practice to get modulation just right. Typically you need to write a bunch of stories with bad modulation before you start to see where you've been making mistakes—and before you can learn the little tricks that make modulation sing. I can give you one quick piece of advice about modulation, though. Nine times out of ten, if your narrative feels like it's out of synch, like things just aren't motoring along at the right pace, the right choice, somewhat paradoxically, is to slow down. Expand a scene, break it down into its component parts and examine those parts. Stretching a crucial scene out to twice its previous length can give it twice as much emphasis.

Character Stakes

Typically when we think of suspense we're thinking about a plot that unfolds piece by piece, but it doesn't end there. Suspense can be built into any element of storytelling—you can build a setting that evokes mystery, and the tone of your story can help build a sense of looming dread or a hopeful desperation.

And of course one of the most powerful methods of building suspense is through the deployment of character stakes. The things your character wants, or fears, or is willing to sacrifice—these are all rich veins of suspense.

When it comes to a character's desires, make sure that what they want seems attainable, but not easy. You don't want your readers scoffing at your protagonist's chances, but you definitely want them to feel the character has earned their rewards. While most stories end with a character being successful in their personal quest, readers need to feel like there's a chance they could fail. It helps, definitely, if your character's desire is something concrete and well-defined. An aimless sense of yearning is certainly a relatable character trait, but it doesn't lend itself to a suspenseful story.

Similarly, a character's fears should be explored

fully and made manifest whenever possible. This doesn't necessarily mean that every story has to have a six foot tall cockroach chasing the hero around, but you do need a focus for the character's dread. Free-floating anxiety and nameless apprehensions don't build suspense very well, so get as specific as you can. Rather than being obsessed with death, maybe the character irrationally fears only pancreatic cancer; instead of being worried they'll be a failure in their profession, maybe imagine a scenario where that failure plays out in a humiliating public fashion.

Examining what a character is willing to sacrifice is one of the best ways of defining them, and an excellent method of building suspense. At the start of the story the question should be entirely academic, but as the plot makes demands on the protagonist, sacrifice asks a series of increasingly nasty questions. By the end of the book your reader should be asking themselves just how far your hero is willing to go to save the world/significant other/idea they have of themselves, etc. Suspense comes both from the question of whether they'll make that sacrifice or not, and also from the increasingly desperate lengths they'll go to in order to not make the sacrifice. Keep in mind that while your natural inclination may be to funnel your character into an unavoidable situation, giving them a little wiggle room both lets them breathe as a character but also keeps the reader guessing. There may be a way out of the central conflict of your story— but is that method of escape worse than facing up to the real problem? Giving your character choices magnifies suspense.

The Man with the Gun

Surprises are the easiest way to build suspense in any story, and also the most dangerous. It's true Raymond Chandler once said "When in doubt have a man come through a door with a gun in his hand," but he didn't actually mean it as good advice—in fact he was describing his frustration with his own stories, and wishing they could have been better (yes, we all feel that way, all the time). Having something random and unexpected will definitely get your readers' attention. It will, however, backfire very quickly. Readers need to feel like the world you've created has rules. They don't have to be the same rules as those of the world we live in—in fact, it's my contention that all fiction is "heightened" or "secondary" to one degree or another. But the rules should be self-consistent, and having a plot twist lurch into your lane with no warning forces you to then do a lot of back-pedaling in order to justify the intrusion.

Which isn't to say you shouldn't do it. There are definitely times in a book when the unexpected and explosive development is warranted. Just be extraordinarily sure that you're doing it at the right time and place. Suspense may be the feeling of wondering what comes next; what kills it best is the belief that what comes next won't make sense. The absolute last thing you want your readers to think is that you're playing silly games with them. Abusing their trust and manipulating them.

Even though, of course, that's exactly what you're doing.

What you need to do.

Oh, hey, look at that—out of nowhere, we're reaching the end of the essay and I'm about to talk about why all fiction is psychological manipulation.

Because that's what we've been talking about this whole time, right? How you can lead your readers around by their noses. How, like the carnival barker, you as a writer offer all manner of promises regardless of what you've actually got in the tent. How you're going to exploit the weak spots in human psychology to keep your readers turning your pages.

Which sounds really bad, doesn't it? On some level, writing fiction breaks down to just lying for money. Tricking your reader into thinking that if they give you some of their precious time and attention, you'll give them something special, when what you're actually selling is just pure snake oil.

Does that make you uneasy? Does it make you feel like maybe there's a better way to earn a living? Maybe it doesn't. Maybe you think your books or stories will be different. That instead of taking advantage of your readers, you're going to create a gentle partnership with them. Offer them unfettered access to the wonderland of your imagination, where they can find such delights that . . .

Sorry, I fell asleep writing that sentence. Where was I? Oh, right, talking about how all fiction is deception and manipulation. Well, the kind of fiction people like to read, anyway. The kind that keeps them entertained.

It's a game. A con. A grift.

And I love it, and I love it when I get gulled, absolutely. For the same reason I like stage magic. Nobody goes to see an illusionist do card tricks thinking they have real powers. We know we're being fooled. Some of us watch the trick thinking we'll see through it, that we're the one who can't be misdirected. Some of us love the weird chill of seeing something impossible and not understanding how it worked.

Your readers are the audience for that show, and you're the magician. Your job is to make them happy by making fools of them. And don't forget to heed the great maxim of all entertainment: always leave them wanting more.

CONVEYING HORROR

RAMSEY CAMPBELL

LET ME START by declaring why I write horror. There's no reason to write anything unless it engages your imagination, and no reason to write horror unless you're conveying what you yourself feel. For the record, I don't strive to impose the experience on the reader; I try to communicate what the situation in the tale and the plight of its no doubt unlucky protagonist feels like to me.

Choosing the best words for the task, especially when you want to impart a sense of the uncanny or of psychological stress, shouldn't be an attempt at imposition. It's rather an acknowledgement that the finest work in our field communicates through the careful selection of language, the structure of the narrative, the pacing of the prose. I believe horror fiction has a continuing tradition, where writers build upon and develop the achievements of their predecessors.

I'll do my best to demonstrate with examples from the classics and from some of my own stuff.

There's nothing wrong with learning from a study of the great works, or even necessarily by imitating them. In most of the arts this isn't perceived as a problem, let alone as contemptible, but it's too often condemned when it comes to fiction writing. I began by trying to pay back some of the pleasure the field had given me, which involved emulating favourites while I learned some craft—enough to turn from imitation to dealing with my own fears and my own experience. Let me first look here at the classics.

Edgar Allan Poe virtually invents the modern horror tale by refining and condensing the Gothic novel into short stories, often intensely focused on the abnormal psychology of a character. He creates or perfects many of our modes, from the unreliable narrator to the melding of crime and horror fiction, from the evocation of the uncanny to the interior examination of maniacs. Here are two openings of his. "The Fall of the House of Usher," melds the psychological and the supernatural. Many classic tales derive directly from a sense of the uncanniness of a landscape, and Poe's opening paragraph suggests that the place may be unnaturally alive. Its influence can be found in many later works, all the way to Stephen King and after.

"During the whole of a dull, dark, and soundless day in the autumn of the year, when the clouds hung oppressively low in the heavens, I had been passing alone, on horseback, through a singularly dreary tract of country; and at length found myself, as the shades of the evening drew on, within view of the melancholy House of Usher. I know not how it was—but, with the first glimpse of the building, a sense of insufferable gloom pervaded my spirit. I say insufferable, for the feeling was unrelieved by any of that half-pleasurable, because poetic, sentiment, with which the mind usually receives even the sternest natural images of the desolate or terrible. I looked upon the scene before me—upon the mere house, and the simple landscape features of the domain—upon the bleak walls—upon the vacant eye-like windows—upon a few rank sedges—and upon a few white trunks of decayed trees—with an utter depression of soul which I can compare to no earthly sensation more properly than to the after-dream of the reveller upon opium—the bitter lapse into everyday life—the hideous dropping off of the veil. There was an iciness, a sinking, a sickening of the heart—an unredeemed dreariness of thought which no goading of the imagination could torture into aught of the sublime. What was it, I paused to think, what was it that so unnerved me in the contemplation of the House of Usher?

It was a mystery all insoluble, nor could I grapple with the shadowy fancies that crowded upon me as I pondered. I was forced to fall back upon the unsatisfactory conclusion, that while, beyond doubt, there are combinations of very simple natural objects which have the power of thus affecting us, still the analysis of this power lies among considerations beyond our depth. It was possible, I reflected, that a mere different arrangement of the particulars of the scene, of the details of the picture, would be sufficient to modify, or perhaps to annihilate its capacity for sorrowful impression.

Acting upon this idea, I reined my horse to the precipitous brink of a black and lurid tarn that lay in unruffled luster by the dwelling, and gazed down—but with a shudder even more thrilling than before—upon the remodelled and inverted images of the gray sedge, and the ghastly tree-stems, and the vacant and eye-like windows."

If you don't know the tale, you've a treat in store. Like all good writing, it gains by being read aloud. Savour the rhythm of the language, the assonance of the words, the emphatic use of alliteration and the echoing of sounds. Poe had a poet's eye and sense of language, and brought them to his prose. Like his successors Lovecraft and Ligotti, he sometimes embeds within his tales a discussion of the aesthetics of terror: see the middle of the paragraph above.

Most pertinently to why we're here, the excerpt demonstrates the power of atmospheric preparation. Nothing has happened so far, and yet the awful house, which shares a soul with its doomed occupants, has been brought to undead life.

While such an opening is appropriate to an atmospheric tale, Poe could be swiftly direct when it suited. Here's how he drops us straight into the mind of a madman in "The Tell-Tale Heart."

"True!—nervous— very, very dreadfully nervous I had been and am; but why will you say that I am mad? The disease had sharpened my senses—not destroyed—not dulled them. Above all was the sense of hearing acute. I heard all things in the heaven and in the earth. I heard many things in hell. How, then, am I mad? Hearken! and observe how healthily— how calmly I can tell you the whole story.

It is impossible to say how first the idea entered my brain; but once conceived, it haunted me day and night. Object there was none. Passion there was none. I loved the old man. He had never wronged me. He had never given me insult. For his gold I had no desire. I think it was his eye! yes, it was this! He had the eye of a vulture—a pale blue eye, with a film over it. Whenever it fell upon me, my blood ran cold; and so by degrees—very gradually—I made up my mind to take the life of the old man, and thus rid myself of the eye forever.

I owe a good deal to this approach. If I'm dealing with the deranged, I believe in sharing their mind with the reader. Sufferers from these conditions generally believe there's nothing wrong with them.

Here's the opening of "The Dead Must Die", my story of a man convinced that those who benefit from blood transfusions are undead and must be exterminated like the vampires he believes they are:.

"As soon as I push the doors open I know I am in the presence of evil. The lobby walls are white as innocence, but the place stinks of deceit. It is crowded with lost souls who wander aimlessly or talk to one another as though they are in church. Sensitivity to atmospheres is yet another gift which the mass of mankind has abandoned. I breathe a prayer and cross the threshold, steeling myself against the unhealthy heat which refutes the pretence of healing, the disinfectant stench bespeaking the presence of corruption, the closeness of so much unredeemed flesh . . . "

By now you may have twigged that he has walked into an ordinary hospital.

Here's an excerpt from *The Booking*, a novella of mine where a bookshop seems inseparable from the psyche of its enigmatic owner, much like the Ushers and their house. The central character approaches it hoping for a job. Some of the following may suggest he has strayed into somewhere stranger than he's looking for. I believe unease of this kind is best conveyed gradually, the better to accumulate power.

"He couldn't help thinking the street resembled a trap, enclosed at one end by the featureless concrete rear of the precinct and at the other by a brick wall at least twice his height, not to mention the lid of a low January sky as dully blank as a dormant computer screen. No doubt the far end was a junction foreshortened by perspective, and in any case there was a way out through the precinct. "It's a job," Kiefer muttered and made for the shop.

He was only yards away when he made out several books propped open on stands in the window. Their pages had curled up like dead leaves, and one book had toppled off its stand to sprawl on its face. The largest item was a single volume of an encyclopaedia, exhibiting a fold-out page that illustrated fossils, which appeared to have added the condition of the paper to their age. Beyond the window display was a large dim room where bookshelves occupied the whole of all three walls and three wide double-sided bookcases took up much of the intervening space. Every shelf was full of books, and however dusty the window and the dimness made them look, Kiefer already felt at home.

The door beside the window was scaly with paint that was well on the way to forgetting its colour. A rusty stain between the upper panels showed where the number of the building used to be. When Kiefer grasped the metal doorknob, crumbs of it clung to his hand. The door stumbled inwards, tripping the clapper of a bell that sounded stuffed with dust and erasing a muddy footprint from a bare floorboard. He hitched up the computer—the strap of the bag was tugging at him like an impatient child—and peered around the shop.

It was even less like a library than he'd suspected. The books weren't arranged by author or by any concept he was able to discern, not subject nor yet title. They weren't even separated into fiction and its opposite, but he wouldn't be surprised if the proprietor knew where every item was. If the books were in the order of one solitary mind, what did that say about the man? Perhaps just that he was no more eccentric than many booksellers, which might explain why he seemed to be hiding from his visitor, and Kiefer was preparing to call out or at least to clear his throat when he realised he was being watched from a back room.

The dusty muffled sunlight didn't reach that far. As Kiefer began to distinguish the room he could have imagined it was forming from the darkness. It contained a desk a good deal broader than the doorway, a piece of furniture so monolithically immobile that it seemed to have lent its stillness to the man seated behind it."

Horror can be conveyed indirectly with real power. The narrator may be unaware of what he's telling us will happen (as in W. F. Harvey's "August Heat", where the narrator reveals his own fate to us without realizing) or consider it not to be horrific, which simply makes it more so (as in Kazuo Ishiguro's, *Never Let Me Go*, to my mind unquestionably horror fiction). The naïve voice can be an especially potent device— narration by someone not fully aware of the implications, especially a child. To my mind the masterpiece of the form is Arthur Machen's "The White People", where the tale is told by a girl just turned adolescent, who lets us realize that she has been initiated into dark magic. Here's a sample.

"I was thirteen, nearly fourteen, when I had a very singular adventure, so strange that the day on which it happened is always called the White Day. My mother had been dead for more than a year, and in the morning I had lessons, but they let me go out for walks in the afternoon. And this afternoon I walked a new way, and a little brook led me into a new country, but I tore my frock getting through some of the difficult places, as the way was through many bushes, and beneath the low branches of trees, and up thorny thickets on the hills, and by dark woods full of creeping thorns. And it was a long, long way. It seemed as if I was going on for ever and ever, and I had to creep by a place like a tunnel where a brook must have been, but all the water had dried up, and the floor was rocky, and the bushes had grown overhead till they met, so that it was quite dark. And I went on and on through that dark place; it was a long, long way. And I came to a hill that I never saw before. I was in a dismal thicket full of black twisted boughs that tore me as I went through them, and I cried out because I was smarting all over, and then I found that I was climbing, and I went up and up a long way, till at last the thicket stopped and I came out crying just under the top of a big bare place, where there were ugly grey stones lying all about on the grass, and here and there a little twisted, stunted tree came out from under a stone, like a snake. And I went up, right to the top, a long way. I never saw such big ugly stones before; they came out of the earth some of them, and some looked as if they had been

245

rolled to where they were, and they went on and on as far as I could see, a long, long way. I looked out from them and saw the country, but it was strange. It was winter time, and there were black terrible woods hanging from the hills all round; it was like seeing a large room hung with black curtains, and the shape of the trees seemed quite different from any I had ever seen before. I was afraid. Then beyond the woods there were other hills round in a great ring, but I had never seen any of them; it all looked black, and everything had a voor over it. It was all so still and silent, and the sky was heavy and grey and sad, like a wicked voorish dome in Deep Dendo. I went on into the dreadful rocks. There were hundreds and hundreds of them. Some were like horrid-grinning men; I could see their faces as if they would jump at me out of the stone, and catch hold of me, and drag me with them back into the rock, so that I should always be there. And there were other rocks that were like animals, creeping, horrible animals, putting out their tongues, and others were like words that I could not say, and others like dead people lying on the grass. I went on among them, though they frightened me, and my heart was full of wicked songs that they put into it; and I wanted to make faces and twist myself about in the way they did, and I went on and on a long way till at last I liked the rocks, and they didn't frighten me anymore. I sang the songs I thought of; songs full of words that must not be spoken or written down. Then I made faces like the faces on the rocks, and I twisted myself about like the twisted ones, and I lay down flat on the ground like the dead ones, and I went up to one that was grinning, and put my arms round him and hugged him."

For what my experience is worth, that excerpt—the beginning of a much longer paragraph—fills me with the kind of dread I find in several of the films (horror films if ever I saw any) of David Lynch. I know few other tales of terror that convey so much by indirection, or suggest so much more than they show. The technique is still with us—see the stories of Thomas Ligotti and Mark Samuels, for instance—and I applaud its revival.

I've had a few tries at the naïve voice myself. Here's a taste, from "The Place of Revelation". A boy is retelling a tale his ambiguously sinister uncle told him, or perhaps it's an experience he's undergone.

"Once there was a boy who went walking in the country on a day like it was today. The grass in the fields looked like feathers where all the birds in the world had been fighting, and all the fallen leaves were showing their bones. The sun was so low every crumb of frost had its own shadow, and his footprints had shadows in when he looked behind him, and walking felt like breaking little bones under his feet. The day was so cold he kept thinking the clouds were bits of ice that had cracked off the sky and dropped on the edge of the earth. The wind kept scratching his face and pulling the last few leaves off the trees, only if the leaves went back he knew they were birds. It was meant to be the shortest day, but it felt as if time had died because everything was too slippery or too empty for it to get hold of. So he thought he'd done everything there was to do and seen everything there was to see when he saw a hole like a gate through a hedge."

"That's the way." Uncle Lucian's eyes have begun to shine like fragments of the moon. "Make it your story."

"He wasn't sure if there was an old gate or the hedge had grown like one. He didn't know it was one of the places where the world is twisted. All he could see was more hedge at the sides of a bendy path. So he followed it round and round, and it felt like going inside a shell. Then he got dizzy with running to find the middle, because it seemed to take hours and the bends never got any smaller. But just when he was thinking he'd stop and turn back if the spiky hedges let him, he came to where the path led all round a pond that was covered with ice. Only the pond oughtn't to have been so big, all the path he'd run round should have squeezed it little. So he was walking round the pond to see if he could find the trick when the sun showed him the flat white faces everywhere under the ice.

"There were children and parents who'd come searching for them, and old people too. They were everyone the maze had brought to the pond, and they were all calling him. Their eyes were opening as slow as holes in the ice and growing too big, and their mouths were moving like fish mouths out of water, and the wind in the hedge was their cold rattly voice telling him he had to stay forever, because he couldn't see the path away from the pond—there was just hedge everywhere he looked. Only then he heard his uncle's voice somewhere in it, telling him he had to walk back in all his footprints like a witch dancing backwards and then he'd be able to escape . . . "

So far all the excerpts have been deliberately paced, but the crucial element is the choice of language. The best tales of terror create their effects by finding the perfect word. As in comedy, timing is crucial too. Showing just enough to suggest far worse is the core of M. R. James, famed for his Edwardian ghost stories but unquestionably for horror too (which he himself said was essential to them).

He's able to convey more horror in an apparently casual glancing phrase than most of us can achieve in a sentence. Often in his tales the horrors are barely glimpsed if even seen. Sometimes he makes his nightmare creatures all the more monstrous by not describing them as such.

Here is an example of his timing, where the prose may lull us into feeling safe. One principle James demonstrates is that in the tale of terror, less can frequently be better. I don't mean that horror should be described as indescribable (a tendency of which Lovecraft is too often unjustly accused); rather that it's ideal to show just enough to suggest far worse. Here's an instance from "Casting the Runes". Note the dry wit, given the rest of the paragraph, of the reticent first sentence.

"The night he passed is not one on which he looks back with any satisfaction. He was in bed and the light was out. He was wondering if the charwoman would come early enough to get him hot water next morning, when he heard the unmistakable sound of his study door opening. No step followed it on the passage floor, but the sound must mean mischief, for he knew that he had shut the door that evening after putting his papers away in his desk. It was rather shame than courage that induced him to slip out into the passage and lean over the banister in his nightgown, listening. No light was visible; no further sound came: only a gust of warm, or even hot air played for an instant round his shins. He went back and decided to lock himself into his room. There was more unpleasantness, however. Either an economical suburban company had decided that their light would not be required in the small hours, and had stopped working, or else something was wrong with the meter; the effect was in any case that the electric light was off. The obvious course was to find a match, and also to consult his watch: he might as well know how many hours of discomfort awaited him. So he put his hand into the well-known nook under the pillow: only, it did not get so far. What he touched was, according to his account, a mouth, with teeth, and with hair about it, and, he declares, not the mouth of a human being. I do not think it is any use to guess what he said or did; but he was in a spare room with the door locked and his ear to it before he was clearly conscious again. And there he spent the rest of a most miserable night, looking every moment for some fumbling at the door: but nothing came."

Crucial to the effect of this passage, I think, is how the moment of horror lurks in the middle of the paragraph, lying low until it seizes the reader. The composition of the prose on the page is essential to the timing. The very gradual realisation adds to the sense of unease.

Now let me take to bits a short story of mine, "Calling Card," and examine some of its working parts. For the record, it was written to a very specific commission: a ghost story set over Christmas and New Year, using locations in and around Liverpool, and about two thousand words in length. I find working on occasion to someone else's specifications can be a useful discipline. You may be amused to learn that the editor who commissioned the tale decided it was too gruesome for his newspaper, but it soon found a home elsewhere. It touches on a peculiarly British tradition, the first foot—the first person to cross your threshold on New Year's Day, said to bring you luck, but not in this case.

"Dorothy Harris stepped off the pavement

and into her hall. As she stooped groaning to pick up the envelopes the front door opened, opened, a yawn that wouldn't be suppressed. She wrestled it shut—she must ask Simon to see to it, though certainly not over Christmas—then she began to open the cards.

Here was Father Christmas, and here he was again, apparently after dieting. Here was a robin like a rosy apple with a beak, and here was an envelope whose handwriting staggered: Simon's and Margery's children, perhaps?

The card showed a church on a snowy hill. The hill was bare except for a smudge of ink. Though the card was unsigned, there was writing within. A Very Happy Christmas And A Prosperous New Year, the message should have said—but now it said A Very Harried Christmas And No New Year. She turned back to the picture, her hands shaking. It wasn't just a smudge of ink; someone had drawn a smeary cross on the hill: a grave.

Though the name on the envelope was a watery blur, the address was certainly hers. Suddenly the house—the kitchen and living-room, the two bedrooms with her memories stacked neatly against the walls—seemed far too large and dim."

The scene is set, then, and the first hint of macabre menace introduced. An apparently circumstantial detail will become vital at the end. Dorothy heads for her daughter's home across the river.

"The bus already sounded like a pub. She sat outside on the ferry, though the bench looked and felt like black ice. Lights fished in the Mersey, gulls drifted down like snowflakes from the muddy sky. A whitish object grabbed the rail, but of course it was only a gull. Nevertheless she was glad that Simon was waiting with the car at Woodside.

As soon as the children had been packed off to bed so that Father Christmas could get to work, she produced the card. It felt wet, almost slimy, though it hadn't before. Simon pointed out what she'd overlooked: the age of the stamp. "We weren't even living there then," Margery said. "You wouldn't think they would bother delivering it after sixty years."

Or was it a gull? I'm told some readers find initial glimpses like this one in my fiction linger even after they've been rationalized. Horror can be all the more disturbing if it is initially misperceived. Part of the business of writing—the best way to avoid cliché—is to make us look afresh at things we may have taken for granted. The hint of the physical—the suddenly wet card—prepares the way for grislier developments. Christmas Day brings no further threat, and Dorothy goes home to host a family meal.

"An insect clung to a tinsel globe on the tree. When she reached out to squash the insect it wasn't there, neither on the globe nor on the floor. Could it have been the reflection of someone thin outside the window? Nobody was there now"

I learned that kind of glancing image from M. R. James, of course. The language is absolutely neutral, and perhaps that adds to its ambiguous menace, which I hope the story is starting to gather. The family visits, and all is fine until they're stepping out of the house.

> "Grandma, someone's left you a present," little Denise cried. Then she cried out, and dropped the package. Perhaps the wind had snatched it from her hands. As the package, which looked wet and mouldy, struck the kerb it broke open. Did its contents scuttle out and sidle away into the dark? Surely that was the play of the wind, which tumbled carton and wrapping away down the street."

We may now have a sense that all sorts of things, especially items we could take for granted, are capable of turning uncannily on us. As the days pass the details mount up. "A blurred voice seemed to creep behind the carols on the radio, lowing out of tune"—and even the banal familiar environment of the local laundrette proves to be no refuge, just a lair of something imperfectly perceived:

> "The Westinghouse Laundromat was deserted. ooo, the washing machines said emptily. There was only herself, and her dervishes of clothes, and a black plastic bag almost as tall as she was. If someone had abandoned it, whatever its lumpy contents were, she could see why, for it was leaking; she smelled stagnant water. It must be a draught

that made it twitch feebly. Nevertheless, if she had been able to turn off her machine she might have fled."

A visit to a friend provides little relief, only a sense that Dorothy can be pursued anywhere:.

"The following day she went to a friend whose flat overlooked Wavertree Park. It was all very convivial—a rainstorm outside made the mince pies more warming, the chat flowed as easily as the whisky—but she kept glancing at the thin figure who stood in the park, unmoved by the downpour. The trails of rain on the window must be lending him their colour, for his skin looked like a snail's . . . No, the man in the park hadn't really looked as though his clothes and his body had merged into a single greyish mass."

From the simply visual we move inevitably (and, I trust, unnervingly) to the physical. Dorothy takes her grandchildren for a Christmas treat, but even crowds of shoppers provide no protection.

"She took them to the aquarium. Piranhas sank stonily, their sides glittering like Christmas cards. Toads were bubbling lumps of tar. Finny humbugs swam, and darting fish wired with light. Had one of the tanks cracked? There seemed to be a stagnant smell . . .
She was glad of the packed crowds in Church Street, even though the children kept

letting go of her hands. But the stagnant smell was trailing her, and once, when she grabbed for little Denise's hand, she clutched someone else's, which felt soft and wet. It must have been nervousness which made her fingers seem to sink into the hand."

Dreams and nightmares are best used sparingly in supernatural fiction, but I think by now in this tale the everyday has become nightmarish, and a dream draws together some of the elements so far.

"That night she returned to the aquarium and found she was locked in. Except for the glow of the tanks, the narrow room was oppressively dark. In the nearest tank a large dead fish floated towards her, out of weeds. Now she was in the tank, her nails scrabbling at the glass, and she saw that it wasn't a fish but a snail-coloured hand, which closed spongily on hers. When she woke, her scream made the house sound very empty."

We've reached New Year's Eve, and the finale. On a visit to her next-door neighbours Dorothy learns the secret of the card.

"After several sherries Dorothy remembered something she'd once heard. "The lady who lived next door before me—didn't she have trouble with her son?"
"He wasn't right in the head. He got so he'd go for anyone, even if he'd never met them

before. She got so scared of him she locked him out one New Year's Eve. They say he threw himself in the river, though they never found the body."

Dorothy goes home to await the family. The climax rediscovers images from earlier and develops or transforms them. If the pace is at all imposed by the restrictions of length, I hope it suggests a rush towards a revelation. Is the final line a black joke? Well, I'm from Liverpool, and our wit is dark.

"The sherries had made her sleepy. Only the ticking of her clock, clipping away the seconds, kept her awake. Twenty past eleven. The splashing from the gutters sounded like wet footsteps pacing outside the window. She had never noticed she could smell the river in her house.

Twenty to twelve. Surely they wouldn't wait until midnight. She switched on the radio for company. A compere was making people laugh; a man was laughing thickly, sounding waterlogged. Was he a drunk in the street? He wasn't on the radio. She mustn't brood; why, she hadn't put out the sherry glasses; that was something to do, to distract her from the intolerably measured counting of the clock, the silenced radio, the emptiness displaying her sounds—

Though the knock seemed enormously loud, she didn't start. They were here at last, though she hadn't heard the car. It was New

Year's Day. She ran, and had reached the front door when the phone shrilled. That startled her so badly that she snatched the door open before lifting the receiver.

Nobody was outside—only a distant uproar of cheers and bells and horns—and Margery was on the phone. "We've been held up, mummy. There was an accident in the tunnel. We'll be over as soon as we can."

Then who had knocked? It must have been a drunk; she heard him stumbling beside the house, thumping on her window. He'd better take himself off, or she would call Mr Harvey to deal with him. But she was still inside the doorway when she saw the object on her step.

Good God, was it a rat? No, just a shoe, so ancient that it looked stuffed with mould. It wasn't mould, only a rotten old sock. There was something in the sock, something that smelled of stagnant water and worse. She stooped to peer at it, and then she was struggling to close the door, fighting to make the latch click, no breath to spare for a scream. She'd had her first foot, and now—hobbling doggedly alongside the house, its hands slithering over the wall—here came the rest of the body."

I hope the examples I've given are sufficiently varied and inspiring. It's time to sum up. The past offers many other fine examples. Lovecraft, for instance, devoted his entire career to trying to develop the perfect form for the weird tale. He constantly experimented with structure and narrative voice, in particular carefully modulating his prose within many of his tales, which is why there's far more to his fiction than the mythos he created and the purple prose that's sometimes used against him, and also why his work is so difficult to represent here: "The Colour out of Space" is the single best introduction to his achievement, I think. But there are as many good techniques as there are good writers—modern ones certainly too.

In, *Rosemary's Baby*, for instance, Ira Levin creates a sense of mounting paranoia by his use of neutral prose—precisely because it doesn't tell us anything is wrong, we're infected with suspicions on behalf of the unaware heroine, and they prove to be all too justified. It's also remarkable as a horror novel told largely in dialogue.

Savour the subtlety of *The Haunting of Hill House*, where Shirley Jackson prepares her spectral terrors with great delicacy, not least in her handling of psychology of character. Nor should we forget Stephen King: take another look, for instance, at *The Shining,* and consider how he prepares the hideous encounter in room 217—in particular how he paces the scene—or the devastating climax of *Revival.*

Examine the extended passage in the dreadful basement rooms of Adam Nevill's *No One Gets Out Alive*, if you can stand back far enough to be objective, and see how the attention to detail produces the suspense, just as Hitchcock often conveyed it by isolating details with close-up and montage. The minutely realistic observation doesn't just bring the moment alive; it lends the fantastic a foundation of realism, exactly what supernatural fiction needs. Track down Alison Moore's gem of understated terror *Eastmouth*, to be found in more than one recent anthology, and appreciate how much it achieves with great restraint and an enviable economy of means.

In a phrase, then, read the classics. In another, learn from them. At its best horror fiction can reach high places that few if any other genres can. Aim higher than you think you can attain. Experiment with technique. Discover what happens if you do without techniques and elements you think your fiction needs. Above all, tell as much of the truth as you can. I hope to hear of you.

UNVEILING THEME THROUGH PLOT: AN ANALYSIS OF NATHANIEL HAWTHORNE'S "THE BIRTHMARK"

STEPHANIE M. WYTOVICH

MORE OFTEN THAN not, writing a story or a poem is like putting together a jigsaw puzzle. Each piece fits (or doesn't fit) together. Eventually through a lot of trial and error, the bigger picture, or theme, starts to reveal itself. When defined in its broadest sense, theme is the central idea or abstract heartbeat of the story. It either directly or indirectly shows us a reoccurring concept that flows through the narrative highlighting the response or message the author wants their reader to leave with, and while theme is never explicitly spelled out for the reader, it is shown through characterization, conflict, iconography, and tone, hence making the plot points of story—exposition, rising action, climax, falling action, and denouement—all the more important to the unveiling at the end.

Let's take for instance Nathaniel Hawthorne's short story, "The Birthmark." Readers are first introduced to Aylmer, "a man of science, an eminent proficient in every branch of natural philosophy, who not long before our story opens had made experience of a spiritual affinity more attractive than any chemical one" (Hawthorne 357).

We learn that despite his proclivity toward science and discovery, that he has fallen in love and newly devoted himself to his bride, Georgianna. One day, Aylmer asks Georgianna whether she has ever considered having the birthmark on her cheek removed. This obsession with the blemish on her face, one that is described as, "a healthy though delicate bloom" lays out the exposition of the plot as readers prepare for the inevitable onslaught of the mark's removal (Hawthorne 358).

The rising action, defined as incidents that create suspense such as, but not limited to, character flaws, decisions, background story etc., is shown through a series of actions that Aylmer uses in an attempt to prove that he will be successful in the mark's removal. Georgianna, being completely smitten and in awe of her husband and his talents, tries to explain to him that she is willing to undergo any risk if it will make him look favorably upon her again.

"Danger is nothing to me; for life, while this hateful mark makes me the object of your horror and disgust, life is a burden when I would fling down with joy" (Hawthorne 360).

In an effort to both meet her demands and prove to himself that he can outwit nature, Aylmer presents three separate experiments to Georgianna: a plant, a portrait, and the elixir of life.

When he shows her the plant, one that preemptively shoots up from the soil and blossoms into a gorgeous flower, he urges her to touch it. When she does, the plant quickly turns a coal-black color only to then shrivel up and die. This is the first instance of foreshadowing, soon followed by the portrait Aylmer attempts to take of Georgianna through a series of light against polished metal. When he goes to check her picture, he notices that her face is, "blurred and indefinable while the minute figure of a hand appeared where the cheek should have been" (Hawthorne 363).

As we continue toward the climax, this acts as the second instance of foreshadowing disaster via another failed attempt at science through his obsession with the mark.

It is at this point in the story when Aylmer shows her what he believes to be the elixir of life, a concoction he's made through his continued studies in alchemy and chemistry. What is interesting about this detail specifically is that he mentions that based on the dosage, it is either eternal life or poison, thus exhibiting his control and god-like demeanor as both man and scientist. Readers, at this point, are starting to see his denied failures as a result of his pride, not to mention this obsession with the mark as an opportunity to achieve the impossibility of physical perfection in his wife. Georgianna's response to these medical feats is one of awe and admiration, and she hardly hesitates to tell her husband yet again that she will take or undergo whatever he chooses for her, regardless if it kills her, if there is a chance she can be free from the mark and looked favorably upon by her husband again.

The climax, or the highest point of tension in the story, comes when Georgianna drinks a potion, and readers are left in suspense as her life is suspended on the page. Hawthorne takes this opportunity to dangle the denouement, or conclusion, of the story through a chance belief in Aylmer's success as it appears the mark is dissolving and paling against her face, the falling action one of hope to make the final delivery of her impeding death hit that much harder.

Before Georgina dies at the end of the story, she says, "do not repent that with so high and pure a feeling, you have rejected the best the earth could offer" (Hawthorne 368). In her final words she surmises to say that his obsession with perfection and war between nature and science has caused him to lose that which was already perfect to being with, birthmark or not: herself. It is now, at the end of the story, that readers are left with the message that one should err against striving for the impossibility of perfection while also being warned against the using science to mess with that which nature has already gifted us. In a lot of ways, it's easy to see Aylmer walking hand-in-hand with Victor Frankenstein as both scientists were driven mad by their obsessions and then forced to live with the repercussions of their pride.

As such, dissecting the theme of a story is not only a great way to dive into a deeper analysis of a work, but it also allows readers a chance to stand on two feet as a literary critic and compare and contrast similar stories at hand to see how a particular theme can be traced and expanded upon within the cannon.

Works Cited:

Hawthorne, Nathaniel. "The Birthmark." *The Art of the Short Story*, edited by Dana Gioia and R.S. Gwynn, Pearson, 2006, pp. 357-368.

Art by Clive Barker

INTERVIEW WITH CLIVE BARKER

TIM CHIZMAR

WHEN I WAS a child I gravitated towards the larger hardcover bound books at my community library. The very highest level of the deviant and forbidden was always his words, always his. I'd look through *The Books of Blood* and quiver in my little boy boots at what sort of man would create this. Who is he? These images came to life in my youthful impressionable mind, what sort of man indeed. My interest in checking out all of his adult fiction brought the ire of the librarian, who told me emphatically I was forbidden to read the works of Clive Barker unless I had a parent say it was okay. With my mother standing across the checkout table a day or two later, that self-imposed dictator of censorship was confronted and as she backed down from her earlier judgment she told my mother something I never forgot, "Well fine—he can read Clive Barker, but know this, he'll either grow up to be a great horror writer, or a serial killer."

I never killed anyone, but I did begin writing, and occasionally I thought of him. I met him in person for the first time at Dark Delicacies, the classic brick and mortar shop dedicated to all things macabre, located in Burbank, California. I remember clearly so desperately wanting to separate myself from the regular fans standing in line, to let him know I wasn't just an admirer but rather a peer. A fellow dark dreamer. However, I was still a peer holding books for him to sign just like everyone else. I had to find a way . . . I decided on a few choice statements to show how I was different. When I had my moment with him, we connected over my unusual musings, and he invited me to his side of table, (it had worked!) I sat next to my guru as he finished signing and doodling art for the rest of the fans. He invited me to pose for a collection of photography, but I chickened out because it was very erotic. We exchanged emails for years after that, advice and notes about the industry as my career blossomed. He even gave me a blurb on my writing, which graced the cover of my first book. Getting to know him as I have I can say without a doubt he is a very giving, charming, and unique individual. Nobody sees the world like this visionary. While at the same time, he is human, and after being bedridden from toxic shock for nearly three years he was the first to tell me that he isn't the man he used to be. No matter, Clive Barker is an artist we all can relate to, and still has the fire in his eyes. Having an excuse to meet back up with him for this book was a joy.

Segments of this interview were recorded over the course of three visits around Halloween 2018, at his home in Beverly Hills, California. I hope you enjoy it.

TIM CHIZMAR: Welcome!

CLIVE BARKER: Isn't it I who should welcome you?

We both laugh.

TC: Very nice to be here with you again.

CB: Very nice indeed.

TC: What is it that you love about the writing process?

CB: Well I don't always love it, it can be a pain in the frickin ass, you know this—there are days where the page seems to recede from you, you know I handwrite everything obviously (*Clive motions to stacks of papers*) and there are days where the pen can't make contact to the paper. Or if it does, it's not a good word that appears, and that happens. Now, on the other hand, there are days when a lucidity that is unearned by any method that I know in your pen: actually head-heart-pen, right? I think that's the three-part journey. Yeah? For me as a handwritten . . . Actually from heart to head to hand. It goes to heart first because if I don't feel it, I have no interest in telling it, does that make sense?

TC: Yes, of course, are you more plot-driven or character-based in your writing?

CB: I don't think there's a difference. If there's no character there's no plot . . . If there's no plot, the characters just stand there.

TC: Please tell me, do your characters ever surprise you?

CB: All the fucking time, absolutely, but that's not the same as difference between plot and characters is it? With respect, plot is a way to move a narrative toward a conclusion which you have either morally, or philosophically, or spiritually predetermined: I want to give stories to people. A river that moves really fast carries larger stones, the stone represents the weight of philosophical spiritual content, the narrative should move forward, yeah? And there should be an inevitability about it, you don't know where it's going, but you know it's going somewhere. You're in the hands of somebody who has begun to tell a tale that he or she is driven to tell. What drives me are three things: Curiosity, curiosity, curiosity. I am spiritually curious—I am sexually curious—geographically curious . . . That is to say that very few of my narratives if any, now that I think of it, happen in the same place . . . I never thought about that before . . . I've written, I dunno, 40 books . . . I don't think I've ever written a story set in the same city. I love new places. I've written about Liverpool, my hometown I think actually twice, once in a short story and once in *Weaveworld,* so I have been back there twice, but by and large I like to go to new places. People are different from each other and very often places are different from each other. I'm astonished that white people write only about white people, largely speaking, broadly speaking, straight people write largely about only straight people, gay men tend to write about other gay men, gay women tend to write about other gay women . . . If I were a wrestler I'd want to write a book about boxing! If I was a boxer I'd want to write about masturbation, I don't know whatever it was going to be. I don't think there's a reason—for me it's journeying. Of one kind or another and you want to journey places you haven't been before. I'm not good in crowds to be perfectly honest. I have to be in some faintly altered state of soul to feel comfortable about wandering around. I can get into an altered state just by getting naked.

TC: I certainly understand that. Tell me, Clive, what advice would you give to young writers? Somebody new, just starting out?

CB: A filmmaker came to Kubrick and said, "I want to make films. Mr. Kubrick what should I do?" Buy a camera, he had said.

TC: I believe James Cameron said that to a fan as well, so in other words, are you saying people just over-think it?

CB: Yeah what is there to think about? If you're gonna write then fucking write.

TC: I love it!

CB: People come up to me at conventions, and say things like I have a great idea for a novel, I say good when did you start writing it? Oh, you're gonna write it? I'll just take 50%. They say that so often, so often, and I say—you really don't get this, do you? Its not about having an idea. T.S. Elliot said it's not good enough to be drunk on a Friday night writing a poem, [when] you have to be sober at 9AM on a Monday morning, writing a poem, writing from an altered state is earned by writing. You don't get drunk and then write, firstly it won't be any good, and secondly you'll be an alcoholic by the end of the week. You've got to work from a place of joy in the process of writing. And the problem with that is that very often the process isn't joyful. Because its hard fucking work . . .

TC: Yes, it sure is.

CB: . . . and, because you mess up, right? You've been to all these places yourself, so we are talking writer-to-writer here. I think you may end up answering this question yourself, because between the two of us, we probably know about all the pitfalls and all the highs. The highs when they come along are mind-blowing, aren't they?

TC: Yes, I was just the guest speaker for a screenwriter event in Hollywood, and it felt like joy.

CB: Although, lets be honest, a screenplay is an invitation to a dance. It's not the dance.

TC: Yes, that's correct, I always say there are three movies, the one you write, the one you shoot, and the one they edit. Three completely different movies.

CB: There's four, the one they review! There's a 5th, the one they review 30yrs after . . .

TC: This is fascinating.

CB: I can testify to that, because *Cabal,* and

Nightbreed, and the Directors Cut came out last year with the 25min they had [initially] cut put back in again, and the movie that people despised, they now adored. Yes, and there's a 6th one! The one they review when you're dead. In other words, what I'm saying is, a movie seems fixed, doesn't it? But it's protean, because people change and people's response [change] as well. People's response to narrative changes. What we thought *Hansel and Gretel* was about when we first heard it is not what *Hansel and Gretel* is about. Right, Its about two children lost in a forest, almost eaten alive, and who were put their by their mother and father. Bruno Bettelheim writes about this, about fairy tales' subtectual life. Now, if that's true of a fairy tale in ten pages long, how much more true is it in a long elaborate short story or a novel? The complexity of possibilities that can and do happen. You know it was Socrates, or some Greek, that said you never step into the same river twice. Yeah that's true, true for two reasons number one, the water has moved on, and number two, you are not the same person who last stepped into that river. So when you start the next sentence of your book, you're not going to be the person you were when you left it. You had a conversation, you got into a depressed state, you got into a joyful state, and you feel angry, you do feel, whatever it is . . . I am given things often in the night, an example: *Brother Plato right or wrong, said the tribe where I belong, is a family of souls in two, me a half another you, lets stay together one tonight, and prove our brother Plato right.*

Now, I woke up in the middle of the night, wrote *that* down, and fell asleep again. I knew I'd written it in the morning, but I didn't have any clue as to where it came from. It's a very elaborate rhyme scheme,

So the first line echoes the last line: *Brother Plato right or wrong* and *prove our brother Plato right*. So the structure, you can't get into it, it's a lot you can't polish, there's nothing to polish, and somebody gave me that. I'm not someone that believes my subconscious is a genius (*he laughs*) I don't, I don't . . . Something is in the air around us, I'm speaking now of everybody, but moreso those who are willing to enhance their creativity with doing it a lot. There's something around us, that is—how do I say this?—It's like somebody doesn't allow access to these things is like a sealed steel ball, somewhere locked in the middle of that steel ball is their soul—you, me . . . We may still be steel balls, but our steel balls are full of holes! Right, the energies which are around us all the time are being drawn in through those holes, to what's in the middle, which is us. All I am doing all the time is making sure the holes are clean and open and wide, and that's the most I can do as an artist. I can't practice it. It's not like a violin. I can just do it, and if I do it often enough, well, meticulously enough, the powers that surround us—the divine things—allow for creation.

TC: What of overt sexuality, which seems to be a reoccurring theme for you in your work . . .

CB: Sexuality is a very fucking complicated thing.

We both laugh.

TC: How do you handle depression, or life's bullshit, in your work?

CB: We all have bad times. Hollywood is based on lies to a large extent. What could be is not necessarily what will be. But we can undo the curse. By large, I believe people don't believe there are ways to undo the curse anymore. I think Trump has something to do with that, our situation globally has something to do with that, that we are watching the world fall apart and nobody seems to give a fuck.

TC: You've worked in so many mediums, comics, books, movies, video games is there any interconnectivity? For example, now everything comes from graphic novels . . .

CB: Pity, isn't it? My point is, I can't paint at the top of my talent in a comic, I can't write a poem in a comic, I can't talk about . . . Look, I love comics, but they are a very limited medium, very limited, aren't they? I fear that the explosion of movies based on comics will kill comics, because people won't want to read static images in which someone who isn't Robert Downey Jr. is playing Iron Man. When was the last time you read *Prince Valiant,* the comic book, or *Flash Gordon*?

TC: Never. I saw Flesh Gordon . . .

CB: So did I. (*laughs*) Serious question, though, my point is these were extraordinary comic books.

TC: Okay.

CB: And you don't know what they are anymore. Yet there's a new *Flash Gordon* on Netflix, in other words ... comics are seen as source material for experiments.

TC: Perhaps they are seen and used as a storyboard.

CB: You are right, they are a storyboard. For me things always come back to books, always. Look at Jack Kirby, I knew Jack very little, but he did six pages a day. When you look at it now, it's awesome, but it does look exactly like what you just said. It looks like storyboards. Yet it isn't. It's the outpourings one of the most extraordinary imaginations of the 20th Century, and if you were to ask somebody who created Iron Man, most people would say Robert Downey Jr.

TC: Wow.

CB: Don't you think? Do you think anybody would say—Oh, ah, Jack Kirby—Do you think anybody would actually say that now?

TC: No the average ticket-going fan . . . I agree.

CB: If we are going by numbers, I think the average ticket-going fan couldn't give a flying fuck what the origins of the material are.

TC: That's a shame

CB: But don't you think it's true?

TC: I'm a Comic-Con guy, so my circle . . .

CB: Yeah, I know you, this isn't about you, and we value *Dr.Strange*. You know who made *Dr.Strange*? Steve Ditko's work redefines what magic is in comic books. His work is groundbreaking, the designs of the environments and not just the characters. How many people know who made *Dr.Strange* ?

TC: Well, that's a shame.

CB: But do you agree?

TC: Sadly, let me ask you another question. You've created video games such as Jericho and others, what is that process like?

CB: I had the best time, because I got to do the designs; I got to do the story. Then the stuff I don't really like, the technical stuff, I didn't have any hand in. I'd have gladly done more but it's a very strange business. I never understood the politics of it. It's like working for a studio in which you never meet the people that head up the studio. I did three in total.

TC: Do you have an ending in mind? Do all the paths lead to the same big bad guy?

CB: There is no ending, is there? Lots of endings, you play it out, in theory it's like a Chess game, no two are exactly alike.

TC: So, you just create the pieces and let them go at it?

CB: It's like making a map for which there are diverse routes. Then you create the characters and say, have at it guys. So much of it is trickery, saying BOO! and I'm not a big fan of that. I've been surprised at how intense some of the games get, though, incredibly violent.

TC: Was it ever your intention for Pinhead to become a sex symbol?

CB: Nooo, not really . . .

TC: I know I should call him the Hell Priest that was never your intention for him to be given that name.

CB: Its fine, everyone knows him that way anyway. I don't find monsters very sexy, I'm thinking if there are any exceptions to that.

TC: Certainly Hellraiser is very sexual, right?

CB: But sexual is not the same as sexy, is it? He's very sexualized but he talks about pain and pleasure in a detached way. You don't get the impression he's getting off every Wednesday. He's very cold, yet you get told what is true by the people who read you, am I right? Its people's response to the work that tells you what the work is. It never occurred to me that these rather ominous figures would ever be attractive. For example: his is not a face you could touch. By his very nature, it's gonna hurt. Not in a good way. Plus, his personality is not fun. For me, to be sexy is to be fun. He is not fun. He is judgmental, he is cold, and I think that nature is opposite to sexy. Not opposite sexual . . .

TC: If I can be honest, I was terrified when I saw him.

CB: When you first saw him? I love that. That's exactly what was intended.

TC: I wasn't "tee hee" scared like with a Freddy Krueger. I was legitimately terrified, because if you're in a room and the box opens and the doorways open, what are you gonna do? You're fucked.

CB: That's interesting. So it was the box that was the first indicator yes? Have you seen the new Sabrina? They used a lot of my paintings. I haven't seen it yet, but they used a version of my box—called a different kind of configuration puzzle box—on the show. For Hellraiser, I had a story about raising powers, but how could I show that without using images we've seen a thousand times? I didn't want to show drawing in chalk while speaking backwards in Latin, or whatever, so eventually I remembered that my grandfather brought back a puzzle box from China, where he was a ships cook. A very simple one, and nothing as elaborate as in the movie, but it was wooden and it was about the same size as the box. It fascinated me, 'cause there was only one way to make it work. I've long since lost it. It was my grandmother's, and she'd passed and so on, but I thought, wow wouldn't that be cool because raising something is the opening of a door and solving a puzzle is in a way an opening of a door. So using this as a symbolic door-opener, like a key almost, made sense. And then I found this guy, Simon Sayce, who's passed away of cancer, but when he was about your age, we sat down and thought how do we make this like nothing that's been seen before? He obsessed on it for months. He gave me something that is as central a part of the mythology as Pinhead is.

TC: The circular story-telling, the way it opens and closes with the passing of the box, I've watched it lots of times and listened to your commentary with Ashley Lawrence. I loved it, but it terrified me, and that's why I went back and revisited it as an adult to see why it scared me so much.

CB: What was the answer?

TC: Loss of power, and the amazing sequence with the engineer chasing her down the hallway, that was just about the most terrifying thing I've ever seen, because it's so close, and the unpredictability of the box and the doorways, I thought for sure it could close before she got to the end!

CB: Yeah, absolutely, it's even set up like it could happen, I felt that—we made that for nine-hundred thousand bucks, which sounded like a shit ton of money when they said it at first, but it wasn't a lot, and I've always felt when you don't have very much, you try harder. It was stuck together with spit and tape.

TC: It's a masterpiece, it really is great.

CB: Well, thank you, I want to offer these three things as putting myself out of the picture for a moment. I was blessed with special effects such that nobody would expect for that scale of picture. Particularly in the designs, in the way I think, Pinhead once seen is never forgotten, I think.

TC: Chatterer too . . .

CB: They are nightmares. I had a great DP who I could persuade to turn lights off. That time movies were over lit, you remember? Look at Poltergeist now. It's like a Disneyland movie. Bright, bright, bright, even something like Fright Night, which is a movie I love, nevertheless, bright! I said to him, I know you're not going to like this, but we are going to turn lights off. There's a shot for instance—I remember this, because we had a big argument over it—close-up of the guy who was playing Frank hunched in the corner of the upstairs room when he's not really fully brought back, and he turns and looks at Julia through the door there, and he says "I need more blood" or something, and there was a lot of light on him, and I said we'll do it your way, but then lets shoot it by turning off everything but one light. It was a rim light shot, basically. In dailies the next day he said, "Okay I'm convinced." We turned off a lot of lights, it had two advantages: it made the thing look bigger, because with a lot of darkness you're not sure what's there. Secondly, it made it look kinda classy. The most important thing I had was Chris Young, I had music.

TC: The music was powerful.

CB: Powerful and bigger, much bigger than a movie of that scale would normally be.

TC: Creepily cheerful, that sound like a toy box.

CB: Absolutely, the little Chinese box from my grandfather had a little "ding, ding, tinkle, tinkle" noise inside it, I mentioned that to Chris and he put that in it. He had a sense of grandeur, when the opening credits go, we were used to Carpenter's two fingers the Halloween deal, no argument about that, it works, but it wasn't big and I had seen The Fury with a John Williams score and it had this magnificence to it, and I think it's a much better film than people give it credit for. I'm not a big DePalma fan across the board, but I think it's a great picture. I thought, wow, if I could get that kind of sound. We had this tiny room with a piano and we went through this for weeks, he instantly got it and wanted to make it as big as possible. We called in favors from everywhere to have a much bigger orchestra than we could afford. As a consequence, the picture grows; it just grows in scale because the music does that for you.

TC: It all just stays with the viewer, with so many layers.

CB: It's about something. It's about a family. I've always said the scariest line in the movie is: "Come to Daddy," because firstly it's not her father, secondly it implies something incestuous is about to happen. It's certainly sexual what he's saying to her, and for one terrible moment you think maybe she'll succumb to this, then she gets to scrape his face and you see there's another body below there. First thing I said on the day of reading the thing, I said to everyone this is not funny.

TC: Why do you think so many people fight horror from being mainstream?

CB: Mainstream horror is only acceptable to reviewers if it doesn't take itself seriously. In other words if it seems to be mocking itself or if it seems to be done for the buck, reviewers say, "That proves me right. This is a worthless genre." The whole idea of coming to peace with horror means that you are taking the idea of horror in the world as something that is real I don't think most people want to think about that. That's okay, because I don't want to say I'm like you, because I'm not like you.

TC: It's a shame people still think horror writers are psychos or crazy.

CB: But let me offer this, if we were normal . . .

TC: You know what Oscar Wilde said? "The only normal people you know are the people you don't know that well?"

CB: Right, right, right, which is the equivalent of Groucho's "I don't want to be a member of a club that would have me as a member."

Shared laugh.

TC: I love Groucho.

CB: So do I.

Art by Clive Barker

WRITING YOUR WORLD

CREATING A UNIVERSE IN JUST A FEW EASY STEPS

KEVIN J. ANDERSON

AT THE BEGINNING of my writing career, when I tackled my first real, full-length novel, I was ambitious, but I didn't really know anything. That didn't stop me, though—I was a writer. I could just make it all up.

The novel was an epic fantasy (of course), the first in a trilogy (also, of course). I drew a map, covered it with obstacles, mountains, rivers, deserts, monster lairs, empty cities, and I turned my characters loose, magic sword and all, on their epic quest from one side of the map to the other.

Having grown up in a small Wisconsin town, I had never seen real mountains, the ocean, jungles, or a large city. I had never been out of the country, or experienced unusual cultures first-hand (honest, I had never even eaten Chinese food). I had a lot of learning to do.

While building my publication credits, I wrote a few brief freelance articles for *Dragon Magazine*, the official Dungeons & Dragons publication, on little historical details of interest to gamers: medieval doctors, real medicinal plants that might be found in the wild, innovative techniques for cleaning armor while on a quest. I also landed an interesting job from my friend and fellow aspiring writer Mike Stackpole. He's now a well-established *New York Times* bestselling author, but at the time he was just a precocious young gamer only a few years older than me, with a small startup gaming company. He produced "Mythospaks"—ready-made worlds, complete with stats, in which RPG players could set their games. Mike hired me to write a Mythospak about a world of my choosing (I selected the setting for my own epic fantasy novel in progress), and he gave me a list of things I needed to describe in order to fully flesh out the environment.

Oh, the things I didn't know about my own world.

It was a revelation, because every answer I developed led to more questions and more descriptions, which set off other descriptions. By the time I was finished and I delivered the completed, Mythospak, my novel was richer and more complex. My world felt real. The characters had a full-color three-dimensional playground instead of a rough sketch. (That novel was, *Gamearth*, my second published novel.)

Over the years I expanded on that ingredients list, turned it into a full-blown toolkit. The process of building the world properly is the most inspirational step in developing a novel, because the answers I come up with lead to some of the best scenes, ideas, and plot twists. I've written an entire book on my methodology, *Worldbuilding: From Small Towns to Entire Universes*, but I'll give the broad strokes here to convey the scope of the project.

The Ingredients

Building a world depends on more than just drawing a map and imagining some terrain. A fully fleshed-out fictional world has cultures and economics, varying climates, religions, arts, politics, social expectations.

This isn't just for exotic, fantastical places. Writing a modern-day, mainstream story set in a real place also requires world-building, because not every reader will be familiar with what you consider to be mundane details. I grew up in a small Midwestern farming town, and the everyday details of local farmers and their schedules, the smell of manure spreaders during springtime, the fields of cabbages, hunting for wild asparagus along the fence line, catching caterpillars, playing with my cousins and receiving hand-me-down clothes that circulated around the family at least three times before they fell into rags. All that was perfectly normal to me and utterly boring, but would it be a truly alien experience to, say, be a stock broker in Manhattan or a dance student in Los Angeles.

Even familiar cities and towns have a unique character. Seattle is different from New York, to Chicago, or New Orleans, or the mining colony on the ice moon of Rigel Seven, or the dragon-infested kingdom of Malgorn. Each has its own feel, its own climate, its own history and culture. A writer has to paint the full picture so your reader has an *experience*, not just a story.

These are my key elements to consider and develop for a fully formed fictional world:
- Geography
- Climate

- Politics
- Economics
- Society
- Religion
- Science
- Arts
- History

Geography

If we're going to build a world, let's start with the *world itself*—the geography, the landscape. Are your characters in a giant desert like Frank Herbert's *Dune*? Is it an ice planet like Hoth from *The Empire Strikes Back*? Is it a lush landscape with forests and mountains like Middle Earth?

Every epic fantasy novel seems to have a big map with suitably spaced hazards from west to east, so the characters can encounter plenty of adventures along the way. Don't succumb to "wistful fictional geography." Rivers start in the mountains and drain toward the sea. Settlements tend to arise where there's a *reason* for a lot of people to gather: rivers or harbors, major crossroads, the site of important resources (wood, iron ore, salt), and there will be roads to connect the various settlements.

Climate

Climate is more than just "It was a cloudy day outside." Climate drives an entire culture.

A civilization that springs up on a lush tropical island, with plentiful water, fish, fruit, and moderate temperatures, will be very different from the culture that develops in an exceedingly harsh equatorial desert or in the frozen sub-arctic tundra.

Do your people live in a land with changing seasons, from hot summers to cold winters, or do they live in a temperate area where hunting, fishing, and agriculture continue throughout the year? When your survival depends on planting at a certain time, harvesting at a certain time, and preserving and storing lots of food for an entire season, your characters will have a different mindset than if they know every day is going to be basically the same.

Climate influences clothing styles and fabrics, and therefore *trade* in the materials to make those clothes. An extremely cold environment requires warm clothing, thick wool, or furs. In a hot and humid climate, clothing would be loose and cool, and traders would focus instead on fabrics like cotton and silk.

Climate has an effect on food and cooking styles. In hot, moist climates where food spoils quickly, the locals tend to make heavily spiced dishes. In colder climates where there is a seasonal component to hunting and fishing, the people have to gather and store a year's worth of food in a fairly short time period: drying, salting, pickling, even freezing.

Politics

Is your society a monarchy? If so, how does the succession run? First-born male child? First-born child of either sex? Does the leadership pass by right of mortal combat among all of the ruler's children, and may the best candidate win? Is the ruler a usurper or tyrant, hated by all the downtrodden people, or is it a rightful king or queen whose rule is not questioned? Or is the land run by a council of elders? A council of nobles? How are they chosen? Through inheritance, or merit, or randomly chosen by nametags drawn out of a cauldron? Are the council members honorable or corrupt? Is it a democracy? How to people vote? Are people literate and knowledgeable enough to vote?

Do your people live in a free culture where they are allowed to poke fun and make biting satirical commentary of the rulers, or are such comments swiftly and violently repressed? Are the laws upheld or are the police and justices subject to bribery? Do people even have a sense of fairness and justice?

Economics

What do people do for a living? How do they pay their bills? How will they acquire the necessities of getting from day to day? Where do they get shelter?

A society has the basics of growing or acquiring food, and then distributing it, which leads to transportation needs and providers, merchants, as well as the subsidiary industries of cooks, restaurants, inns, and on and on. The same goes for resources: woodcutters, lumber mills, carpenters, and miners, smelters, blacksmiths, and quarry workers, stonecutters, masons. Everything *in* your society was created and built by someone.

Is there some special commodity that's unique to the city or land—like the spice in *Dune*, for example. Or, closer to home, we have petroleum, buried under a harsh desert inhabited by often hostile people or out in the wild, storm-whipped North Sea.

Society

The social structure creates a framework for everything your characters do. How are people treated in your fictional world? Are they happy and pursuing dreams in their everyday life, or do they live in a repressive world, tight-lipped and fearful at any moment?

Is your population treated equally, or is there a rigid class system? If there is general equality among the sexes and races, then your character interactions can proceed however you like. A strict class system, however, adds an entirely different set of complications to your plot and characters.

How do people interact inside and outside of their classes? Are there extremely differentiated castes, or just a general spectrum from the powerful to the powerless? The wealthy and the poor? They will *act* differently toward one another.

How are women treated? Are they considered objects of great beauty? Held inside a noble house and never let outside? Or forced to cover up every part of their skin so that no other men can be jealous? Are they kept barefoot and pregnant, or are they equal partners in society? Are they allowed to be educated? Are they revered and worshipped as in a great matriarchy?

Do your people have large families, or are they limited (perhaps by the government) to one or two offspring?

How are children treated? How does your society treat the sick and poor? Are there beggars in the streets, or can anyone find a job to earn room and board when needed? Are the sick cared for with benevolent healers, or are they abandoned, left to die? What about the elderly? Are they revered or considered a burden and a waste of resources?

How does communication work in your society, particularly long-distance communication? How is news spread? By courier? Newspaper? Telepathy? Spell mirrors? How do people know about the rest of their world?

How does the military fit into society? Does the ruler hire mercenary forces or security troops when she feels the need? Or is there a large (and expensive) standing army at all times?

On the flip side of warfare and defense, what do the people do for *fun*? What are the main leisure activities? Are there interesting sports, perhaps some that require individual exercise and physical prowess, or others that have become team sports? And what about drugs? Are they commonplace and socially accepted, like caffeine, alcohol, or tobacco . . . or are they potent and illegal?

Religion

Religion (or rival religions) is one of the primary drivers in a world, shaping many aspects of culture and society. What sort of god or gods do the people worship? Are they benevolent paternal or maternal figures, or are they scary monsters that demand sacrifices? Or are the "gods" mere philosophical concepts for comfort and enlightenment, like an esoteric Higher Power.

Even if the gods themselves don't have walk-on

roles in your story, the organized religion may be powerful enough to dominate much of the world. Is your religion powerful and monolithic, like the Catholic Church in Europe in the Middle Ages? Or are there various churches, sects, cults, and traditions? If so, how are the others tolerated? Is there a grab-bag of cults all vying for new members, or are any new religions forced to meet in secret back rooms or else face persecution?

What about the priests and the priesthood? Are they respected? Are they allowed to marry and have children? Are they literate?

Science

How do people think the world works? Do they know where the sun goes at night? When your characters hear thunder in the sky, do they believe gods are battling in the clouds, or do they know it's caused by hot and cold air masses colliding in the atmosphere?

Does everyone have a basic scientific understanding, or are scientists—alchemists, astronomers—revered and mysterious, like high priests or magicians?

How widespread is education? Is it open and available to everyone, or just to an elite? Does everyone know how to read and write? Do they understand mathematics? Or is such knowledge limited to a secret cabal of experts?

What is the state of medicine, and hence, what is the state of biological knowledge? Are there large hospitals and medical schools with dissection laboratories, or are there just local healers using traditional remedies and "old wives tale" knowledge passed from generation to generation? Are women allowed to be educated? And if so, are there specific professions in which they specialize? Can they be doctors or just midwives?

How is information disseminated? Is there the printing press? Are books widely available in free libraries to anyone who wants to read them (again, assuming they can all read)? Or do secret societies keep treasure troves of repressed information? Are there elaborate scientific societies and universities, or just crackpot inventors working in a shed behind the garage?

Arts

Artistic expression is what gives a society its "look and feel."

Start with architecture. When your character arrives in a new city, what does she see? Think of the graceful domes and minaret spires of Istanbul, or the cold and blocky buildings of Soviet-era Warsaw, the soaring stone castles and cathedrals in Europe, the wooden churches of Scandinavia, the low adobe pueblos of the American Southwest. Are the buildings painted with bright frescoes, brilliant primary colors, or are they subdued—grays, whites, tans? Are the buildings themselves considered beautiful, or just utilitarian?

Is there a specific style of music? Do the minstrels play folk songs, or impassioned religious hymns, or do they sing thinly disguised commentary on current events? Do they play interesting musical instruments—flutes, drums, stringed instruments? Accordions?

Art—decorations, paintings, sculptures, music, writing, and poetry—is an indicator of the extent of free expression. Are people allowed to be imaginative and even eccentric in creating new works? That sort of thing happens only in a free *and prosperous* society. In a squalid subsistence-farming village or in a nomadic tribe in the drought-stricken Serengeti, you won't find many people supporting themselves through poetry or portrait painting.

History

Your world has a history, and even if the characters don't know all the names and dates, they will have a general awareness of where they come from and what happened before. What happened before your story starts? Has there been a long-standing peace and your people are relaxed and confident of where they'll be in a year or a decade, or have the characters lived through an endless succession of political upheavals and the resulting social turmoil?

Is your story set in a newly formed colony, or do they live in an ancient city steeped in centuries of history and traditions?

Were your people recently conquered and now live under disliked overlords, or are they the conquerors themselves? Remember, winners and losers will have an entirely different version of what happened.

The Finishing Touches

No matter how much meticulous detail you put into developing your world: *Don't Include Everything!* World-building details are like seasoning thrown in to enhance, but not overwhelm, the flavor of your story.

You don't have to answer every one of these questions for the world you're creating—but at least think about them, especially the ones that have something to do with your specific story and characters.

When you start turning over the creative rocks and looking at what might scurry out, the very answers you concoct might spark story ideas or new characters, or just interesting background details that will make your world stand out.

SPEAK UP: THE WRITER'S VOICE

ROBERT FORD

LET'S TALK FOR a bit, you and I.

Pull up a bar stool and order something. Drinks are on me. Don't worry, I'm not going to ask what your sign is or if you come here often. That's not my shtick.

I want to tell you something. Something . . . *horrible.*

A writer's voice is tone and style and rhythm. It's grammar and structure, but it's not *only* those things. It's the writer's unique way of *telling* a story. It's what breathes life into the work itself. Take out the writer's voice and what you're reading becomes void of personality. It stops engaging the reader and is about as effective as a lab report.

As a writer, your personality and delivery is your fingerprints on the work. Carry personal experiences into your words. Readers want to see and feel what the characters are going through—and you're the only one who can deliver that to them.

Nurtured and developed, a writer's voice is what keeps readers coming back to new work. It's the way *you* write and tell a story: the cadence and word choices, the overall rhythm and attitude. *No one else* can tell a particular story like *you* can. So own it.

Let's talk about cadence for a moment. When you're writing a story, that's the flow of sentences and structure of how you put things together. While you're reading another writer's work, take a step back from being a reader and study it as a writer. You'll start to notice patterns in the work and how that writer handles things.

During action scenes or moments of high tension, the sentences are usually much shorter. Adjectives are dumped in favor of brevity. Kill and burn every adverb (in general, this is a damned good rule) in lieu of a better word. The story is tighter so the reader moves faster through the material. It's a subconscious trick that triggers the reader into actually feeling what the character is feeling.

One or two short sentences followed by a free-form piece helps create a flow and rhythm to your work. When it feels right, it feels right and you'll know it. The pieces jog together to fit like a puzzle.

Word choices in your work also help differentiate your specific voice. Stephen King has often been referred to as "blue collar horror" because, for the most part, his work is very easy to read, with few lofty words—however, he does season his work with some upper-end vocabulary for the reader, and I think that's important.

Tone and attitude are the last pieces that make up your voice. These components are sometimes a little more intangible than others because they come from your outlook on the world as a person. It's the way *you* express yourself.

Do you curse a lot in real life? Do your everyday metaphors lean toward the Deep South like an apple tree in a high wind? Or are your sentences and word choices coming from the sun-baked asphalt of a city?

Write *your* story. Be vulnerable and raw and let your readers see you for who you are. After all, that's what they're paying for. Write from the heart and be *you.*

I see you shaking your head over there. I see the question floating in those dark eyes. I'm talking about the *writer's* voice, not the *character's* voice. There's a big difference.

If you happen to be writing a character who has grown up on the streets of Philadelphia and has never seen the other side of the Schuylkill River, obviously, you can't have them speak as if they're from backwoods Alabama, of course not. Those are the choices you make for their dialogue and thoughts—*as a character.* But your writing voice is still what's delivering the goods.

I've written about hit men and prostitutes, con men and feral children, but my voice was the vehicle delivering the goods. There's a scene in the movie, *Reservoir Dogs,* where the actor Tim Roth is playing an undercover cop and is getting trained on telling a funny backstory so he's believable to the group he's infiltrating. He's told in training it's like learning a joke—you learn the joke, add inflections and tell it your own way. In that process, it becomes your own.

Your work might include a serial killer or racist in the south or an aging cop caught up in a case. Give those characters personality and flaws and put them through hell so the reader can go along for the ride. Deliver their emotions truthfully and sincerely to their character, but write it your way. Again, when it feels right, you'll know it.

There are so many writers who have such an incredibly distinct voice. Stephen King. Elmore Leonard, and hell, he's on the sidelines as a screenwriter, but throw in Quentin Tarantino as well.

Let's paint a scene.

It's a Saturday, barely past lunchtime and all those writerly fellas mentioned above are sitting on a few well-worn but incredibly uncomfortable chairs in the lobby of a bank. The air conditioning inside is a welcome relief to the blistering August heat.

Four men rush inside into the bank lobby. All of them dressed in tactical gear and holding automatic weapons.

Annnnnnd go! How would each of those writers tell that story? King would focus on the minute sensory details as he described the scene, and perhaps get inside their heads. Leonard would have some of the crispest dialogue you've ever read, communicating the action and the character's personalities. Quentin would tell the story with ultra-violence that still somehow resonates with the everyday man.

Now, how would *you* describe that scene?

Developing your voice as a writer takes time and effort. Most writers, early in their career, emulate their heroes and start mimicking their style—often it's not even on purpose. There's nothing wrong with that, it's natural, but your work will definitely be compared to that writer's voice, and sometimes not in a good way. Don't get me wrong, when you get your first good review comparing you to your idol.

Oh my god. Yes, it makes you all fluttery inside.

Because it's comparing you to your hero. It feels damn good, but there also might be times when your work is described as a watered down version of (insert author-hero here). You have to eventually develop your *own* style and voice.

Why?

Because if you don't, you'll *always* be in their shadow. You've emulated them enough to be mentioned in comparison. The first time, it's great. The third and fifth time might be great, too. But after that? Guess what?

You're not *in* someone's shadow anymore. You've *become* the shadow.

There's only going to be one Stephen King. One Joe Lansdale. One Elmore Leonard. One Tarantino.

And only one you.

So, how do you develop your voice?

Read. Read your ass off. Go through the mistakes of writing. Mimic your heroes. Write your stories in their voice. Get *complimented* on how much you sound like them. Get *rejected* because of how much you sound like them.

Keep going. Eventually you'll shed those comparisons like a favorite old flannel shirt and you'll move on to your own groove.

Sell your first story. Get reviewed. Get compared. Eventually your reviews will be focused on *you* because you'll stand out as unique and different from the others.

Don't forget, as you're developing your own style and voice, the need for a good editor is so incredibly important. You can't sharpen a blade by running it over a whetstone once or twice, and you can't improve your writing unless you continue to hone your style with good editing. It helps to have another set of eyes on your work to cut out unnecessary parts. It will tighten your work, refining it *and* your voice.

Early on, I got into the mindset of trying to write a story as if I was sitting at a diner with a friend and relaying it in person. I always read my work out loud to hear if it sounds right—that helps *immensely* to understand if the words flow into the rhythm I want. When you're writing dialogue, I find reading the lines out loud to be a crucial part of ensuring they sound natural. You'll also clearly begin to see the things you can edit. Try it once and you'll see you can probably delete a ton of speech tags.

Over time, you'll find your own cadence, rhythm, and structure. With close to seven billion people on the planet, you are the only one who can tell your story *your* way.

Now it's your turn. I'll keep the bar tab running but I'm not leaving. I'm here and I'm listening. Tell me something. Tell me a story.

Tell me something . . . *horrible.*

WRITING A BETTER WORLD

CHRISTOPHER GOLDEN

I RETURNED FROM the DFW Writers' Conference, deeply tired but very happy to have spent several days with such a diverse group of writers. I'm so grateful for the invitation and for the enthusiasm and kindness shown to me by organizers, attendees, and other guests alike. (Most of all, I had to thank Jennifer Duggins for both her efforts and her effervescent presence.) I was inspired, both by the people I met and by the fact that DFW Con is a place where writers of every literary stripe gather in mutual respect and encouragement, no one thinking their brand or style is any more legitimate than any other. For writers, that kind of camaraderie is food for the soul.

When Jennifer contacted me to ask if I'd deliver their Sunday keynote, I was a little nervous. It's not something I've done a lot of. But then she told me the theme was "Writing for a Better World," and I was in.

Several people have asked me to post the text of that speech. So here it is, for those of you who may be interested. Thanks for reading.

We never really grow up. Never really leave behind the children we were, or forget the lessons we learned then—at least not for long. We *change*, though. THAT, we do. Common wisdom suggests that people do not change, but we do. We *can*. And the simplest and most difficult way to do that is to choose it.

As a kid, and later in college, and later in adulthood, I have met people who have accused me of being perhaps a bit over-earnest. There's a dichotomy there, because anyone who knows me will tell you that I am one sarcastic son of a bitch. Growing up in New England, you learn sarcasm around the same time you learn to walk. That's just sparring. Keeping your wit sharpened. But when it comes to things I care about, I am often painfully sincere. Some people are made uncomfortable by that sincerity. Others distrust it, presuming it hides some ulterior motive. Still others deride sincerity as terminally uncool. Well I'm guilty of giving a damn. And I'm not ashamed.

Which is why I can begin, un-ironically, with this.

When Robin Williams died and I learned the heartbreaking truth about his pain, I wanted to make sure my children knew him from something other than *Aladdin*. I pulled out the film of his that had most inspired me, the Peter Weir film, *Dead Poets Society*, about an English teacher who inspires a group of boys at an American boarding school in 1959. Williams's character, John Keating, not only helps the boys to face their troubles, he inspires them to care about one another and to aspire to a better future, to dream about the roles they might play in achieving it for themselves.

In the moment that resonated with me most, Keating challenges the boys to interpret the meaning of the Walt Whitman poem, "O Me! O Life!" In this moment, the teacher lays his heart bare not with confession or personal revelation, but with bold earnestness . . . utter sincerity. He inspires these boys because they can see and feel how much his message *to them*, means *to him*. The pertinent lines of Whitman's poem come at the end, and Keating reads these lines aloud.

"The question, O me! So sad, recurring—What good amid these, O me, O life?

Answer.

That you are here. That life exists, and identity. That the powerful play goes on, and you may contribute a verse."

Keating repeats that last line.

"That the powerful play goes on, and you may contribute a verse."

I am no literary stalwart. I'm a storyteller, mostly a genre writer. I write horror and fantasy, science-fiction and mystery and comic books. Many would not consider these serious works, but despite my sincerity I never made it my goal to set the literary world on fire. I have only ever wanted to tell stories. To entertain. I don't write about politics, but I also don't try to erase my convictions from the page. When we put words on the page and we know those words will be read by others, even if all we really want is to tell stories that people will enjoy, we need to remember the influence that fiction can have. All you need to do is think back to the books that helped to formulate who you are. That influence is undeniable. Without it, none of you would be sitting in this room.

Epiphanies come at the strangest times. I'm terrible with chronology, but if memory serves this one came not long after 9/11. I was being interviewed about horror and the usual question came up, "What scares you the most?"

Because I'm an over-earnest son of a bitch, I took the question very seriously.

"Nothing scares me," I said, "more than the fact that we've finally reached the point when politicians have stopped bothering to pretend they *aren't* lying to us."

That sort of sentiment doesn't make its way into my work very often, but when it does, you end up with something like *Tin Men*, a military SF thriller that came out last year. I won't bore you with the pitch, but suffice to say it's full of the things about the future we're building that scare the shit out of me. And it asks, from a wide variety of angles, a question that echoes in my mind all the time.

What do we stand for?

What do I stand for?

What do *you* stand for?

Which always leads me to think about the characters I'm putting into my work, the stories I'm writing, and what they're saying to my readers. What do I owe them? What do we owe our readers?

The answer, of course, is honesty. And, if we can achieve it, inspiration.

I'm not suggesting that we go easy on our readers. They'd hate that, and so would we.

The good guys don't need to win. We don't owe our readers that. But we do owe our readers and society an acknowledgement that when the good guys lose, it is a loss. Maybe even a tragedy. There will always be those writers and readers and critics who disagree, but I believe that fiction ought to have a fundamental moral center, a narrative awareness that acknowledges certain behaviors as wrong, unsavory, even evil.

I'm not suggesting that we shy away from the darkest stories, from the most profound tragedies, from characters so evil they make the reader cringe, hold their breath, sleep with the light on. But only a glimpse of light will allow readers to recognize the depth of real darkness, to feel the depth of genuine tragedy, to recognize true evil.

Of course, no two of us will share precisely the same moral code or frame of reference. Given the current political climate in this country, that may be truer than ever. But let's begin at least by agreeing on this much—we believe in freedom, equality, and the right to go about our business without being raped or murdered. I'm sure we can add plenty to that, but let's keep it as our baseline. I'm not inside your heads. I can't know what you believe or what you hold sacred. The only thing I can do is talk about my own experience, and what it means to me, and how I hope it applies to you.

Our society is changing, and like it or not, we are changing with it. Life is a series of both epiphanies and gradual realizations. I am not going to change the kinds of stories I write, or the fact that I write them mainly to entertain myself and to entertain readers who want to come along for the ride. But over the years there has been a certain evolution for me, and I want to talk to you about that.

I want to talk about representation and presentation. About the world we live in, and the worlds we create in our writing. About being a thoughtful citizen of the literary realm.

I started my first novel as a senior in college. When writing that novel—*Of Saints and Shadows*—I did a number of things that were outside the mainstream without even realizing I was doing them. One of those things was to make Meaghan Gallagher, the book's female lead, bisexual. I started writing it in 1988 or '89 and sold it to Ace/Berkley in 1992. I'd love to claim that I was being thoughtful or proactive in some way by making that character bi, but it honestly never occurred to me that it was something especially odd for a mainstream book. It fit the plot, made the character more interesting. When I asked a few writers to read it, hoping for blurbs, one of them came back with very kind words, but also mentioned that he could never have written that character . . . that he wouldn't have dared. To this day I'm not sure if he was worried about backlash from the publisher or from readers who might be offended by the inclusion of the character.

I'd been around gay people my entire life: my older sister, Erin, my uncle Sonny, assorted cousins, one of my mother's dearest friends. I still remember a fight my parents had when I was very young, when my mother claimed she didn't know anyone who was gay and my incredulous father shouted at her a litany of the people in her life who were, in fact, gay. I remember thinking, even as young as I was then, ah, well, that explains a lot. I remember the sadness that permeated my sister's life during the height of the AIDS epidemic, when so many men she knew were dying. I remember my mother telling me, one night, that if I ever told anyone else that my sister was gay, she'd never speak to me again. She was emotional that night. She didn't mean it. And she's long since come around, enough to host my sister's wedding at her house. But the moment stayed with me.

Still, I had no agenda back when I was writing, *Of Saints and Shadows*. LGBT people were simply a part of my world, and my fiction reflected that world. By the second novel, *Angel Souls and Devil Hearts*, two of the leads were female vampires in a mature, committed, complex relationship, one a lesbian and the other bi. Gay characters have continued to appear in my work in the decades since then. They're just a part of my world, and they're a part of your world, too. Which is why they belong in our fictional worlds.

But there's more to representation than just presentation.

In *Of Saints and Shadows* and its sequels, Peter Octavian starts out as a private detective who just happens to be a vampire. The fact that he's a vampire is not the all-consuming focus of his character. Likewise, Meaghan Gallagher is a law firm paralegal who just happens to be bisexual. Whether you present diversity in your fiction for some higher purpose or simply because it's how you present the world we all live in, character must come first. Sexual preference *isn't* character. Gender *isn't* character. Race *isn't* character. Those are among many things that inform character, but they are not in and of themselves character, and if you use them as some kind of shorthand to suggest a type, you should think about your goal with that choice. Are you relying on the prejudice and presumptions of others to fill in details?

I've talked very generally about introducing gay and lesbian characters into my work because that was the first time anyone pointed out to me that there was anything unusual or requiring thought about presenting people with experiences other than my own. But Meaghan Gallagher isn't just bisexual, she's also a woman. This may come as a shock to you, but I am neither of those things. It's no coincidence that the main protagonists in most of my adult novels are straight white cisgender males. It's an easy, comfortable place for me to begin. The ground is stable underfoot when I'm starting with a straight white cis guy, and when you're not actively thinking about representation, then it's easy to default back to whatever your personal stable ground might be.

My young adult novels are a bit different. The majority of them feature teenage girl protagonists. Some of my friends will tell you that's because I'm a teenage girl at heart, and they're probably not too far off the mark. But when I write these girls, I'm thinking character first. Jenna Blake, the protagonist of my ten-book Body of Evidence series, is a young college student dealing with imminent adulthood and the way that creates new conflict between her divorced parents. She's also struggling with the way her aversion to blood complicates her desire to become a surgeon someday. Her boss is disabled. Her roommate is Japanese. Her co-worker is a gay man in a committed relationship. Her first serious boyfriend is black. Maybe I was thinking a bit about diversity by then, but I was more focused on my own college experience and the people who populated my world then. They are all characters first. They're *people*, first.

In recent years, I've changed. And that's what I really want to talk to you about today. That change, and why I think we should all be changing, now and for the rest of our lives.

I published two novels in 2015, *Dead Ringers,* and the aforementioned *Tin Men.* Of the three women with major roles in *Dead Ringers*—two of whom I would call the central characters—one is black, one is Indian, and one is a Chinese woman with a pregnant wife. *Tin Men,* is similarly diverse, though most of the time the characters' minds are trapped inside robot bodies.

I'll be honest with you. Though I've made greater efforts toward diversity in my fictional worlds, those efforts fall far short of a crusade or even political correctness. I'm not on a mission. It's still just representing my world, and my shifting perception of it, the things I'm learning. Maybe because of that, I'm naïve. Certainly I felt a bit naïve when I read one of the reviews of *Tin Men* and, in reference to the main character, Kate Wade, the reviewer actually wrote these words, "Why do you have to say she's black?"

Yep. Think on that a moment. "Why do you have to say she's black?"

Naturally my first instinct was to bristle at this, thinking the reviewer must be a racist whose nostrils flared in disdain at the presence of a disabled black woman as the true hero of this military science-fiction thriller. Actually, though, this criticism was coming from the other side of the argument, suggesting in some way that I still don't understand that we ought not to mention the race of a character at all.

I'm not criticizing that position. I simply don't understand it. And I sure as hell don't agree with it.

Now, before I continue, let me say this.

There are people who view writers of one race as

unfit to present the experience of characters of another. The same thing holds true for gender, sexual preference, religion, etc., and I think that's valid and honest. On a long list of words I might use to define myself, one of them is, "Feminist." But I am well aware that men raising their voices to fight other men over the rights of women is a double-edged sword. So I don't want to speak *in place of* a woman, but if I can do something to help quiet the voices speaking against her, I want to do that.

My point is that I don't feel fully qualified to present the true experience of a woman, or a person of color, or someone in the LGBT community, but I am a human being, and I do understand pain and love and hope. If I can't present the true experience of diverse characters, I can at least present those characters with thoughtfulness and respect. I can present diverse characters with humanity.

So let's get back to, *Tin Men,* for a second, and the reviewer who wondered why I had to say Kate Wade was black.

And let's go back much further than that.

I didn't grow up in a particularly enlightened environment. I had the advantage of having diversity in my world, but as a kid, I did and said things that are painful to remember. I laughed at every off color joke and retold most of them, more than once, never understanding how much pain lived inside the words I spoke.

But I learned. I'm far from perfect, but I like to think that the arc of my life is bending toward kindness and fairness and respect. I believe deeply—despite all of the ugliness we see happening out there and all of the people who benefit from sowing the seeds of fear and hatred—that the arc of our society is also bending in that direction.

When I read that review asking why I had to say Kate Wade was black . . . I answered the question. I wrote a blog about it, and I want to share some of that with you now, because I think, in many ways, that blog is why I'm here, at this conference, where the theme is, "Writing for a better world."

We live in the age of outrage, and people will always find a reason to burn.

I have to say Kate is black because most of my readers will otherwise assume she's white, and I want them to envision a world where the most formidable character, the most competent, the one they'll all follow (including the guy you assume is the protagonist), is a black woman with no legs.

I have to say she's black (just a couple of times, not enough to belabor the point but enough so you can see her in your head, particularly since most of the novel she's inside a robot) because if they ever make the movie, I want to create an environment where it would be difficult for studio executives to cast a white actress.

When *Tin Men* was in development as a film, the screenwriters attached to the project created a presentation for the studios they would be pitching it to. The presentation included photos of actors meant to represent the cast, to give the studios some visuals to hang onto while the writers spun out the story for them. Guess what? The image they chose to represent Kate Wade was of a white woman.

I refused to allow it. They argued that it didn't make a difference; that once the movie was greenlit, the producers and director could cast whoever they wanted. I insisted that it did matter, because by doing this, by pitching the character to them as white, they would be giving the studios very clear permission to ignore the race of the character as written. We would be telling the studios that we were in favor of erasing people of color in favor of white faces. And that is something we simply can't do.

A few weeks ago, I watched a very old film called, *Gentleman's Agreement*, starring Gregory Peck. Peck stars as Phil Green, a journalist who—after moving to a new city—decides to write an expose about anti-Semitism by presenting himself to his new co-workers and acquaintances and the world as a person of the Jewish faith. It's uncomfortable viewing for many reasons, but the title of the film comes from a conversation in which Green's fiancée is trying to defend herself against the suggestion that she herself might be anti-Semitic. A Jewish friend uses gentle inquiry to bring her around to the realization that no matter how much she FEELS horrified by the behavior of her society friends and acquaintances, by staying silent, she is tacitly approving and encouraging the behavior she claims to loathe.

Why do I have to say she's black?

Because there are people who don't want her to be.

There are people who don't want their protagonists to be anything but what they are, just as there are people who want you to be afraid of anyone different from you and who think the very idea that those different people want to be treated equally is an affront to common decency. Those people need someone to explain to them the meaning of the phrase common decency, but they're out there. Some of you might agree more with them than you do with me, though I hope not.

So many people, ordinary people with hearts just as tender as yours and dreams just as big, suffer from the messages they receive from the world, messages that tell them they are worth less than others, or even that their differences make them abominations. Freaks. When the real abominations are those who would use those differences as an excuse to harm or ostracize them, to crush their spirits. Those messages from the world lead to depression and suicide as a byproduct of cruelty and heartlessness inflicted for no reason other than that some people don't fit into the box others expect them to.

Earlier, I talked about entertaining people. I said I'm nothing but a storyteller, and that's always been true. Always will be. But entertainment, my friends, can change the world. It has always had that power. The way LGBT lives have been presented in entertainment has contributed mightily to acceptance in our society, and by that I mean the presentation of LGBT people as humans, just like anyone else.

The arc of social change is bending toward acceptance of our differences, but we aren't there yet. This year, all over the country, people frightened of those differences are doing everything in their power to spread that fear, to spread hatred and bigotry in hopes that those things will make otherwise decent human beings ignore the injustice inherent in a society where some of us are afforded rights and privileges and protections that are not afforded to others. There is no way to view this as anything other than the panic of those who would do anything to protect their ability to discriminate, to spread hatred, without recrimination.

This pushback against progress has led us to a hateful, paranoid environment perfectly constructed to nurture the injustices typified by the racial strife in Ferguson, Missouri and elsewhere . . . the anti-Muslim fearmongering . . . and the hysteria over allowing trans people to use the bathroom appropriate for the identity of their hearts.

If we're meant to be writing for a better world, then that means a better world for everyone; a world where every person is judged by their words and their actions, by what they bring to society's table. If we're writing for a better world, then we need to reflect the real world around us, in all of its motley beauty. We need to approach the world and its people with love, not hate. With kindness, not judgment. If we do not understand the lives that different people lead, then it is incumbent upon us as writers to do our research, to go and learn, to educate ourselves.

We cannot represent the true experience of people whose lives are fundamentally different from our own, because we have never lived their lives. We can never know what they know, or feel what they feel.

We can respect it. We can honor their lives and fears, their pain and their love. We can reflect that in our work. Let me be clear. The messages the world is sending are destroying people's lives, maybe even inspiring them to take their lives, and we have the power to help change those messages.

Change the message.

Write for a better world.

"The question, O me! So sad, recurring—What good amid these, O me, O life?

Answer.

That you are here. That life exists, and identity. That the powerful play goes on, and you may contribute a verse."

—Christopher Golden
Fort Worth, Texas
April 24th, 2016

SHAPING THE IDEAS: GETTING THINGS FROM YOUR HEAD TO THE PAPER OR ON SCREEN

DEL HOWISON

IN 2017 CRYSTAL LAKE PUBLISHING released the nonfiction book about the art of storytelling in the horror genre, *Where Nightmares Come From*. It went on to not only be nominated for a Bram Stoker Award, but bedside reading for every creative writer. In it I wrote a chapter where I put together an imaginary roundtable discussion with writer/directors **Fred Dekker, Tom Holland, Amber Benson** and **Kevin Tenney**. It was entitled, *Creating Magic from a Blank Piece of Paper*.

I say "imaginary roundtable" because in a real roundtable discussion you sit a very talented group of individuals at a big table, turn on the recorder and fire away with questions. Gathering a group like that together in Hollywood is like trying to net krakens. So I turned the idea on its head. I wrote up the questions that I wanted answers to and sent them to each person in the roundtable. Everybody received the same questions. They would have no input on what the other participants had to say. I wanted the unvarnished individual response about the way that they worked. I did not want any outside influence.

I then compiled those answer together under the guise of a roundtable discussion (as if they were all together at one time) and wrote the interview. What I thought would be interesting and mildly insightful turned out to be fascinating. Knowing that their responses would be up against their fellow artists caused them to keep the bar high. High enough, at least, that I was asked to do it again.

So here you have it. You hold in your hand what can be credibly called *Where Nightmares Come From Vol. 2* even if the title is changed before publication. This time we go a little deeper into the creation process, not just where do the ideas come from but how do you manage them and mold them into what you would like them to say? How do you make it different? How do you make it stand out? How do you make it honest?

The group of artists I have assembled for this second imaginary roundtable is, once again, stellar. Here is a thumbnail sketch of each of our participants. **Heather Graham Pozzessere** is a New York Times best-selling American writer, who writes horror, romance, thriller, and mystery. She writes under, both her maiden name **Heather Graham** and under the pseudonym **Shannon Drake**. She was awarded a Lifetime Achievement Award by the Romance Writers of America along with countless others. When I was a trustee for the Horror Writers Association Heather was the Vice President. In 2009, when Editor Jeff Gelb and I were putting together the anthology *Dark Delicacies III: Haunted*, I asked Heather for a horror story for the book. She blessed me with: *Mist on the Bayou.*

Writer/Director **Mick Garris** was an easy choice for this roundtable. Creative artist in several areas Mick's first forays into writing were in journalism, reviews, and as a press agent. In the late 1970's he created and served as the on-screen host for a Los Angeles cable access interview program show called "Fantasy Film Festival," that aired on L.A.'s legendary Z-Channel which was an early precursor of what was to come. His big break came through Steven Spielberg in 1985 as one of the writers and story editors for the television series: *Amazing Stories.* Mick's first book was a short story collection: *A Life in the Cinema* in 2000. Mick also joined Heather Graham in writing a story for: *Dark Delicacies III: Haunted* by treating us all to the gruesome short story *Tyler's Last Act.*

Writer **Steve Niles** is well known to fans of graphic novels, horror stories and screenplays. Several of his graphic novels have been optioned for film but he is probably most noted for the film translation of his vampire graphic novel *30 Days of Night.* His character Cal McDonald is featured prominently in the *Criminal Macabre* series of graphic novels. But he has also turned some of those adventures into straight prose novels and short stories two of which, *All My Bloody Things* and *The Y Incision* found homes in the *Dark Delicacies* and *Dark Delicacies II: Fear* anthologies respectively. Steve also had a long relationship with the late **Bernie Wrightson** as friends and partners in many graphic novels.

Award-winning author **Maria Alexander** is a

novelist, short story writer, screenwriter, poet and virtual world designer. Her novel, *Mr. Wicker,* won the Bram Stoker Award (2014) for Best first novel and her book *Snowed* (2016) received a Stoker for Best Young Adult Novel. Her short story, *Though Thy Lips Are Pale*, which appeared in the anthology *Dark Delicacies III: Haunted*, was singled out for an honorable mention by Editor **Ellen Datlow** in, *Best Horror of the Year, Vol. 2.*

Just to toss the applecart around a bit I have also added in Screenwriter/Filmmaker **Mark Savage**. Mark hails from Australia where he made and sold his first feature, *Marauders,* at the age of 24. He has also written and produced for television. His specialty is thrillers, horror, crime, cult, action and exploitation-themed films. His film, *Defenceless,* won the Best Film, Best Director, and Best Actress awards at the 2005 Melbourne Underground Film Festival. His film, *120/80: Stressed to Kill,* starring **Bill Oberst Jr**, and **Armand Assante** is a black comedy about middle-age crisis. He is also known for his film documentary of **Jackie Chan,** *Beyond Mr. Nice Guy.*

Del Howison—With all the different areas of creativity you have found yourself working in how do you discover or create new venues? Do you need new avenues or entrances into creativity to keep creation fresh and the excitement of writing alive?

Heather Graham—Places and people-they are never the same. I do a workshop in which all the participants start with the same sentence and they pick characters and adjectives from a mixed bowl. I'm always amazed by what writers come up with—and how many venues a simple statement can allow.

"The blood dripped slowly down the wall."

For one writer, it was comedic horror—she was a zombie trying to go vegetarian but her neighbor zombies kept throwing their leftovers into her yard. She married a human, and was trying to behave, but, alas, found out her husband was having an affair with the zombie next door. When a bloody hand flew her way the next time, she let her emotions go and feasted on her husband's brains.

For another writer, it was a serious murder mystery. For another, sheer horror as werewolves ripped into Congress. (Go figure.)

For another, a comedy. A make-up artist with a crush on an actor was having a disastrous time -she flipped her supply of stage blood all over him in her attempts to appear cool and sophisticated.

I read non-fiction and fiction genres out there, and I love all of them. The concept of switching around is something that I believe has helped keep me excited about whatever I'm working on through the years. It is, of course, important these days to establish a "brand". But, then, you can establish another one, too.

Steve Niles—I always need new ways to tell a story, but not matter what avenues are there. It's writing comics that I prefer over anything else. I fall into ruts easily. My life has been pretty up and down the last few years with floods and fires and such, all of this finds their way into my new comics.

Maria Alexander—I don't really chose the venue, it

chooses me. Creativity is volcanic, ever rumbling and effervescing. Unstoppable. In fact, if I try to avoid it or put it off, the effects on my mental health are deeply negative. So it's a poem, a story or sometimes even music, I just obey the muse and do it.

Mark Savage—Personally, I'm always drawn to concepts and stories that allow me to explore our duality. For me, genre is the frame in which a human story is told. Inconsistent human behavior drives drama. The challenge of each project is not to repeat. I always have too many ideas and not enough time to fully flesh them out.

On one hand, that's good—it gives me time to test a project's staying power as drama. If it (the story) runs out of steam or I run out of passion for it, I won't waste further time with it. The ideas that persist, sometimes for years, tend to percolate and become richer.

In the past I've written some plays, too, but I didn't stick with that medium, it felt limiting. I enjoy the magic of film and prose narrative where you can jump quickly from place to place or time zone to time zone. That's not so easy on stage.

Each new project is a challenge because it begs to be told differently. With hundreds of thousands of movies already in existence, the desire to do something different is always pressing on one's conscience. If I don't think I can bring a fresh approach to a premise, I don't commit too much time to it. Sometimes you have to begin writing to learn how worthwhile or pointless the idea is. Some projects simply don't work as films, but they might work as novels, short stories, or plays. A concept or idea needs to earn the time you're going to spend with it.

Mick Garris—Anything I write or shoot is new, and it feels like a rebirth with each new creation. As I write books and fiction, write and direct for movies and television, and host my own interview podcast, I am always doing something new, and looking for "new" in anything I approach. It's the reason that I now do the occasional "director for hire" job in series television. I was really surprised to find out how much I enjoy working on someone else's show, and how much I keep learning and evolving from it.

Del Howison—How do you work differently if it is your own material as opposed to somebody else's piece that you are adapting or even historical material that you are molding into a creative piece? Do you prefer one over the other (original as opposed to being based on something that already exists)?

Mick Garris—I like both, actually, but I work in totally different ways. In adaptations (especially of the work of others, as I have adapted my own fiction to the screen, as well), I go through the material scrupulously, everything is outlined, I pay careful attention to structure and even dialogue. If it's something very well known, as with (Stephen) King material, I want to make sure that I'm delivering what I believe the audience wants from the book, even though they are completely different media.

When I'm writing something original, particularly on spec, I never outline. I just start with an idea on page one, and write until it's over. I love the freedom of creating something as it goes along.

Steve Niles—I definitely approach these differently. My own material, I think of ideas, or an idea comes to me and I usually sit on it for days, sometimes weeks, going over the story in my head. It might change while I'm writing. I can go inside the story and the characters might move into something different. The ending might change. It's all open as I write.

If it's someone else's material, I have the story; it's there and set in place. I just need to shape it into a story that works.

You know it depends on where I am in my life. Sometimes, I have no ideas coming to me. So working on someone else's work might be better for that time. If I'm feeling really creative, I would prefer to be working on something original.

Maria Alexander—I prefer something from Scratch, but the challenge of taking a person who already exists such as Julie d'Aubigny aka La Maupin is very exciting because I've felt such a close connection to her for decades. Fortunately for me, we don't know that much about her. Many of the stories passed around about her are purely apocryphal. So, I still get to exercise my creativity as I mold her past and character.

Mark Savage—If it's my own material, I obsess initially over point of view—am I telling the story from the point of view that gets the most from the material? Is there a better approach, a better angle? A story can be harmed or enriched by your choice of whose story it is. The information the character gives you—what you know and what you don't know—draws you into the story. Every piece of information is a choice. Point of view determines those choices. When it's my own material, the point of view is a pressing one.

When adapting an existing work, short story or novel, several choices have already been made by the writer. In the short story or novel form, the story is clearly working; that's why you were drawn to it in the first place. But when adapting it for a new form such as a movie, you're aware that the narrative elements that work on the page (interior monologues, for example) might not work on the screen. I find myself reading interior thoughts of characters and wondering how and if those thoughts can be physicalized (made cinematic) for the betterment of the movie.

Initially, it's important to understand why the story works in the first place; you need to clearly identify what attracted you to the story. Can what attracted you carry itself into the new medium? Or is what attracted you best left in its original form? I definitely believe that many stories meant to be read are best left in that format. Not everything will make a great movie. And not every movie can be smoothly adapted into novel form.

I don't prefer original work over adaptations or vice versa. The advantage of adapting an existing story is it gives you a structure that works (at least in the novel form), and gives you characters already developed and juxtaposed against each other. The symphony of characters is already in place. In a sense, the adaptation comes with welcome limitations; you have a ready-made circle to work within.

With an original work, the possibilities are endless. Despite limitless possibilities appearing attractive, they also bring a certain degree of option anxiety; you have so many places to go, so many ways to fuck things up, too.

Ultimately, I'm attracted to an engaging premise and conflicted, psychologically complex characters.

Heather Graham—I haven't adapted anyone's material, but, I often base work on historical stories—nothing is ever more frightening, wild, intriguing, or as bizarre as events that have really occurred. I also believe that if you ground work in truth, readers will follow you into what-might-have-been with greater ease. I also love places and people and sometimes incredibly sad or often unbelievable things that have really happened. As we all know, life parallels art, or art parallels life, and sometimes they even coincide.

Del Howison—Have you been approached with an idea or type of project that you felt wasn't for you and you turned it down? Have you ever, later, reached back to that idea?

Steve Niles—I've been approached with all kinds of projects that weren't for me, usually slasher or horror with a lot of sexual stuff thrown in that's just not my kind of thing. I can say after a couple of them I wondered if I might have damaged future business relationships by saying no to them, but I don't think I ever came back to them later.

Mick Garris—Yes, I've turned down much more than I've accepted over the years, and no, have never gone back to it. I keep facing forward.

Heather Graham—Once, I had written a reverse time-travel—a Civil War soldier fell back in time and found himself in the middle of a re-enactment. At the time, it didn't appeal to the editors. But a few years later, I was asked for the novel—the concept of such ideas selling had come around. Now, I sometimes think of ideas I had that I had never followed through on, but, hey, I'm still breathing, so, I may get to them!

Maria Alexander—Many years ago, when my former agent was shopping, *The Goth Girl's Guide to Loving Relationships,* we had an editor for one of the big publishers ask if I could just write it as a straight dating guide, no winking, nudging or humor. I couldn't do that. I still can't imagine doing that. The whole point was to use my subculture to subvert mainstream culture's ideas of dating through humor. Good girls use *Rules*. Goth girls use *Ropes*. But real dating guides were so popular back then that I can understand why everyone was looking for the next big hit and not satire. I've not gone back to this idea, but I could be tempted.

Mark Savage—I've been approached with projects that were far too general for my tastes. Sometimes, a producer assumes you'll like a clichéd horror idea just because they know you like horror. The truth is, people who create horror are less likely to embrace clichéd horror than those whose tastes lie elsewhere. I'm mostly attracted to stories that mix genres, or don't fit neatly into a genre box.

I recently was approached to rewrite and direct a script that felt like a copy of a popular urban crime thriller. I discussed changes that would have made the film less like the film it was imitating, but the producers insisted on dialogue and plot polishes only. I declined the project.

Another project I like a lot became less attractive when the producer insisted on casting his son in the lead role. I insisted on auditioning the son and found him to be less than a convincing actor. Despite liking the script, I declined the project because it would have been destroyed by the casting choice. If the son had been in a smaller supporting role, he could have been incorporated into the story without harming the project. Casting is so important; it can make or break your movie, and your investment. In good conscience, I can't take on a movie already handicapped financially by a poor casting decision.

I have never gone back to an idea I rejected, but I have gone back to an idea that I couldn't raise financing for at the time. Many projects are more viable as time passes or culture changes. Good ideas have a universal appeal. For me, it always comes back to the characters and how they drive the story.

Del Howison—Do you revisit ideas you had that you were writing early on but dropped because your skill set hadn't gotten there yet or you didn't know how to approach it?

Maria Alexander—My YA novel, *Snowed,* is the grownup version of my flash fiction piece, *Coming Home.* I knew even when I wrote, *Coming Home,* that it could be much more. But at the time, I was just starting to write short stories. Some would agree that it's a great start, but I just didn't know yet how to develop and deepen certain ideas. I have a book that, when I tell people about it, they absolutely love the idea, but it's been stuck halfway in second draft because I've simply not had the bandwidth or resources to research the real-world aspects in the story. But if anyone reading this has friends with officers in San Francisco's Robbery/Homicide Division, this thing could actually happen.

Mark Savage—Yes, I have revisited some good premises I didn't have the chops to make the most of when I was young and inexperienced. Some of the premises weren't so good. Some were.

When you return to something after a decade or more, your life experience adds immeasurably to the internal dialogue you're having about ways to improve, enrich, or restructure it. In the early days, I was more obsessed with plot than character, and I'd sometimes create plot turns that were inconsistent with the characters making them. I was betraying my own characters. Now, at least, I understand what I was doing, and my loyalty towards consistency is paramount.

Steve Niles—Oh yeah, most ideas float around for some years. When I was first starting out, I had lots of stories but couldn't get them all down. I can look at some old things I started and maybe not want to revisit them because they don't seem that good to me later.

Mick Garris—I have never really gone back to old ideas, as they were important in their time, and, for the most part, as life changes, so do the stories and ideas. And the more you live—fall in and out of love, travel, find passions, have your heart broken, lose people close to you—the more your life deepens, the better the artist you become, and the deeper and more relatable your art . . . one hopes.

Del Howison—Is there one thing new writers should know about beginning writing that will change as their skills mature?

Mark Savage—There are probably many things beginning writes should know. First, unless you *need* to write, *must* write, do something else. What changes in your writing reflects the changes in your life. The two are not separate.

Writing about what you know (a misunderstood cliché) is about writing the feelings you've felt. Feelings are universal. If you've lived and loved thoroughly, you'll have something interesting to write about.

It takes a while to stop imitating what you love and find your own voice. It takes even longer to be comfortable with your own voice. But you need to find that unique voice.

Steve Niles—I always tell writers to just write. I was writing for about 20 years before I actually sold something. You have to stick with it if you want to be a writer. There aren't any short cuts, writing itself should be the reward.

Heather Graham—You always hear "write what you know." But! I think it's also incredibly important to write what you love. There is where your passion lies. Be excited about your work—remember, you have to be excited if you want others to be excited as well.

Del Howison—Are you always looking for new ways to approach your projects or does the project pretty well dictate the approach?

Mick Garris—Well, both. Filmmaking is always in an evolutionary state, and I like to keep on top of what's possible in the technology of visual storytelling. But I don't want style to get in the way of story. That said, story dictates the approach in filmmaking. In fiction, there are far fewer rules, and I love to play with language.

Maria Alexander—The level of my obsession dictates the approach. I can only write a book because I'm deeply obsessed with a story and its characters. I might write a short story to blow off steam or process something that's bothering me. Same for poetry. But books, yeah, I'm inescapably absorbed. And that's good!

Heather Graham—I usually begin with a place, a person, or an idea that intrigues me. A book out now— *Fade to Black*—started finding shape in my mind at Monsterpalooza and continued at a comic con. The mystery of Edgar Allan Poe fascinated me and I used that research in a novel last year, *Wicked Deeds*. No matter what we're writing—even outlandish sci-fi or fantasy—we're mimicking life, and life will always supply us with ideas.

Mark Savage—Project dictates approach. I don't like to force style on a project. As I stated before, point of view is a choice, and it definitely impacts the story positively or negatively. I'm always questioning how the story should be told. What should be included? What should be left out? What should be implied but not seen? As project dictates approach for me, the first question is always: Whose point of view is this? Then: What point of view expresses the dramatic tensions?

Steve Niles—I don't look for it, I just have to go with it when the creative juices get started. Every story has its own way. Sometimes I just start writing and it flows while I'm typing, other time I have to think about it for weeks before writing it down. Sometimes I type out an outline, though that can derail the story while I'm in the thick of it. It can be helpful if I really need to shape a story from beginning to end, but most times I just go with an idea and let it flow.

Del Howison—Some people love research and some hate it. Where do you stand beyond it being a necessary evil? Has research on a project ever accidentally taken you off the project and into a new idea because of what you discovered?

Heather Graham—The problem with research is

that one book/site might give you a bit of information that makes you want more information . . . and, at the end of the day, you're still fascinated by the different paths your research is taking you down. And, sometimes, it's a tough call. You wind up with way more information than you really needed—and you have to remember that your novel doesn't need big info dump any more than it needs omission of necessary bits and pieces.

Maria Alexander—Research has so far never derailed me, but it can sometimes remind me of old projects that never got off the ground. It can be hard to resist revisiting those projects, but I know the level of research for those old projects vastly outweighs the newer ones. So it's not too hard to stay focused.

Mark Savage—I really enjoy the research component of writing, and have found that the more you research, the more the project expands into areas you never imagined. Research is adding branches to your idea. It's never a negative thing. And though you might discard 80% of your research, the 20% you use gives the story enormous gravity, authenticity, and richness.

Research has sometimes shifted the focus or point of view of a story. When you've been attacking the material from one direction, research suddenly opens up various points of attack, and sometimes directs you to an element, originally dismissed, that suddenly becomes extremely important and interesting. When researching the life of a hitman for my, *Sensitive New Age Killer* aka *Hitman's Hero*, information uncovered about the hitman's personal habits (via an interview with a detective) opened up a part of his life that had direct impact on his failures. At that point, more clichéd aspects about his life were thankfully eliminated and we focused on the more private side of his warped personality.

Steve Niles—I hate deep research overall for a story's sake as I think it can damage a story if I take too much time trying to be correct historically or scientifically. With horror there's a lot of suspension of disbelief as it is. I like to learn a minimal amount needed so I can get back to writing and I can let the story take shape. I think sometimes I've gotten ideas after spending time researching something because I found it interesting. I really got into watching tons of, *Cosmos*, the planets and Universe documentaries, which got me writing a number of comics set in outer space.

Mick Garris—I've had some projects, including a Jack the ripper story, that required lots of research, but it was inspired by a Ripper tour in London, and the research was a lot of fun. But mostly, ideas come from the heart and the head with me, and are not usually filled with research, though it's become so easy with the internet over the decades. Probably the most research I've ever done on a project was on Salem for *Hocus Pocus*.

Del Howison—As a writer what is your biggest struggle and what is your greatest enjoyment?

Mick Garris—Well, in filmmaking, the biggest struggle is fighting time. There is never enough time, and you really have to settle more than you want to. Technical complications, temperamental actors, difficult animals, new and untried visual effects and the like can be a major source of frustration and struggle. That said, the greatest joy is, as happened to me recently directing a very emotional scene on a TV show, seeing the cast in tears as one of them is slowly losing her life, and seeing the crew around them, including myself, tearing up, believing the very heartfelt scene being shot on a soundstage truly comes to life . . . and, in this case, death.

Heather Graham—I think we all struggle—and that it continues through our work, be it our first, second, or onward. Threading important information is always a challenge. But, at first, we have all our original ideas and concepts. As we go onward, we have to keep striving to be fresh. We do become more comfortable with structure. From what I've seen, the best authors were and remain readers—we write because we've so loved and continue to love the written word. I think the greatest enjoyment possible is when someone tells you that a book brought them through a very hard time in his or her life—that's the sweetest validation ever!

Steve Niles—These days my biggest struggle is coming up with new ideas. My greatest enjoyment is when I do get a really good idea and start flowing with it.

Maria Alexander—The biggest struggle will always be finding time to write. My greatest enjoyment is falling in love with characters, although hearing from kids who loved *Snowed* has really been amazing. I adore my adult fans, but when kids take time to read and share with adult authors how much they enjoyed something, there's nothing quite like it. I hope they enjoy *Snowbound* just as much!

Mark Savage—My biggest struggle as a writer has been to make a living writing that which is closest to my true nature. I stuck at that, and it's paid off. But it would have been far easier to write publisher-and-producer-pleasing crap.

The greatest enjoyment is seeing something I have written impact people in a movie theater. To touch hearts is a rare pleasure.

Artwork by Luke Spooner

THE NITTY GRITTY

ON RESEARCH

BEV VINCENT

RESEARCH IS A time-consuming task that many writers abhor. As authors of fiction, we love to make things up. We aren't actual slaves to the dictum "write what you know," and if we don't understand exactly how something works, what difference does it make?

Why should we be concerned with getting every little detail right? We can make something up that sounds good, can't we?

We're lying to our readers from word one, and they know it. They enter into a contract with us and willingly suspend disbelief. They're shelling out their hard-earned cash fully aware that in return we are offering something made out of whole cloth. They want to be swept away by our fantasies. If they wanted facts and truths, they could read the newspaper (well, maybe) or a work of non-fiction (again, maybe!).

Consider this (he says, in his best Rod Serling voice): While our words are filling their heads, our readers are in our hands. We manipulate their emotions. We conjure images that become as vivid in their minds as they were in ours when we set them down on paper. All they ask in return is that we play fair. If we say World War II ended in 1948, we'd better be writing alternate history. If we're too lazy to look up the facts, the fine wires that suspend readers' bridges of disbelief unravel and snap.

But research is a drag, right?

Stephen King has said he does just enough so he can lie *convincingly*, and in that adverb resides the core of the matter. We need to make sure we don't write things that are so obviously wrong that they destroy our carefully constructed fictions, and that often means we have to learn specific facts about things we aren't familiar with, and that means we have to do research. It can be fun, under the right conditions, but often it's a pain. What could make it easier?

I'm going to lead you down the garden path for a bit, as one of my university professors used to say. Bear with me.

When I was a kid, our television picked up only one station. (That's not exactly true. There was also a French station, but we didn't watch it unless there was a hockey game on, and only then with the volume turned down.) Among the memorable programs from that era were three British series that used so-called "supermarionation" technology—creepy puppets with big rolling eyes and mouths that clicked like teeth when they closed. *Stingray*, *The Thunderbirds* and *Joe 90* all featured characters who were part of acronymic organizations that fended off evil creatures and/or empires.

In the latter, the protagonist, Joe McLaine, was a nine-year-old super-spy with WIN, the World Intelligence Network. (I wasn't sure about this detail, so I looked it up. Research in action!) Who'd suspect a kid of being a Most Special Agent? Whenever he needed a particular skill to complete a mission, he sat on a chair inside this gizmo that resembled an enormous, multicolored eggbeater. The machine, invented by his father, was known as the BIG RAT, a strangled acronym meaning Brain Impulse Galvanoscope: Record And Transfer, also called the "rat trap."

The ability Joe needed (deep sea diving, piloting a jet, brain surgery, whatever) had been copied to tape from the minds of experts in the field and implanted temporarily in his brain by a set of electrodes on his temples. So long as Joe wore a pair of special spectacles (early Google glasses?) he could retain and use the knowledge.

As a writer, I wish I had access to something like the BIG RAT. I often find myself in need of expertise in certain subjects, but only for the amount of time it takes to write a story or book. I guess, in a way, the internet is our BIG RAT. If I'm in the middle of working on something and I need a specific piece of information—the biographical details of a historical figure, the exact location of a building, the name for the ceremonial dagger used in Wicca rituals —I go online and look it up. The trick is in knowing when you have all you need and to avoid getting bogged down. Information can be seductive, and the internet is full of rabbit holes waiting for you to tumble through them, never to return.

Here's an example: In my short story "Screaming Jenny," the main character is a freight train engineer. Now, I've been around trains all my life. I grew up less than a mile from the main rail line through Eastern

Canada. We frequently sat at a level crossing waiting for the red caboose to go by so we could continue on our way into town, and I used to know exactly how many railcars made up a mile of train. I took trains back and forth to university many times, and I've traveled all over Europe via rail.

But I've never met an engineer, have never been on a freight train, and had no idea what the inside of a modern locomotive cab looked like. It was important to the story that I know these things, not because I was writing a technical manual, but because the protagonist knew them. They were second nature to him. Many readers probably wouldn't blink if I had him gripping a steering wheel or stepping on a gas pedal instead of moving a lever to change the speed of the train, but these mistakes would ruin the effect for those who knew I'd gotten it wrong.

So I did my research. I sat in my BIG RAT and filled my head full of locomotive knowledge. I found animated schematics and videos from locomotive cabs. I googled *"day in the life" locomotive engineer* and found interviews with people who drive trains, and even a page about a day in the life of a train. In essence, I transferred knowledge provided by experts in the field directly into my brain, and then used that information to carry out my mission: write a story.

If you stood me next to a locomotive (so long as I was wearing my special electrode-bearing glasses), I think I could find my way up the ladder (8 feet tall) into the cab. I'd know enough to throw the main switch and all the circuit breakers to power up the system. I might even be able to start the diesel engine and get the train moving. Certainly, though, after a couple of days of research, I knew enough so my main character could perform most tasks of his routine existence while at the same time coexisting with the plot of the story.

The secret is to not let the details overwhelm the tale. It's not important that all the fruits of your research end up in the story; instead, they add color while at the same time getting our minds thinking in new directions. I often put a lot more in the first draft than survives upon revision. I'm proud of my research.

For a week, I bored my wife to tears with train trivia. Did you know that a typical freight train weighs over two million pounds and that it can take two miles to stop? Did you know that the area of contact between a train wheel and the track is smaller than a dime? I do—or I did while I was working on the story. Six months later, I had replaced much of that trivia with something else. The average speed of an unladen European swallow, perhaps.

The stuff I learn is almost never the focus of the story. It's the window dressing that makes everything else seem real. Without it, my stories would be as starkly staged as Lars von Trier's movie, *Dogville*. Readers have to do more work if the walls are all imaginary and the doors non-existent.

Geography is a big part of our research. How often do we watch or read something and shake our heads at some detail that doesn't ring true?

Dan Brown totally fluffed the geography of Paris in *The Da Vinci Code*. Unless you've been there, you probably wouldn't know, but I have been and it temporarily took me out of the story. That's not to say that if you set a short story in Prague (as I did, for a *Doctor Who* anthology) you have to get on a plane and head for the Czech Republic, but I did enough research so people familiar with the local geography wouldn't totally hate me for making it all up.

You know all those travelogues people post on their blogs, complete with candid photos? Pure gold when it comes to location research. Pictures truly are worth thousands of words, and are a great substitute for a costly trip to Europe.

My werewolf story, "Silvery Moon," deals with a group of hikers on a mountain trail. At a certain point I had to decide whether the locale was going to be fictitious or not. No one would have complained if I'd opted for the former. The exact location isn't crucial to the story.

However, the story came more alive for me after about ten minutes researching hiking trails where people could conceivably be away from civilization for a few days. For no particular reason other than it fit my scenario, I selected the Beartooth Mountains. A Google image search produced countless photographs of the environs. I could imagine myself there. I could hear the babbling brooks, smell the particular kinds of vegetation in that area, hear the wildlife, and see the jagged, lunar mountaintops, all details I worked into the story to strengthen the threads suspending that bridge of disbelief.

I've done quite a bit of traveling over the years, and I try to record my impressions from my journeys in case I ever decide to set a story in one of these exotic locations. I always take a journal to make notes, and I often record video snippets or take photographs to document the locales. I've set tales in Switzerland, Japan, Australia, Hong Kong and Canada, and I once drove all the way across Texas with a video camera mounted to the dashboard to do location research—because there's only so much you can learn from the internet. A few snapshots and Google Earth maps of a locality might be enough for a short story, but in this case I was writing a novel and things went so much better after I visited the place where the book was set. You learn things like how often trains go through the middle of town, disrupting its normal calm, what color the mountains turn when the sun sets, and how rundown the part of town south of the tracks is compared to the way it looks on the computer.

I like getting details right. Stephen King set *Cell* in Boston instead of Manhattan because he knows Boston better and he anticipated all the letters he would get if his characters left Manhattan via routes anyone familiar with the city would never use. Readers are quick to let you know when you get it wrong—witness the Dark Tower fans who knew that the A Train doesn't go to the station where Odetta Holmes lost her legs.

Research takes many other forms.

I've gone to lectures and attended Citizens' Police Academy. I've watched documentaries and read books about pertinent topics. I've taken mornings off from work to sit in a courtroom and watch jury selection.

Much of what I've learned has worn off, except for the material I've captured in my notebooks, on video, audio or digital film. Like Joe 90, when the immediate need for the expertise goes, the details slowly dissipate. Except for the ones I've used as part of the palette in painting the sets for a story.

Sometimes the story arises from the research. My

story, "Rule Number One," in, *The Blue Religion*, edited by Michael Connelly of *Bosch* fame, happened because of my first police ride along. I knew I wanted to write about cops on the beat, but I had no ideas for a story yet, so for eight hours I sat up front with a Houston Police Department officer as he went about his tour of duty, handling everything from moving violations to domestic situations to reports of prostitution. I was a sponge, soaking up details and atmosphere so that when the time came to write a story I would have a greater familiarity with the setting. I recorded everything he said. I was hoping there would be an incident that would inspire a story.

My view of a police officer's routine was absurdly tainted by the TV show *COPS*, but I quickly came to understand that the reality is far more mundane and at the same time far richer and deeper than what's shown on "reality" programs like that one. If I had written a story where the cop rushes from one interesting, exciting, nerve-wracking event to another, many readers wouldn't have batted an eye, but those in the know would have laughed me off the page. What I didn't expect was that, instead of expanding upon any one particular incident, I would end up writing a story about a police ride along that goes off the rails in an interesting way. The title itself came from something the officer said to me.

So, while it may be a pain, research is a necessary part of the job. It would all be so much easier if I could sit in that BIG RAT for a few minutes and then wear my special goggles while I write. I have to wear glasses anyway. As long as the prescription was right, I'd be good to go.

EDITING THROUGH FEAR: CUTTING AND STITCHING STORIES

JESSICA MARIE BAUMGARTNER

ROLL YOUR EYES. Grumble under your breath. It's time to talk editing.

Forget all the crap about, "practice makes perfect." Yes practice is important, but to keep your work from committing suicide, an author needs editing skills. Get used to it. Editing *is* writing. Rewrites, cuts, additions, technical skills, grammar, and style: all of these are the tools of a great writer.

There will always be truth to the, "all good writers have good editors," adage, but before you pass your work onto someone else, please make sure it's not too crappy. Shitty first drafts are expected, but that first draft is nowhere near a finished product.

I no longer advertise my editing services because I found that there is far more bad writing than good. It breaks you down, almost makes you fear reading at times. Just yesterday I sat back rubbing my eyes cursing the words, "was," and "had."

A keen eye can be developed. I was not born an editor. I am dyslexic.

True story.

Reading and writing does not teach anyone how to edit or train their brain. That comes from experience. Working with skilled editors and knowledgeable authors is imperative to shaping a great story. Workshops and classes are everywhere. Whether on-site or online, writers have more resources than ever.

There can be no excuses. If I shrugged every time I submitted a piece and said, "Well, I'm dyslexic," I would never have gotten as far as this, nor would I keep getting better. That in itself is the first lesson of editing, check your feelings at the door. Pride has nothing to do with edits.

My college English 101 professor always warned me, "Never get married to your work." This advice serves me well every day. In order to find success in publishing, one must appease a certain amount of readers. Your fate is in their hands. To weigh the odds in your favor, have fun with writing, but be a heartless editor. The story has to grow and change in order to breathe properly.

I often joke that editing turns me into a sociopath. It's true. I have learned to enjoy cutting up my work and sewing the bloodied pieces back together. When finished your creature arises fresh and ready to face every mob. Torches still blaze. Tensions tighten and constrict creativity, but finding the balance between technical skills and imagination will drive back the ignorant and bring forth a new dawn.

I'm not going to yell about how you should lock your work away for at least six months before you do the first self-edit. It should be common knowledge at this point. From a person whose brain doesn't always work properly, I can attest that this method is solid, but it isn't always realistic. Like this piece, for instance; I started writing it 2 months before my deadline, so of course, the rules get broken for special circumstances.

What I wish to address are the nitty gritty details. Those little beasties that get caught in the lines and trip your story's flow. Damn devils. But the "devil is in the details," am I right?

So let's explore them.

Rewrites are often necessary. I'm an author who never puts in enough detail, so I often have to go back and add more description, deeper thoughts, and further explore the scene later. It sucks. It's grueling work that frustrates you until you want to quit.

Luckily this issue can be alleviated with experience. If you know your weaknesses you can tackle them head on. Most writers don't skimp like I do, this is good because it's easier to hack a manuscript to bits and restructure it with what is already there.

Shaving things down is all about saying goodbye to explanatory sentences that fulfill nothing more than an author's overinflated ego. We love to write our ideologies into our stories. I've read more unnecessary rants on society, politics, religion, and right versus wrong, than anyone should ever have to stomach. Cut that shit out.

The only time preaching flies is when done in a subtle manner. Metaphor is the perfect way to allow a few gems in. It also works when delivered from the mouths of your characters. Don't tell me, "Her people had suffered too many atrocities to let this one go." Show me her anger, the pain in her eyes. Then write a realistic line that conveys what that means to her specifically.

Every word matters. Phrasing counts. How your characters speak and move is one of the main ingredients of concocting a potent story. Too many writers forget the power of conversation. If there isn't dialogue within the first 2-3 pages of your story, your characters aren't speaking enough.

Even if they are introduced alone, the power of *thought* should take over. Internal speech is just as important as every other element of writing. With that comes the horrid addition . . . tags. Those damn anchors. They can sink your sentences if you're not careful.

The most modern rule of dialogue tags is to always stick with, "said" or "asked." Please do not have your characters: expostulate, exclaim, announce, demand, beg, respond, suggest, remark, petition, question, etc. Before you slam this book on the ground and say, "Screw you," let me explain.

Dialogue tags suck.

These annoying additions slow down your story and are often redundant. If the reader knows what is going on in the story, and you did your job showing instead of telling, they will feel the emotion being portrayed. "Said" and "asked" are simple tags that the brain filters out. We don't get tripped up on them. They are perfect in their simplicity.

Long winded tags, on the other hand, destroy the story's rhythm. It kills the melody of your dialogue and breaks concentration. If you hate this idea, I would suggest two things: One, get over yourself. Editors have been saying this for years. If you want to be a pro, you have to work like one. Two, there is a workaround. Instead of adding a tag, write out an action instead. Actions drive the words forward and paint a picture.

Painting with words comes together as you play with your style and find what works for you, but please do not use, "That's my writing style," as an excuse. Bad grammar is not a writing style. Only Cormac McCarthy is allowed to claim that and it's because his writing is incomparable.

Spelling matters. Everyone has spell check. Unless you are writing dialogue and doing light accents, stick to the rules. I rarely find too many spelling issues; it is punctuation that's the problem.

I am in love with semi-colons. They melt my heart and make my world. Vonnegut can bite me.

Even so, these big bold marks need to be used sparingly and at the proper spots. Heavy use weighs down the page and is not pleasing to the eye or the brain. Everything in publishing is about balance and flow.

The only thing uglier than pages of semi-colons is multiple exclamations. They're enticing. Everyone thinks their characters need them, but 99.9% of the time they are wasting space. You have cute happy ones that beg to be worked in. The angry ones demand attention. I love good old fashioned "surprise" ones meant to shock everyone.

Unfortunately, they're over actors. Expressions and actions will shape a better story than bland punctuation. Don't give me punctuation; show me the light in a child's eyes, the pinched features of an angry face.

You get one shot at a poignant exclamation. Maybe two in longer works. Anything beyond that is overkill.

Don't argue in favor of the exceptions. It's true. Overuse of these silly additions is an amateur move. I know —I used them more than anyone when I started out.

Sentence length is also a doozy. Nobody wants to read a series of words that have five-hundred commas, don't set any good pacing, and flat out do nothing to keep the reader interested while going on and on and on about something already stated in the previous paragraph which is littered with clichés, extra words, bad grammar, and weak points.

It's disgusting. Yuck.

Spread them like butter. Smooth long statements along with short slick ones. Mix them together to make everything fresh. My recent edits are chunked full of obese statements that are likely to give anyone an asthma attack. There is a time and a place for long flights of fancy and large helpings of sponge cake writing.

To make a story palatable for the reader you need these editing tricks. I haven't even gotten to the worst of it yet. We're almost there. I promise.

Formatting is a big word for those of us who ever experienced the trauma of reading slush piles. You're eyes burn, your brain throbs. The computer sometimes looks like it is breathing. There are standard fonts, sizes, and margins that are easier to read and it matters.

Always check the guidelines of where you are publishing before you send your work. If no guidelines are listed, stick to the William Shunn manuscript rules. It will work in your favor. Keeping up with industry standards shows a level of professionalism people respond to.

Speaking of professionalism, I'm going to reveal my biggest personal pet peeve. This is it. The *one*.

All editors find hiccups and patterns that annoy them. Each of us has that single annoying habit we wish we could pluck out of a writer by magic. If I could stop author from doing anything, it would be to get them to avoid "was" sentences, "had" sentences, and "as" sentences.

Anyone can write, "It was," "she was," "he was." And "were" also falls into this category. It takes real skill to find more intelligent ways to tell a story. When writing for children, "she had," and "they had," works, but everything has already been written. It is an author's job to keep the reading interesting and to do that they must go further.

Try harder.

There is a giant list of words to avoid in writing. I'm not going to sit here and tell you to get rid of: that, very, so, much, and so on. Any class, workshop, or good editor will. The reason, "was," and "had," grate on me is because I find them in nearly every sentence of every self-published novel, and plenty of pieces published by small and independent presses.

Most of the red marks I give during edits are based on these. Not just because they are underdeveloped, but because they set the author up for "telling" instead of "showing." Sure, "She was beautiful," is nice. Nice is good, but readers deserve more. "She stood like a pillar of beauty. Her hair rippled around her face revealing bright eyes and soft lips," is better.

That's just off the top of my head, but you get the idea.

Sometimes the easy stuff fits, but not often. Same

with "as" sentences. These are growing in popularity and just make me want to jab my eye with a pen. "As she blah, blah, blah . . . " "He glanced back as blah, blah, blah . . . " Again, it works *sometimes*, but not often, and definitely not all of the time.

I don't say any of this to destroy anyone. Editing is all about polishing. It exists to improve. Some jobs are bigger than others.

I've been on both sides of submission calls and feel for everyone who has the courage to submit their work to an agent, magazine, or publisher. Accepting your role in the writing world is often difficult. No matter how terrifying rejections are, having your work torn apart by someone is rare. Just do your best. Breathe!

But wait, there's more:

And now to put my writing where my words are, have a sample. For this specific piece I dug up one of the first stories I ever published. It found a home with, *Quantum Muse,* years ago. There was no pay, no print edition. Just a simple online fantasy story for anyone to read.

Bold = cuts
Italics = add ins

The Last Dive
By Jessica Baumgartner
(Aww, this was before my middle name demanded to be seen)

"The water's a little rough today." The scuba guide told

(Should be "said"—end sentence here.) Julie and Collin as (Cut this out and start a better sentence.) h (Capital H)e led *Julie and Colin (NOW introduce characters)* **them out on (Cut this out)** to the beach with the other divers. "Nothing we can't handle. Once you get down there you won't notice it at all."

Julie **was a bit nervous as they walked (Cut this out and SHOW her nervous behavior instead of saying "Julie was"** *dragged her feet (Add to show her hesitation)* on the weathered dock**. (End sentence here to build tension)** *She bit her lip and stared at (Add in to show more apprehension)* **that led to (Cut)** the boat . Collin grabbed her hand and squeezed it. "You'll be fine, you're P.A.D.I. certified and I'm here with you."

"Thanks," Julie **said (End sentence here and use action to drive story forward) as they found cut this "as sentence" out and fix** *She followed him to a pair of (add this to give the story more umph)* **their (Cut this word)** seats in the boat.

She had Cut "had" sentence beginning) *I used to love water, she thought. (Add to let the character speak for herself)* **ever since she was (cut "was sentence" set up)** *As a (Break the as rule 1 time only)* little **kid (Cut and expand thought)** *girl she always looked forward to (add for more depth)* swimming and boating **every summer (Cut for better flow)** with her family **(End sentence here to prepare for reveal)** *That was before the accident. (Add in 1 "was sentence" in an impactful sentence)* **Until (Cut this)** *Just after she turned*

(Better way to start sentence) **was (Cut that nasty "was")** eleven years old *she lost her parents to that chilling water (This lays it all out without giving away too much or telling the reader what to feel).*

LEAPING INTO THE ABYSS

GREG CHAPMAN

WRITING A NOVEL is daunting, and not something that should be taken lightly. Which is why I put off writing my first novel for almost six years. So how do you begin such a venture? When is the right time to leap into the abyss and spill your soul onto the page?

The timing is up to the individual, but I'll aim to share the how, and the why, of my decision to take the plunge. I'll also provide some insight into how I brought my novel into being; from concept to characters, to the writing style and the themes I weaved into the plot. Hopefully, my experiences will be useful to authors looking to try their hand at writing their own debut novel.

Prologue

It was about a decade ago that I started pursuing horror writing, and during those ten years, I'd mainly penned short stories and novellas. By the time I decided it was "time" to try writing a novel (again), I'd had five novella-length works and a collection of short stories published. I had written a novel before—an

80,000 word dark fantasy piece that I submitted to a publisher only to have it rejected. The experience left me deflated, to say the least. It was a real blow to my confidence, not because I believed the work was good, but I felt like I'd wasted my time and energy.

A writer doesn't devote themselves to a task as much as sacrifice themselves to it. So my desire to try another was wearing thin. Yet, writing was, and still is, a part of me. I don't feel complete unless I am using my imagination and telling stories. Writing is more than a compulsion. It's as vital as drawing breath in order to stay alive. It was inevitable that I would tackle the task again when I regained my confidence and found a project to inspire me.

In my "day job" as a newspaper reporter, I'd amassed quite a few ideas for stories, but I didn't have time to put them on paper. Between my 8 to 5 job at the paper and raising two young children, the idea of dedicating myself to another novel was painful. The thought of being rejected again also led me to put it off. But the ideas still came and over time, one idea in particular began to niggle at me. It was a half-formed body in the backyard of my mind, demanding to be unearthed.

One such story I reported on for the newspaper involved a victim of a home invasion. As he reached for the phone to call the police, an intruder, armed with a machete, had almost taken the poor man's hand. There was speculation the intruder had been after drugs or drug money. A few months later, we found our way back to the same address after the police were alerted to a foul smell emanating from the property. The stench of that story lingered with me, so much so that I would use it six years later as the foundation for my novel, *Hollow House*.

The Premise

The first novel I wrote, the dark fantasy piece, was too large in scope, and contained some fundamental flaws that I didn't know how to fix without a complete rewrite, so I decided (albeit reluctantly) to downscale my ideas. I settled on writing a haunted house story.

Obviously, haunted house stories are a dime a dozen (an Amazon.com search of "haunted house" in the books category provides more than 8,000 titles). I agonised for many months on how to make my story "original". I remembered the follow up investigative report for the newspaper, how I spoke to the neighbours as the pervading smell of death floated around us. I remembered watching the forensics experts and wondering what it would be like to be inside the house. It was these sights, sensations and interactions that I used as the basis of my story.

Building the House

I read countless novels on people entering supposed haunted houses and I didn't want to recycle that concept. In recalling the real-life story, what fascinated me were the neighbouring houses and the people who resided there. I asked myself, "What if the neighbours didn't go into my haunted house, but instead it haunted theirs?

The Residents

One of the fundamentals of writing convincing and believable horror fiction is creating convincing and believable characters. Emotion, specifically the emotion of fear, is what drives a horror story—it's the blood in the veins of your story. Before I put pen to paper, I started to shape the characters in my fictional street. Through my years as a reporter, I'd met hundreds of people and drawn on that knowledge to create my characters.

I knew early on that my main protagonist was going to be a journalist. I wanted to use my own experiences to enhance the level of believability. The other neighbours came more slowly. The majority of characters I intentionally made common; a broken family, a couple (the journalist and his wife), and an elderly couple. There was one character who was truly out of the ordinary who I added to mix things up—a sociopathic loner.

I made a list of their names and ages and thought about each of their eccentricities and backgrounds. Was it a happy marriage between the journalist and his wife, for example? These had to be real people with real problems. As an artist I could easily visualize each of these characters, but I chose not to focus on their appearance, but rather their behaviors towards each other, and of course, the creepy abandoned house. If you think about the street where you live for a moment; how much do you know about your neighbours? You might know their names and faces, but can you ever really know them, or what goes on behind the walls of their homes?

It was this idea that became the skeleton of my story. Each neighbouring house had to have a story of its own before my haunted house reached out to infect them. I gave each of the inhabitants of the central houses around, *Hollow House,* a psychological flaw: one was afflicted by domestic violence, another the aftermath of an attempted teenage suicide, and, of course, there was one a bit further down the street where an emerging serial killer lurked.

I focused on telling my tale from the outside in, rather than the other way around. I used my reporter protagonist to slowly reveal the central mystery of the unidentified body in the house, while I used the other characters to reveal its "power".

Other writers might use the hero's journey to tell their story, with each piece of the puzzle leading to the next and so on, and that would likely work for a new writer. My goal, as with all of my storytelling, is to play with tropes and twist the narrative to enhance the feeling that not all is at it seems. New authors might find it more manageable to follow the path of least resistance, but one should always strive to have the occasional bend in the road (or dead end) along the way.

My decision to have Ben, the newspaper reporter, as the main protagonist was deliberate because in the back of my mind was the adage, "write what you know." It gave me a level of confidence that helped prepare me for the task of writing a novel. Although I had other flawed characters revealing the scary house on the corner, Ben sought the *origins* of the haunted house. Each character had a part to play in the grand design of my horrible house.

I thought a lot about the families, the kids, and the elderly couple and less on the haunted house because real identifiable characters were vital to making the supernatural goings-on more believable. Domestic violence, teenage suicide, parental abuse—all these things happen in our neighbourhoods. If we're willing to accept the knowledge of such horrible things occurring in our communities, would it be so hard to imagine the possibility of supernatural horrors being included as well?

Weaving the Threads Together

I regard my writing style as succinct, something I inherited from my days as a newspaper reporter. With, *Hollow House,* I wanted to focus heavily on characterization and dialog and provide just tiny amounts of information to keep the reader engaged—a slow burning horror story.

Below is the opening page from the novel. It was put in as a prologue to set the atmosphere. It gives you an idea of the sparseness of my prose:

The stench of putrefaction leaked from the Kemper House into the air over Willow Street for three days before any of the neighbours noticed it. The residents went about their daily regimen: rising from sleep, going to work and school in the city, renewing the cycle with each dawn, ignorant to the rot growing inside the centuries old house at number 72.

Willow Street never noticed the stink because they'd forgotten the house was even there. The Gothic Revival two-storey dwelling was invisible to them, despite its dilapidation. It was a meaningless edifice of split wood and grimy windows, twisted gutters and a queer metal mailbox overflowing with weeks of junk-mail. To its neighbours, the Kemper House had died a long time ago and been left an empty vessel.

They were wrong.

One of my peers, fellow Australian author Brett McBean highlighted my no frills style when he described the novel as a "taut, unnerving and often heartbreaking look at the horrors that surround us and the madness within."

Because of the great number of characters, I purposely kept my chapters as brief as possible. *Hollow House,* is on the short-end of novel-length works, but again this was deliberate. Characterizations and themes were key to creating a modern gothic piece.

Multiple perspectives allowed me to provide different pieces of the puzzle from different angles—and explore the social themes that were important to me. As observed by Bram Stoker Award-winning author Lisa Morton who said, "the real hauntings in Greg Chapman's compelling, unnerving *Hollow House* don't happen in the title structure, but in the finely-observed families surrounding it." If anything, the novel is about the sense of emptiness that can pervade in every house—if we let it.

The Process

I work 8 to 5 Monday to Friday, which meant I was writing, *Hollow House,* during lunch breaks and after hours. I am also a dad and at the time I was writing the novel, my children were still in primary school.

Therefore, my actual writing time was scarce. To complicate matters I wrote, and still write, all of my longer works freehand in notebooks. I feel a disconnection when I try writing directly through a keyboard. The words flow better when I have a pen in my hand. It's the true tool of a writer and the scratch of a pen on paper is music to my ears and keeps me going.

I aimed to write at least five to six handwritten pages a day. Most of the time I met this goal, occasionally I exceeded it. One thing I will say is that as hard as the prospect of writing a novel is, if you can write one page a day, by the end of year you'll have a 365 page novel. With those same rough calculations, I believe I was writing 2-2,500 words at least three to four times a week. All in all, it took about six months to write and review the first rough draft.

My novel didn't require a great deal of research, which meant I could focus solely on the story and its characters. It was the characters and the belief that I was writing something unique that spurred me on. I started to fall for the characters in a way. I strived to make them real and in some cases, unlikeable. I believe that it's the flaws that make us who we are. I knew what was going to happen to each character and every chapter was just a cog in the wheel.

Every day before I started writing I would read the previous chapter. I edited as I went, making notes here and there, finessing and in some cases, rewriting. After completing the first draft, I sent it off to one or two beta readers who I trusted to be honest, and they were. Toward the end of the book, there was a section where one character (possessed by the entity from the house) returns home to torment others. There were a few problems, my beta reader found that the entity was a bit too much of a cardboard cut-out villain, but I was able to address this fairly quickly and not lose my tempo. Beta readers are the best asset any novelist can have.

Translating my scratchy writing into a word document is a necessary evil, but it does allow me to maintain that "edit-as-I-go" approach. I also find that seeing the story unfolding as I type, cements that sense of achievement, that notion that I've created a story, even if it doesn't see publication.

I believe that if you set yourself a word goal and focus on just getting your story down on paper, or on screen, and not worry about where your story "fits" you'll have not only a readable novel, but an honest one.

Road to Publication

Surprisingly I sent *Hollow House* to its ultimate publisher on a whim. I knew of their reputation and I found the courage to just contact them outside of normal channels. My manuscript (which carried the working title "The Temple of Folly") was ready and I had a synopsis and the confidence that the story would appeal to them. The publisher happened to be open to submissions at the time, and they knew of me and my writing.

The acceptance of the manuscript came back about a month later. As a previously published author and artist and a member of both the Australian Horror Writers Association and the Horror Writers

Association, my presence within the horror genre community put me in good stead. The acceptance was a real vindication for me taking that chance to invest in a new novel. In the end, though, I feel it was the confidence in my story that led to the acceptance.

Yet the acceptance was when the hard work really began. I was assigned a fantastic editor and over a five-month period she and I went through the story with a fine-toothed comb, finding ways to make it even more impactful.

Hollow House, was published in July 2016 and was well received by readers and critics alike.

Epilogue

The key thing I discovered during the experience of writing my first novel is to write with confidence in something you believe in. Horror is so much more than just bloodshed. It speaks to our faults as human beings whilst opening our eyes to a plethora of possibilities. I never set out to write a novel that would put me on the bestseller list, I just wanted to tell the best horror story I could, one that readers would enjoy and remember. If you become a writer just to make money, you'll likely fail because your heart isn't truly in it.

Go with your gut instinct. The haunted house idea was a tried and true trope, but I went ahead with it, anyway. My aim was solely to make it my own. It was a sound decision.

The majority of reviews for *Hollow House* have been very complimentary and the work was ultimately nominated for a Bram Stoker Award in 2016 for

Superior Achievement in a First Novel. Again, this was proof that my instincts and confidence were right. As a reporter, I believed that I always had to look for that fresh angle and that training has benefitted me greatly in my fiction writing. It's important that, as a writer, you take some risks and be ambitious with your imagination, but most of all love what you do.

Although, *Hollow House,* didn't win a Stoker Award, I'm still extremely proud it was my first novel.

My method may not be how you would approach writing and that's okay, but my last piece of advice would be to surrender to the story you feel you are compelled to write . . . just don't wait for six years to put it on paper.

EDIT YOUR ANTHOLOGY IN YOUR BASEMENT FOR FUN AND PROFIT ... OR NOT

TOM MONTELEONE

LOTS OF WRITERS, especially in genre fiction, get the idea they could edit an anthology and do a good job of it.

There are probably several reasons for such a notion: The short story remains alive and fairly well in the genres of science fiction, horror, and dark fantasy. Despite many publishers' claims that anthologies do not sell, there always seems to be a plethora of them announced, edited, and published every year. And most importantly, most writers think it's *easy*.

The editors of this worthy tome asked me to discuss the process of creating an anthology, and since you've read this far, you should be able to figure I'm here to tell you the endeavor is a mixed bag at best. Yeah, there're plenty of anthologies published every year, but you should be asking yourselves how many of them are really all that good.

As they say, "your mileage will vary."

Part of the reason for that is the way the genre anthology came in to being in the first place. There are several types and ways they are assembled, compiled, or (least of all) actually *edited*. It's probably a good idea to examine these different types in a little detail to not only understand their true natures, but also to hip you to what you're getting into when you decide you want to be the "editor" of any of the different types. So here goes.

The Theme Anthology

This is hands-down the most prevalent and popular type of anthology appearing among all the genres, especially horror, science fiction, fantasy, mystery, and thrillers. The idea is to come up with a gimmick or shtick or *theme* around which you can find enough stories that examine in some fashion said theme. Over the years, I have been invited to participate in a plethora of story-gatherings such as cities of the future, robots, ghosts, vampires, zombies, dinosaurs, sports, magic, religion, conspiracies, alternate history, haunted houses, computers, time travel, freak shows, weird music, weird artists, weird hotels, weird taverns, weird carnivals, weird lighthouses, weird Halloweens, weird Christmases, weird children, and more than one weird serial killer.

I think you get the idea.

If you can come up with the right, catchy, kitsch-y theme for an anthology, you may be able to find enough material to put together a good book. The interesting angle is there are *two* ways to make it happen.

The first is a *reprint anthology*, which makes you more of a compiler than a true editor because you start out by selecting a theme, then go about picking out previously published stories that fit and define your theme. If you have a vast enough knowledge of the genres and have read a significant number of stories that define generations of fiction, you have the tools available to be very discerning as you pick and choose pieces that most aptly examine the theme you want to showcase. You are in complete control of this process and you don't need to have your inbox or your mailbox jammed tight with material you know you don't need to read.

The second course of action requires you wear a more tightly-fitting editor's hat. After you settle upon a theme for your anthology, you have to put out the word (through market reports and announcements in newsletters and social media) that you're looking for *original, never-before-published* stories that will fit within your covers and parameters. If your theme is not overly restrictive (such as *Great Stories about Toasters and Particle Accelerators*), you will most likely be tasked with reading hundreds of submissions—of which most will be familiar, predictable, and thus unacceptable. The upside is that you will eventually encounter at least twenty or so stories that deliver what you need for a good book.

Okay, that covers the most familiar types of anthologies, but there is one more general category with two subsets we need to discuss. And these are probably more interesting as well as certainly more challenging.

The Non-Theme Anthology

As the name suggests, these are compilations of stories that adhere to no particular gimmick or concept, and again, there are *two* types.

The easier iteration of the two is the *reprint* anthology with some generic title such as *Scary Tales,* or *Stories to Read in the Middle of the Night*, or *Macabre Offerings,* or *Space Operas,* or *Midnight Snacks*, etc. Your job, as editor, is the fairly straightforward task of picking out stories you really like that can reside beneath the large and billowy tent delineated by your title. I've read countless anthologies such as this, and (as you should expect) some are more successful than others. The primary reason for this lies at the feet of the editor who completes the project with the drive and energy necessary to create a striking package, or with the uninspired obligation to drag a book of stories across the finish line. You can accomplish your task either by relying on your inherent knowledge of the extant stories already in print—from which you can gather up the stuff you need . . . or you can solicit reprint material from the vast body of writers who are looking for reprint sales anywhere they can get them.

The second type of non-themed anthology is the main heat of this type of book. It is the book that gathers together original stories that have *not* been tailored to fit any theme or category, and have *not* appeared elsewhere before. It is the anthology that seeks out the best stories available—regardless of the concepts presented or territory explored. The best original non-themed anthologies have no restrictions, no taboos, and oddly enough no real guidelines. (Lots of writers have asked me for guidelines for our *Borderlands* series, and I always tell them other than being totally original and avoiding tired familiar tropes, there *are* no guidelines.)

This type of anthology is the most challenging for both editors and writers. If you are throwing the submission doors wide, and you have successfully gotten the word out you are open to submissions, you are going to get a *lot* of stories to read. For *Borderlands 5* and *6,* we received more than 700 stories for each volume. With those kinds of numbers, the submissions can pile up in a hurry and you can fall behind in your reading *very* fast. To keep up with the influx of material, you have to set up a reading schedule and stick to it. You have to not only have discipline, but also a consistent critical eye.

That means always try to do your reading at the same time each day, and make it a comfortable setting that offers few distractions. Don't try to squeeze a story or two in between other tasks. Give every story the same amount of attention and focus. In my early days of reading original story submissions, I would count the number of pages and give the writer at least *half* the total to get me involved. I soon realized the folly of that policy, and learned how to spot the failings of a story within the first 3-4 pages. When you are reading hundreds of manuscripts, you don't have the time to be leisurely—you have to be discerning, sometimes harsh, and always unrelenting in your reasons for rejecting the majority of the stories you get.

So what are the things you need to watch out for?

Allow me, as the poet once said, to "count the ways."

Bad dialogue

This is one of the most obvious flaws in a story because you can't hide it, and it just kind of calls attention to itself like your shirt-tail sticking out of the unzipped fly in your pants. There're two things your writers need to know about dialogue: 1.) when to employ it for maximum benefit; and, 2.) making it sound *real*. I always tell new writers you *must* read your dialogue aloud to yourself . . . and I'm *not* kidding. They simply *have* to do this until they are certain they have developed a great ear for the way people really talk. (It's very obvious when writers refuse to do this). And try this: even if you hate them, go to a few stage plays (or at least *read* them). The dialogue in an effective play carries the plot, creates the characters, and controls the pacing. Your writers could do a lot worse.

Dumb Luck, Coincidence, and Worse

This is a serious plot problem. Look for narratives that make *logical* sense. Remember: plot is a series of plausible, dramatic moments, caused by complication, which must be resolved or allowed to grow into a *worse* complication. Things must happen in good stories out of a natural progression of events and situations. Some of the biggest (and most painfully obvious) offenders are: (a) *Luck*. Never accept this as an explanation why anything happened. (b) *Coincidence*. This is very similar to luck, and is only worse when you encounter a character actually exclaiming "what a coincidence!" (c) *Author's Convenience*. This is the *worst* plot offense—your writer gives *no* reason for why something has just happened, other than the unspoken one that he or she desperately *needed* it to.

Clichés

Two major reasons stories fail in this category: (a) *Trite Expressions* "rear their ugly heads" and you should always notice them. These are things that should have vanished when your writers were revising their first drafts. All writers get lazy once in a while and drop in a cliché or a shop-worn phrase just to keep the narrative going. If you're reading an otherwise good piece of fiction, just excise them like the tumors they are. Trite, over-familiar writing is a signal of two things: lazy writing or inept ability. You need to decide which is obtained with each story submitted. (b) *Stereotypes*. A close relative of the trite expression is the stereotyped character. You know who they are, so I won't bother mentioning the hard-boiled detective or the hen-pecked husband or the unfulfilled housewife or? Once you've read enough stories, you will be able to spot this kind of weak and lazy writing.

Structure

This is really about how a narrative is put together and how it allows a story to unfold. Don't confuse it with plot. It's more about the overall effect the story has on the reader. Structure is all about traditional storytelling, Beginning, Middle, and End, and how a writer may vary them. Some of the most common errors associated with Structure are: (a) *Slow Beginnings*. If a story loses you at the start of the tale, it will probably never get you back. (b) *Sagging Middles*. If the story starts digressing, adding subplots, too much backfill and flashback, it will lose energy and direction. This is the kind of writing that causes readers to put a story down, and "forget" to pick it back up again. (c) *Unsatisfying Endings*. Coming up with a good ending is one of the biggest challenges in modern storytelling because readers are getting very sophisticated, especially readers of horror and suspense. There can be lots of reasons why an ending doesn't work.

A very common error is when the writer wraps things up too fast and too neatly. Another occurs when the ending just kind of fizzles out with people dying or disappearing and no real resolution is at hand. Look closely at the way stories hit the finish line. Endings must resolve enough questions and problems to satisfy your audience's need for (some kind) of order in the universe. A common error is to assume it had to be a, "SURPRISE!" ending. Big mistake, that. (d) *Loose Ends*. These are issues, problems, questions, etc. which arise in a story, and are just plain *forgotten* about when you reach the last page. You either need your writer to resolve these issues or remove them if you want to accept the submission.

Language, Style, and Execution

These are probably the least flashy of the stuff you look for in a good acceptable professional story, but they remain no less valid. A possible early flag that signals a rejection slip on the horizon is a writer's inability to tell a story at a level, which is literate and compelling.

A great story or an original idea, when presented in a manner which has no sparkle or life can be just as much a failure as a story told in bloated, purple prose. What I'm getting at is a general *dullness*. It's hard to describe, but we know it when we encounter it. Sometimes it can be a lack of fresh descriptions or challenging imagery; at others, a dependency on the plainest words, as if the writer was consciously avoiding *any* esoteric vocabulary.

Other symptoms can be an avoidance of metaphors and similes, or *anything* that smacks of the lyrical or the poetic. We're not saying you need to look for prose that sings like Keats or Shelley, but you should pay attention to the overall *feel* of a story. Granted, this is more subjective than anything else, but you should develop some basic radar to detect dull, albeit syntactically correct, writing.

Once you have achieved a comfort-level in how you read submissions and know what you're looking for, you're going to need to establish your own system for how you *reject* the majority of the stuff you read. Some editors have a little standard form letter or note they cut and paste into their emails or insert into a return envelope. Others write a personal email for every rejection. Something Elizabeth has employed with great success is a checklist which delineates many of the reasons why we reject stories. It's quick, easy, and usually accurate. We used to stuff them in the return envelopes, but thanks to email we plug it into the reply. The only time we actually write a personal response is when we accept the story, or ask for revisions, or tell the writer they came close to a sale, but missed for the following specific reason(s).

Now, every once in a while, we've seen our personal notes elicit replies from the writers we hadn't expected and *certainly* didn't appreciate.

Let me elucidate.

One story we rejected concerned a couple driving across the English countryside that accidentally ran their vehicle into a ditch, become lost, and asked for directions from a guy walking along the road. He told them how to reach their destination along with an admonition to *not stop anywhere else along the way.* (Cue scary music here). It turned out that they *did* stop at a weird little village, whereupon they learn they can never leave, and (cue the REALLY scary music) that's because they're: Dead!

Can you say ho-hum?

Yeah, well, so could we. Elizabeth typed out a note, telling the writer that while the story was well-written, it was predictable and used the old ghosts-who-don't-know-they're-ghosts shtick. Not for us, right?

Several hours later, we got a pissy reply which focused on a typo Elizabeth committed to the subject line of her email: she'd made the second letter in the first word of the story's title a CAP instead of lowercase. The writer's exact words were:

Dear Elizabeth,

Thanks for your message, which comes as a relief.

Your inability to spell the name of my MS correctly leads me to suspect that stories that "stretch the imagination" also stretch the rules of grammar and syntax, and in this regard I am, faithfully, traditional.

Yeah, I'll bet it was a real "relief" she wasn't plagued with the pesky task of cashing our checks or appearing in on the signature page with Farris, King, Little, Straub, Strieber, et al.

What an asshole.

Just to make sure she was relieved of any such duties in the future, Elizabeth kept a printout of her note on the bulletin board by her reading chair.

The second example concerns a story we received from a well-enough-known writer. We gave her story a thorough read, and found it not at all what we wanted. Believing that true professionals always want to know why a story does not sell, we pointed out the more glaring and obvious ones—several of which concerned egregious violations of logic, as well as an amateurish (not even rudimentary) understanding of human anatomy and survey-course psychology. In essence, the story didn't work for a variety of reasons. Not long after sending off our thoughts, we received a note informing us that (a) she had been writing for 20 years, (b) hadn't gotten a rejection slip in a *long* time, and (c) three additional, lame paragraphs attempting to defend the points we found wanting in her story, and furthermore to *educate* us on the possibilities of her comic-book-science methodologies being plausible and accurate.

Her email was frankly embarrassing and stunningly un-professional.

The third and final anecdote involves a reply from a guy I've known in the field for 20 years, who'd appeared in a previous volume of, *Borderlands*. He sent us a story that was very well-written, but either didn't work for us, or we were far too obtuse to "get it".

Regardless, we didn't buy it, and sent him a note in an effort to explain why.

He sent an email back, little more than a line, which snidely suggested that since we didn't get/like/buy his story, then, perhaps we weren't as visionary and hip as we thought we were.

It frankly surprised me.

So I sent him back a very un-snide reply, "Your note is curious. We've always liked you and your work. Why would you want to change that?"

Funny, but now that I think back on it, he never answered me.

Now, the question remains: why would any writer who gets a rejection note he or she disagrees with, feel like it's okay to fire off a responding salvo? I think the ease and immediacy of email encourages this behavior, but I'm here to tell you, don't let your writers get away with it.

Tell them you have this really big bulletin board, and there's always room for another note from a writer who has this burning need to remind you what a complete mook he or she is.

Now, get down the basement and start editing.

WHEN IT'S THEIR WORLD: WRITING FOR THE THEMED ANTHOLOGY

LISA MORTON

LET'S SAY YOU'RE a writer who is looking to make some short story sales; maybe you're just starting out, and your novel is still working its way through your head, so short fiction seems like a good way to get to practice your craft in the meantime. Or maybe you're a pro who wants to exercise those short fiction muscles a little, so you've been perusing some markets. Either way, you've just come across a listing for an anthology paying well above pro rates, and the theme is vampires vs. Sherlock Holmes. Let's further suggest that this is a completely excellent opportunity: good pay, a respected publisher, a fine editor, top-notch authors already involved.

If you're like most writers, you'll probably have one of the following responses:

I'm not sure I can work with someone else's ideas.

I have my own ideas and visions; why should I try to bend my writing to someone else's stuff?

Sounds great! Sign me up!

Of course answering #1 and #2 above are the

primary point of this article, but those who answered with response #3 might want to read on as well for a few important tips.

Let's start by laying out a few hard facts about the publishing industry. Anthologies are a tough sell, especially to the major publishers. They require a decent investment going in—since there are a large number of contributors to be paid, as well as editors—and they rarely sell as well as novels. Most agents will tell you that they need two things to sell an anthology to a major publisher: Big names, and a marketable concept. Smaller presses may not be able to afford some of those big names, but they need to be able to promote their books just as the big guys do. This is why themed anthologies are increasingly popular, whereas non-themed anthologies are becoming about as scarce as Mothman sightings. And for you, the writer looking to make short story sales, this means that—at least until you become a big name—you need to learn the fine art of writing for themed anthologies.

So, let's get down to business. Maybe you fall into category number one in my list above—you're the writer who simply isn't sure if you can successfully play with someone else's concept. Here's the best way to answer that concern: study up a little more on the theme. In the above example of an anthology themed around vampires vs. Sherlock Holmes, for example, you should start by brushing up on your Sherlockiana. Read some of Sir Arthur Conan Doyle's classic stories, but try to read them beyond mere entertainment. Study the characters, the settings, Doyle's style. If, after reading some of the original Holmes stories, you're still not sure, then maybe try googling "vampires vs. Sherlock Holmes" and take a look at what's already been done in that arena. You might even check out some critical analysis of the Holmes stories, or perhaps read some biographical material on Doyle to better understand what led him to produce these tales.

If you're thinking this sounds like a lot of research for a short story . . . well, then, maybe this isn't the right themed anthology for you. If, on the other hand, you're an expert on, say, ghost legends of the southwest, then a market call for regional ghost stories should require little research on your part. Every themed anthology won't be right for every writer.

But if you're happy with the prospect of (re)reading some terrific detective fiction (and why shouldn't you be?), then you should enjoy the research angle of this.

So you've studied up on Holmes and maybe vampires; what's next?

My advice—ironically—is to steer as far away from what you've just read as possible. Remember that plenty of other writers are going to submit to this anthology, too, so how do you stand apart from the crowd? One way is to not copy any of what's already been done; think, instead, about what you *haven't* read. Did Sherlock Holmes fight an Asian vampire in any of the stories? Did Dr. Watson have to drive a stake through the heart of an old friend? Is any other writer likely to try a story told from the point-of-view of a vampire trying to hire Holmes to solve a murder?

Now, let's look at the second response some writers might have: *I have my own ideas and visions; why should I try to bend my writing to someone else's stuff?*

Here's a question to that question: *Why not think of it instead as bending someone else's stuff to your ideas and vision?*

Let's say you've done the research and you've got the idea now for your vampires vs. Sherlock story. Maybe you've been interested recently in writing stories that explore feminism in horror fiction; or maybe you've already begun to garner a reputation as a writer who is finding fresh ways to spin classic tropes. In either case, you should enjoy the challenge of applying your personal writing obsessions to this story. Remake Sherlock Holmes in *your* image. Make the vampire *your* personal creation. Set up *your* swing-set on Doyle's playground.

Some writers might balk at a very broadly-themed anthology because it's a type of writing they've never tried before. Maybe everything you've written has been horror for adult readers, so why even respond to a call for young adult short stories? Consider the following: 1.) because it will expose your name and work to a whole different audience and potentially garner more readers for your other work (at least after they grow up a bit!); 2.) it will broaden your skills as a writer; and 3.) young adult (or YA) fiction is hot, and it's likely that it will pay more than most horror markets. And if that last point sounds crass to you . . . well, so is having to worry about paying your next electricity bill. If you are serious about pursuing a career as a writer, you will likely be forced to deal with many crass issues, most far less interesting than thinking about writing a story outside of your usual genre. You might even be pleasantly surprised to discover that not only do you enjoy writing in these other arenas, but you're actually *good* at it.

Here's where we're going to look at response #3: the writer who thinks this all sounds great and dives right in. Just consider one last thing before you sit down at the keyboard: if the unthinkable happens and the editor doesn't buy your story, are you left with something so odd and specific that you'll have a hard time finding another market for it? Are you going to be competing with all the other Sherlock vs. vampires stories that also didn't make it into the intended anthology? Did you just waste a lot of time researching and crafting a 6,000 word short story that's now unsalable?

That's going to be less of a problem if you've followed some of the suggestions above and really made this story your own. You might also consider a rewrite before you start submitting this story elsewhere; in this particular example, think about replacing the instantly-identifiable Sherlock Holmes with your own original character. Your story will no longer be sharing Sherlock with all those other unsold tales.

Here's one tip that's also a plea (because I've edited a few themed anthologies and/or themed magazine issues, and hope to edit a few more in the future): Do *not*, for even one tiny second, think you can get away with simply inserting a reference to the theme into an existing short story. Trust me—editors can spot that from a mile away. As a Halloween expert, I've edited several Halloween-themed anthologies/magazines, and I can't tell you how many times I read stories that included no more than one brief mention of October 31st. Not only will you be instantly rejected, but you actually run the risk of angering the editor enough that they will remember your name. If an editor rejects your story, you want them to remember you because you came *really* close, not because you wasted their time with a glaring attempt at cramming a theme into a story you couldn't sell anywhere else.

After you have a few themed-anthology sales under your belt (and congratulations!), you may find editors coming to you with direct invites into their next themed projects. Some of these may be closer to shared-world (or "mosaic") novels, in which the book's theme is actually an overall plot. In these situations, the editor will provide you with a detailed description of the theme, possibly including very specific suggestions for what your story (or "chapter") should include.

You may even be given a list of the other writers involved in the book and encouraged to share information with them. Contributing to a book like this can be especially challenging, since there might a dozen other authors creating their stories at the same time that you are creating yours. This is when you need to be—on top of a talented and adaptable writer—a skilled communicator. Work with your editor. With these projects, the editor will usually encourage his writers to run ideas past her/him before starting the story, because the last thing the editor wants is to have to turn down a piece from an obviously gifted writer only because it doesn't fit into the book. Depending on how detailed the overall plot or background of the book is, the editor may also suggest significant rewrites to the story once it's done, and it will be your job as a writer to comply promptly and efficiently to those requests.

Here's something to remember about editors: they are bosses, and like the boss in any other business, they want employees who are easy to work with and who get the job done. If you respond to rewrite requests by using ALL CAPS TO SHRIEK AT THE EDITOR, they're not going to be anxious to invite you into their next book. If you strongly disagree with the editor's rewrite suggestions, then reply—in a friendly, polite tone!—with your own suggestions. Editors are smart enough to recognize something good; it's likely to be their name on the spine of the book, and they want the best book. Some pleasant back-and-forth just may lead to your editor responding, "Hey, you know what? Your idea is great—let's go with that."

If your goal is to have a long-term career as a writer, then it's likely that at some point or other you will be asked to write in someone else's universe, whether it's a short story for a themed anthology, or a chapter for a shared-world or "mosaic" novel. In either case, you absolutely can produce a work of fiction that bears your particular stamp and stands as something you can be proud of. Developing the ability to work with pre-existing material can be a useful skill in the writer's permanent toolkit.

ROUNDTABLE INTERVIEW

JOHN PALISANO

THE STATE OF the world has us in a very different environment than we've ever been in before. Artists and writers have a lot more to consider than just creating their works in a vacuum, high atop some lofty hill. With the rise of social media, there are new areas to navigate and consider when following the call.

Where does this all lead? In the end, where is the written word's place in all of this? In this roundtable interview, we speak to David J. Schow, Linda A. Addison, Tonya Hurley, Cody Goodfellow and Mary SanGiovanni to find out what their perspectives are.

How important is the first draft?

David J Schow: You have to start somewhere, and many nascent and wannabe writers are impatient with drafts that aren't "perfect" right out of the gate. I don't know who first said "writing is re-writing," but it's desperately true—and you've got to get a string around your entire story before you jump in and start mutilating it, usually for the better. This can take a long time. In the newer publishing paradigms, there's no room for reflection—no interest or space or time to let an idea ferment. Everybody's in a big hurry to be seen . . . even if their work sucks, they frequently have enough buddies to prop up their egos in a kind of anti-creative circle jerk. I can't tell you how many newer things I've read where I thought, "if only they'd given this the benefit of one . . . more . . . draft."

Tonya Hurley: The first draft is the most important for the writer—it's where your ideas flow most freely, where characters are developed and themes are explored—where you don't have to worry about what your editor or publisher might think. It's the most fun you'll have as a writer in my opinion. The first draft is yours and yours alone. It's where you find your voice.

Linda D. Addison: Without a finished first draft there is no final publication possible. I advocate whatever it takes to get to "The End". The real building is done in the rewrite for me. I tend to rush to the end so I can get the idea/story out, sometimes not even taking the time to give the characters names (C1=character 1, etc.) and when I know something bad should happen but didn't know what, I would put a comment "***SOMETHING BAD HAPPENS***" and keep marching to the end. Finishing the first draft allows the subconscious to flesh out the details for the rewrite.

Mary SanGiovanni: For me, it's pretty important. I tend to edit as I go, sometimes several times, to get what I want to say down, in a way I want to say it. I do rounds of editing and copyediting after, but for me, the first draft is more than the bare bones—it's the structure without the architectural accents.

Cody Goodfellow: It's essential. Without it, you're not a writer, just a liar. What stops most aspiring writers, myself included, is the sense that the first draft must be perfect, the Thing Itself, and the Perfect becomes the enemy of the Good. It's almost impossible to puke out a perfect text, but if a writer narrows their focus on an overwhelming project down to describing the story in one sentence, and then elaborating upon it, they'll begin to get the thing out of their head, one word at a time. In no other medium can describing the thing you want to create eventually create the thing itself.

In the age of constant connection, how does one stay focused?

David J. Schow: Don't blame the internet. The conspiracy against getting meaningful work done has always been the conspiracy of distraction—whatever breaks your concentration. Forget looking good, forget being social, forget all that happy-crappy. I think it was Jessamyn West who was credited with saying: "Writing is a solitary occupation. Family, friends, and society are the natural enemies of the writer. He must be alone, uninterrupted, and slightly savage if he is to sustain and complete an undertaking." Lock the door, forget social media, and don't let anyone come near. Forget breaks, forget excuses—burn on that fucker until it's done.

Tonya Hurley: Distractions are always an issue and staying focused requires discipline especially with social media taking up so much time personally and professionally. Focus is a skill an author needs to develop these days as much as any other. It's a constant struggle because having an active online presence is thought to raise an author's profile, but at what expense?

Linda D. Addison: I've had to limit how much time I spend on social media and emails each day. I give myself an hour first thing to respond to business/important messages/emails. I don't answer phone calls, texts until I take breaks during the day (to let my eyes rest). Basically I don't jump to respond to each way that we can get messages from people now and depend on people to leave messages that I can respond to later. I've found from past experiences that it's too easy to lose time to browsing online instead of writing.

Also, focusing on one project in a day has become very important. Multitasking is an illusion, jump around between too many things in a day can leave you feeling like nothing's been done at the end of a busy day.

Mary SanGiovanni: Sometimes, I need to unplug. Social media and the dramas which are often pervasive there can be a sinkhole if you let it. Sometimes, I just shut it all down and do something real-world for a few days. It's like coming off sugar, sort of––after a while, you don't have a craving for it, and you can get other stuff done, like writing, spending time with family and friends, etc. Lately, there is a lot of polarizing politics on social media, which makes it a little easier to disconnect from time to time. I wish it wasn't that way,

but part of mental health is choosing your battles——
and choosing when to walk away.

Cody Goodfellow: I used to feel like I was promoting
my work and career by engaging on social media, but
really, I was just scratching the itch of a need for
validation as a writer. Telling people about the project
you're working on or hoping to work on gets you a
crumb of that cookie, but it's an illusion fooling
nobody, producing nothing anyone else will consume,
perpetuating an illusion of creation. Writing is by
definition a solitary pursuit, and you must make a
friend of solitude and silence, if you're going to write,
and not just pretend to be a writer.

It seems as soon as a writer finishes a draft,
they can upload their work and sell it on any
number of platforms. Why should writers
wait and go through traditional publishing?

David J. Schow: It's entirely your choice, but the
most obvious reason is to enjoy the benefit of actual,
professional editing. It's rarer these days, but for all
the things still wrong with "traditional" publishing, at
least you know 50 sets of eyes have looked over your
work—not your pals, not your Mom, and not a bunch
of earnest embryos. You can have a card-table
lemonade stand in front of your house, or you can have
a branded national lemon-flavored franchise that
probably has a lot of artificial junk in the mix . . . there
are advantages and downsides both ways. There is a
residual good feeling that comes from having
impressed some total strangers with your work to the

point where they would send you actual money for it; I don't know—maybe that's been buried by now.

Tonya Hurley: How one chooses to publish their work has changed drastically with the pervasiveness of the internet and all sorts of technology. Like musicians and filmmakers, the author now has much more control. It can be very empowering. However, marketing is an important part of any book release and publishers have much better resources than any individual writer. There is something to be said for the traditional process as long as you stay very involved.

Linda D. Addison: First of all I don't look for a market when I finish a draft because my drafts are pretty rough, fiction in particular. There are very few authors who finish a draft and don't need to rewrite to create a well-written piece. Once it's rewritten as well as possible I suggest letting it sit a bit so you can give it a final read after a little distance, even if only one day. If you have a critique/writing group, this would be a good time for them to review it.

Then it's up to the vision the author has for their work/career as to where they want to see their work published. For me, I've sold pieces to online magazines, anthologies as well as books published by traditional outlets.

Mary SanGiovanni: There is a vetting process in traditional publishing that a lot of people in the business and, frankly, a lot of readers, see as a gatekeeping process for quality. While this opinion seems to be changing somewhat as time goes on, there are still other benefits to traditional publishing. If you're working with reputable publishers, you get money up front. For working writers whose sole or majority income streams come from writing, this is absolutely important.

Also, in my experience, traditional publishing often has the means to reach a larger audience with promotional efforts—they can send out review copies, get Bookbubs for your book, run blog tours with cover reveals or content about the book, and can offer distribution to stores that might not otherwise carry the book. We as writers are, if we're lucky, aware of the community of die-hard fans of our genre, but a stable writing career involves reaching a wider audience—— the beach readers, the airport casual shoppers, the people who like spooky books but don't even know horror conventions exist. Traditional publishing sometimes has ways of reaching those people that the average writer doesn't.

Cody Goodfellow: I self-published my first novel without even querying traditional publishers, because I was badly burned by my first contracted projects. I worked for a CD-ROM zine that spectacularly melted down due to hype and embezzlement, and had my first book delayed for ten years, rewritten without my permission, and eventually released without a proper contract, so I was paranoid and determined to retain control of every aspect of the process. The book was well-received by a handful of people, but never got the kind of attention it might have if I'd gone the traditional route, because readers are justifiably mistrustful of self-publishing.

It's easy to get drunk on the DIY aesthetic and convince yourself you're winning when your self-published or micro-press release lights up the dozen or so friends on Facebook the algorithms actually let see your celebratory posts, and to lose sight of how woefully short that tiny success is from even the weakest of indie release numbers. It's crushing to consider how small that bubble really is, and how vast the potential audience who will remain oblivious to, or skeptical about, your release. But if your ultimate goal is real success, and not just a specious self-esteem boost, you need to aim for the highest market that might accept your work, and to heed any feedback they see fit to give, always looking to get into that better market than you feel will let you in, always working to not just meet, but crush their standards.

Are there any essential books writers should have on their bookshelves?

David J. Schow: Books on how to write? Banish them.

Tonya Hurley: What's essential depends very much on the person. It helps to have a basic grounding in the classics, if for no other reason than to understand plot, character development and so on. For horror writers the staples are Frankenstein, Dracula, Horace Walpole stories, Edward Gorey books, Poe, H.P. Lovecraft and Shirley Jackson's collected works, Stephen King and of course William Peter Blatty's The Exorcist as well as the sci-fi queen Ursula K. Le Guin.

I also think collected scripts and teleplays by

writers like Rod Serling, Richard Matheson and the great Charles Beaumont have a lot to teach about horror and fantasy storytelling. With that said, I think that any writer that inspires you is essential—different authors speak to different audiences. The most important thing is that you read, period, that you find your own voice and tell your stories.

Linda D. Addison: Some of the physical books that are in easy reach for me: *Welcome to Hell: A Working Guide for the Beginning Writer* by Tom Piccirilli. This is a wonderful book about the experience of being a writer, whether you're a beginner or not from the late Piccirilli. I find it comforting to dip into often as a reminder of this thing of being a storyteller in a world that doesn't always honor us. It's filled with information about the things to look out for, the ups and downs of writing.

The Art and Craft of Poetry by Michael R. Collings: a fantastic book to try out new forms, Collings does a great job of explaining forms, with examples and exercises.

Writing the Other by Nisi Shawl & Cynthia Ward: excellent guidelines when developing characters that embrace a worldview.

Writing Down the Bones: Freeing the Writer Within by Natalie Goldberg: filled with good exercises.

Per magazines on writing skills and business: I subscribe to *Locus* and *Poets & Writers*. Two magazines I read consistently are *The Writer* and *Writer's Digest*; these days I buy them for a specific subject.

For quick questions/clarification about using

commas, etc. now I find many answers online. Books that have helped me: *The Chicago Manual of Style, The Elements of Style by William Strunk Jr., The Sense of Style by Steven Pinker*.

Linda D. Addison: When sending work to an editor it shouldn't be assumed they will fix errors. I have always worked to send the best version of my work out. It's important to have a good understanding of: dialogue format, professional formats for submission (fiction, non-fiction and poetry); this is VIP when sending work to editors who will have to merge your work into a document with other stories, it can be very difficult if requiring extra formatting work to be done by editors. There are many sites with information about this, the one I often refer to is http://www.shunn.net/format/

Point of view, past/present/future . . . tenses, use of commas, colons, semicolons, dashes (hyphen (-), en dash (–), and em dash (—)). It's fine to break rules, but it's very important to know what the rules are first and have a good reason for breaking them.

Mary SanGiovanni: For horror writers, I think the HOWDUNIT SERIES of books are invaluable. They're books about the scientific processes of body trauma, cause of death, etc. written in layman's terms specifically for writers. Here's the full list: https://www.thriftbooks.com/series/howdunit-series/38270

I also think Stephen King's, *On Writing*, and David Morrell's, *Writing Horror*, are great. As far as fiction . . . there are too many to list. *Ghost Story*, by Peter

Straub, *The Shining,* and, *It* by Stephen King, *Alone with the Horrors,* by Ramsey Campbell, *A Glow of Candles and Other Stories,* by Charles L. Grant, *The Wine-Dark Sea,* by Robert Aickman, and of course, collections by Edgar Allen Poe and HP Lovecraft are all essential, but there are many, many more.

Cody Goodfellow: Besides, *Elements of Style,* or an equivalent guide to proper grammar and usage, I don't know that any one book is essential. Certainly for writers of horror, King's *On Writing* is useful, but not as a model to be emulated. (I tried maxing out on drugs to write a bestseller, but lamentably, I'm the only one who remembers the results.) I feel that too many horror writers consume everything in the field and seek to do something similar, which is death in a genre predicated on surprise and shock, generating herds of mediocre books that turn horror into comfort food lit.

I don't learn anything from writing unless it's so good, that it hurts to read. It should make your brain feel like your muscles feel, after a punishing workout. I've been far more inspired and empowered to write greater horror fiction by reading masterful literature outside the genre, than by the best horror masterpieces.

Diversity has become a very important aspect in the publishing world. In what ways can authors contribute and reflect this?

David J. Schow: The best way is to champion someone you may feel has been suppressed or ignored. Be wary of "diversity" becoming just another flavor-of-the-week buzzword. If it's worthy, if it's good, the work will come forth somehow, some way. Talent should be the only arbiter.

Tonya Hurley: Diversity is an important value but not the only value so each author has to measure whether they are remaining true to themselves, their story and their characters or if they are trying to force a certain percentage of this or that into a story to satisfy an editor or a reader for that matter. I think the best way to address diversity is to make room for more voices in the marketplace. To provide even more choice for readers and for readers to open themselves up to different kinds of stories and not just the ones they are most comfortable with—to broaden the range of what's available to readers and to realize that the best stories are universal and part of the total human experience.

Linda D. Addison: Keep in mind that diversity isn't just writing black characters, it's about looking at the planet and seeing that humans come in all different backgrounds, physical, etc. I'm a huge supporter of trying out a worldview with storytelling. We live with so many fascinating humans, I'm continually interested in having my characters reflect that fact. Humans basically all have similar traits of pain, joy, desire which are changed through the lens of their life.

I mentioned a book above that can be helpful (*Writing the Other* by Nisi Shawl & Cynthia Ward) as well as reading articles online. You don't have to get a PhD in another group to write characters from their point of view but doing some due diligence will help you avoid writing cliched characters.

For example, in my story, *Finding Water to Catch Fire*, in The Beauty of Death anthology (Independent Legions Publishing) I wanted to have the main character in a wheelchair. To make it as real as possible: went through a video online for how to use a wheelchair while in my desk chair that has wheels (paying attention to the descriptive words used), read blogs by people in wheelchairs per how they felt towards non-wheelchair people's reactions and the challenges of moving around in spaces that don't include wheelchair access, watched videos on self-defense when in a wheelchair because there was going to be a confrontation in my story.

The only thing I didn't get a chance to do because of the deadline, which I wish I had, was have the story read by someone in a wheelchair to make sure I didn't make any mistakes. This is an important step if you have time.

Mary SanGiovanni: I think it's important to raise the visibility and awareness of marginalized voices in horror by cross-promotion. Publishing is a business, and I think the best way to reach publishers and agents, and thereby readers, is to show time and again the talent and commercial viability of those marginalized writers. I think it's important to reinforce the universal appeal of their fiction as well as celebrating the variations in experience and point of view.

The movies, *The Descent,* and, *Get Out,* do this masterfully. I think "normalizing" the presence of multicultural casts of characters with taste, empathy, and realism reinforces the connectedness of the human race, and the universal horrors which transcend race, gender, sex, orientation, religion, and everything else. I believe if editors and publishers make at least some attempt to be diverse and marginalized writers keep storming the gates of traditionally all-white male hetero publishing, I think we can meet in the middle and bring a beautifully varied array of books which simultaneously touch the readers' most primal instincts of terror or horror while introducing—and in many ways, humanizing—diverse points of view to those unfamiliar with them.

Cody Goodfellow: Despite our best efforts to champion diversity and inclusivity, the reality is that this will always be an overwhelmingly white and male field, with an overwhelmingly white audience. Writing takes time that only fanatically devoted or well-educated, well-off people can afford to spare, and writing and reading horror and dark fantasy is a pretty bourgeois, middle-class European pursuit.

To overturn this hidebound conventional wisdom, we need to listen to and read other voices, seek out and embrace experiences and friends outside our own cultural and economic bubbles, and reflect them sincerely and empathetically in our writing. We have the unique capacity to step into other lives, and thus, the obligation to do so in lives unlike our own. To do so without exploiting or misappropriating other cultures, genders or ethnic or religious groups is daunting, but so is writing in the first place.

Is it important to join a critique group? What are the positives and negatives of doing so?

David J. Schow: Not in my wheelhouse, so I can't say.

Tonya Hurley: I know lots of writers who are involved in critic groups and they get a lot out of them. You have to gauge what's best for you as a writer. For me, I think the best writing occurs when I'm writing to please and entertain myself. After I have a draft on paper I have a few friends I trust to read it and give me their feedback—that's what seems to work for me.

Linda D. Addison: A critique group can be an invaluable polishing resource. I've been involved with one that came together in 1990 (Circles in the Hair, CITH) after a bunch of us took a workshop at the New School University taught by Shawna McCarthy and wanted to continue meeting and learning to write better.

Our group took additional workshops with authors like Nancy Kress, Terry Bisson and developed an approach that involved the following: 1.) feedback should try to cover the following (adapted from *Critiquers Checklist* by Grace Ackerman): Story Line, Characters, Setting, Dialogue, Details & Mechanics. 2.) state *What works* & *What doesn't* (with suggestions on how to improve, if possible). 3.) when we meet in person (since I'm no longer in NY I get my feedback by email): each person gives feedback in no more than five minutes (not line edits, that's noted in the manuscript). The author doesn't respond until all members are finished with feedback; which they may do to answer questions, etc.

4.) if there's a consensus on something then it may

mean the author isn't communicating that well. 5.) in the end the author is Creator of the work and can ignore all feedback that doesn't make sense to them.

CITH has made an incredible difference in improving my writing—light years!

This is a cautionary tale. It doesn't help if: the author isn't open to hear others reactions to their work without taking it personal, members just say: *This is great!* or *This sucks!* and aren't willing to learn how to give useful feedback, or energy goes away from helping improve writing and becomes a battle of egos.

Mary SanGiovanni: I think critique groups are valuable until you've found your own "voice" in writing. Finding your particular voice is a matter of developing certain basic competency skills in commercial fiction writing—telling a story with a beginning/middle/end, showing and not telling, actually finishing work, understanding dialogue, atmosphere, and characterization and how to use them. The way you do that competently and effectively as a writer naturally becomes a part of your style—your voice.

I think critique groups are good with helping you develop that—with this caveats in mind, of course. 1.) The critique partners should know how to critique. Blithe, generalized statements like "I liked it" or "I hated it" don't help at all unless a person can explain why. 2.) The critique group should be made up of people just as good a writer as you, if not better. Why would you get medical advice from a florist or even a med student when you can get it from a doctor? 3.) Ideally you should have a critique group where different members have different strengths in storytelling and writing. 4.) Ideally, the group should understand what you want to accomplish with your writing. I've seen many critique groups go waaay off the rails if any of these components was missing.

Cody Goodfellow: At some point in one's development, it's very useful, if one can find a group with complementary levels of mastery or better, and a sincere desire to improve by absorbing criticism. Criticism should sting, and you must learn to associate that sting, like the brain-ache of challenging reading, with growth.

No matter how insecure you feel about your writing, a group that just unconditionally cheers you on without offering substantive feedback isn't doing you any favors, instead probably weakening your sense of how far you've still got to go. Almost anyone can point out when something isn't working, but peer readers who can offer constructive criticism that helps you fix the problem are pearls beyond price.

Does an author need to go to college in order to learn how to write well? Are there any other ways to learn?

David J. Schow: Learn by doing, not by trying to find handbooks or shortcuts or some freeze-dried instant methodology. I'm paraphrasing whoever first said this, but these days, "there's no place to go to be bad," and thus develop toward your own strengths in an organic way. Pulps used to serve such a function. After that, tie-ins and novelizations were a great earn-while-you-learn boot camp (frequently predicated on one's personal survival, which is the greatest incentive of all).

I'm a college dropout, by the way. Three semesters and out. Nine years after that, the same university I quit hired me to come back and lecture to classes . . . about writing. They paid me more than my whole grant/loan/scholarship deal was worth in the first place.

Tonya Hurley: In my case, college and continued education in general, gave me the confidence I needed to write. I don't think it taught me how to write because I'm not sure that can be taught. I wouldn't say it was necessary to learn how to tell a good story but it was very useful in telling a good story well. Again, it depends on the writer—some great authors never graduate high school and others have doctorates.

Linda D. Addison: I didn't go to college to learn to write. I did go to college and earn a B.S. in Mathematics and ultimately made my day job in software development.

Learning to write well, for me, has been an ongoing process since I was in junior high school and decided I wanted to see my work in print, before that I made up stories and poetry and read everything I could. I noticed early on that there was much I had to learn (and am still learning) about grammar, dialogue, etc. so I focus on reading about how to improve in those areas. I've taken workshops given by published authors and editors, read mountains of magazines and books about process and other authors' experiences.

Made a rewrite list of things to look out for that I know are my issues after first drafts (passive voice, white room syndrome, etc.).

I also have been blessed with being part of a writer's group CITH (Circles in the Hair) that came together after a workshop at New School University in 1990. For my fiction in particular, CITH has been pivotal in improving my writing.

In the end, college/workshops/writer's groups and books can help an author improve their writing skills, but I don't know if they can create the storyteller that has to be born in the soul.

Cody Goodfellow: I learned how to write persuasively and structure complex arguments in college, but I've often felt that deep reading and life experience could have brought me these skills, and college mostly provided me with the skills to deal with college by the time I graduated, and little else.

Mary SanGiovanni: I'm a big believer in educating our writers, in offering them every possible avenue of philosophical exploration, social experience, and academic training as college will allow. I think if writers have the opportunity to attend something like Seton Hill's Writing Popular Fiction Master's program, that they absolutely take it. All that being said, I don't think it's necessary to go to college to learn to write well. Some of the most phenomenal writers throughout history, both in this genre and out, have barely made it through high school. I think what makes a person learn to write well is to learn to read well—to read critically, to pick up both the surface story and the subtle nuances, the themes, the symbolism, the techniques of great writing. While not all great writers are college graduates, all great writers are avid readers.

How does a writer know they're a writer?

David J. Schow: Hard question, because I'm sure you're surrounded by people who are all absolutely convinced they're writers already. They say so on Facebook—constantly—and have little printed books to enforce their claims.

There's this movie called, *Hearts of the West*, where Jeff Bridges asks ex-pulp writer Andy Griffith the same question, basically. And Griffith says you're a writer when someone *else* says you're a writer. Harlan Ellison used to quote this all the time.

That seemed a little foggy to me, so in my arrogance, I modified it. You're a writer when *a writer says* you're a writer. And by that I mean a writer you respect. Without being coached or prompted or bribed. It may not happen fast, but if you're any damned good, sooner or later one of those writers is going to call you a colleague, and mean it legitimately. There's no feeling in the world that can match that . . . except maybe for the part I said before about getting money from total strangers.

Tonya Hurley: By writing. Writers write. There isn't any more to it.

Linda D. Addison: There's a perception you're only a writer if you've had a certain number of things published or making a defined level of income from writing.

Writing is a creative process that unwinds from the soul. If you're creating work with a beginning/middle/end, then you're a writer. If you find stories/poems, etc. going through your mind while you're doing the other things that life requires and can't wait to find a slice of time to write them down, then you're a writer. Early in my career I stopped writing because I didn't think this was for me. I was tired of collection rejections. What happened is for the weeks/months after that I was so unhappy inside and felt like a pressure cooker without release. That's when I surrendered to being a writer, no matter what the outer world does in return.

Being paid or published is something else, but that can't happen if you're not writing in the first place.

Mary SanGiovanni: If the world were falling apart, if you were suddenly alone on the planet and the world had become a giant, deserted island—if you still feel the compulsive need to tell stories, then you're a writer.

Cody Goodfellow: If you can't watch Barton Fink without composing a unique scenario for a Wallace Beery wrestling picture and shouting it at the screen the way other people shout warnings at victims in slasher movies, you're a writer. (Also, if you watch Barton Fink more than once.)

But seriously, if you process the world in stories, if you delight in noticing what no others notice and putting ineffable impressions into words, and if you don't know how to do anything else, you're probably a writer.

SELL YOUR SCRIPT, KEEP YOUR SOUL AND BEWARE OF SHEEP IN WOLVES' CLOTHING

PAUL MOORE

SCREENPLAYS: **NINETY PAGES** of *who, what, when* and *where*. They are a straightforward blueprint that informs the director who they should cast, the actors what to say, the camera where to go and the editor when to cut, half the words of a novel.

The recipe for horror is simple. Take a clever concept, add compelling characters, snappy dialogue, douse with a generous helping of jump scares, gore and garnish with twist ending. It's a basic formula that even a novice chef or neophyte bartender could follow, right?

If you were expecting the answer to be, *no*, you were wrong. If you were hoping for, *yes*, I hate to disappoint you. The answer to the key, secret, ingredient lies in an often used French phrase: *je ne sais quoi*.

The direct English translation: *I don't know what.*

And that is the plain, beautiful, ugly truth.

Nobody really knows what makes a great screenplay. How many movies have you seen that followed the above formula to the letter and still turned out to be near misses or lifeless duds?

I would hazard the answer is: *Too many.*

On the other side of the coin, how many films have you seen that ignored all of the above and were thrilling successes?

I would venture that answer sounds something like: *Not as many as I'd like, but more than I expected.*

The first thing you need to do when writing a screenplay (or novel) is take the rules and conventional wisdom you learned in the myriad of English and film classes you attended in high school, college and seminars, collect them and store them somewhere in the back of your brain. Tuck them in that mental basement somewhere between such thoughts as: *One more shot of Jägermeister never hurt anybody* and *I should use a condom, but what's the worst that could happen?*

Please take note, I did not ask you to *forget* them. Much of that information is important and will come in very useful . . . later. However in the beginning of the process, they are more likely to cause problems than provide solutions.

No two screenwriters begin in the same place. Some take meticulous notes, others work from outlines on note cards, still others write treatments or work from inspirational material such as photos or music. Some just crank up the laptop and take the plunge. There is no "right" or "wrong" at that stage of the process. There are suggested methods, but in the end, it is what works best for each individual.

There is only one rule that truly matters. Whatever you write, it has to be *compelling*. You are not just writing a great story. You are writing a hybrid entity, something that needs to appeal to artists, businessmen, accountants and the public at large. Those are all distinctly different audiences with distinctly different definitions of what constitutes a successful screenplay.

So, the question becomes: *How do I satisfy multiple masters with a single script?*

Another way to look at it is: *How do a I throw a party that everyone can enjoy?*

You start with the invitation.

The *invitation* is literally the first ten pages of your script. If you are not writing for an independent production where your name will be preceded by *written, directed, produced and edited by* (insert name of person who just squandered $30,000 of their parents money), then these are the most important pages in your screenplay. Anyone not required to read your script in its entirety will determine its potential worth in the five to ten pages. If they are not enthralled and captivated by some element of those, they will pull another from the stack. If they have nothing else to read, then the wrong person is reading your script.

This is the reason so many horror movies open with an isolated scene in which a hapless character runs afoul the antagonist and meets an untimely demise before the opening credits roll. On the surface, this decision appears to be a statement to the audience: *Here's a taste of what's to come, so please bear with us as we introduce a few characters and set the stage. We promise the blood will flow soon.* In actuality, that statement is for the producers.

Even if your script is a slow burn, it would be wise

to consider opening the story with the proverbial *gut punch*. Do not get me wrong, I am a huge proponent of deliberately paced, cerebral horror films. I would never suggest tossing in some hack scenes of blood and boobs just to keep the viewers in the cheap scenes entertained. Now that being said, it is important to remember that whatever you add can be removed.

It is extraordinarily rare for a submitted draft of a script to survive preproduction without any changes or revisions. Sensationalizing the first few pages of your screenplay might seem like the act of *selling out*, but it is actually the acting of *selling your script*.

During the pre-production phase of the film, screenwriters inevitably receive *notes*. These suggestions can come from just about anyone involved with the production. Usually these are provided by the producers and the director, however if the lead actors are big enough names with genuine clout, you will likely hear from them as well.

It can be an infuriating process. Filled with suggestions that range from predictable: *Instead of the hero sacrificing himself to save his girlfriend, let's make it look like he's dead only to have him emerge from the lake into her waiting arms. But as they hug, his eyes glow red showing the soul of the killer jumped into his body!* to the absurd; *Instead of the curse being attached to a centuries old heirloom, maybe it could be a gypsy curse on a fidget spinner. Those are insanely popular with our target audience!*

However, the process does have its benefits.

This is the time you can rewrite your opening to something more suitable to the story you are telling. In the sales industry, this is called the *bait and switch*.

In the screenwriting trade, it is called *showing them what they want, but giving them what they need.*

Be prepared to argue your case, but I have found that most producers (and especially directors) are more open to restructuring once the film is green lighted and you have established a creative relationship with them. Make no mistake, you will have to acquiesce to some of the changes, but you can leverage the lesser of the evils for the greater good.

Speaking of killing two birds with one machete, developing strong characters is a *win* for everybody involved. Too often in genre films, characters are neglected in favor of plot mechanics. To be fair, in certain sub-genres that is completely acceptable. I doubt there is a single person who bought a ticket to *Friday the 13th: Jason Takes Manhattan* expecting a Bergman-level study of marital tensions slowly shredding the humanity of two disparate souls. If someone actually did that, I would have paid triple the ticket price just to sit next to them as Jason sliced through a gallery of clichéd, cardboard characters as he prowled the alleyways of the city.

Also for the record, just typing that last sentence has all but assured that I will be revisiting that film as soon as I finish writing this.

We all know that creating three-dimensional characters goes a long way in helping an audience connect with a film. It also goes a long way toward helping that film resonate with an audience after the credits roll. One has to look no further than films like: *The Exorcist, The Witch, The Babadook, Rosemary's Baby, The Descent, It Follows, Carrie* or *Heredity,* to find evidence that audiences respond to having an emotional investment to characters being menaced onscreen. However, there is another group of people who appreciate that level of depth beyond the average moviegoer . . .

Actors.

A-list, B-list or neophytes looking to make a name for themselves all covet roles that are more substantial than a paycheck bearing one or two digits followed by several zeroes. In fact it has been my experience that if the role is truly interesting and challenging, a few of those zeroes (but not all) tend to disappear, a simple, but often overlooked truth about actors.

They love to act. It is why they do what they do. Never underestimate the value of a substantial role.

I have witnessed and experienced the intoxicating effect that a well-written character has on actors who are tired of being typecast and pigeonholed. If you put genuine work into the script, characters and relationships, they will champion the project. They will petition producers, financiers and the press to get the film made and seen by a wide audience. In a world where social media is a dominant force, there is no better ally than an enthusiastic actor.

So the question then becomes: *The actors love it, my friends and family say that I make Quentin Tarantino look like Alan Smithee, but the producers are hesitant. They say "too much talk, not enough stalk." Do I sacrifice all of this wonderful character work for more jump scares and severed limbs? Or do I stand my ground and look for another buyer?*

That is an excellent question I just imagined you asked me. And the answer is: *neither*. There are myriad of complex and critical elements needed to create a strong horror script. Vibrant characters, an intriguing and well-paced plot, marquee set-pieces, snappy (but natural) dialogue, an iconic antagonist, etc . . . All of the above can be summarized one simple word that is easy to understand, but can be surprisingly difficult to achieve.

Balance.

Too much action, gore, sex and an over reliance on jump scares usually leads your script into the hands of cheap producers only interested in turning a quick buck. Too little emphasis on those same elements typically means that the only producers interested in tackling your script are art house, auteur driven producers who are not cheap, just poor. However, walking that tenuous line can land you in the coveted position of being *in demand.* Most producers seek something that draws in the dedicated, horror fan base, but still appeals to throngs of squealing teenagers.

Because in the end, it is all about money.

Everyone involved desires critical acclaim, artistic integrity and social relevance (even the producers). However it takes spending money to realize those goals and if that money is not returned exponentially, your fifteen minutes of fame will be fourteen minutes and fifty-nine seconds shorter than you expected. In the film industry, there are no participation trophies. There is only first, second and third place.

First place walks the red carpet while second and third place compare who had more "meetings" over a plate of cold fries at 3:00 AM at Mel's Diner. If you are unclear as to what exactly constitutes a *meeting*, I will do my best to explain it succinctly.

If you have a successfully produced script and

legitimate agent, a *meeting* is pitch session with a studio vetted producer interested in cultivating or exploiting your talent. If you have a film that played well at the *LA Shock-o-Rama and Spooky Clambake*, then your meeting will be with a "producer" who uses a gift card to buy you a coffee at Starbucks and promises a fast-track to fame just before driving away in his Toyota Yaris.

Balance is the difference between crossing the finish line with your arms held high or your head held low. So, how does one person armed with a laptop and head full of dark thoughts break reach the finish line ahead of all the other dark dreamers toiling away in windowless bars and under-lit coffee shops across America's heartland? To unravel that particular Gordian knot, one has to return to the fundamentals of horror screenwriting.

The *genre contract*.

Simply put, the genre contract is the unspoken agreement between the filmmakers and the audience. In its broadest interpretation, it means that people who buy a ticket to a horror film expect to be scared. If the trailer, commercials and poster promise a movie that will give them sleepless nights or unending nightmares, then the audience forks over their hard earned cash with the impression that they are boarding a terrifying thrill ride. If the movie succeeds in fulfilling that promise, everyone wins. If it fails to live up to the hype, the producers still get their money, but the duped moviegoer walks away feeling like a stiffed whore: disrespected, unloved, two hours older and twenty dollars poorer for their time.

However, that is an example of the genre contract

in its most rudimentary form. The complete contract is sufficiently more nuanced as each sub-genre carries its own specific set of elements and guidelines. For example, the ghost film.

The popularity of films focusing on supernatural apparitions, hauntings and cursed souls has been on the rise for the last decade. American audiences' appetites were whetted with the flood of J-Horror remakes in the mid-2000s and their hunger has risen to almost ravenous levels once production companies such as Blumhouse began creating their own quality, original content. Not only has this generated an obscene amount of money, it has also cemented the audiences' expectations of ghost film.

For instance, the vast majority of ghost films are rated PG-13. On the surface, this is a financial decision. The PG-13 rating opens the movie to a wider audience and, more importantly, to its target audience, teenagers, specifically teenage girls. However, there is another reason that most of these films are granted that less constrictive rating and it has to do with the genre contract.

Audiences do not expect excessive gore from ghost films. Their goal is not to shock the moviegoer with copious amounts of viscera and bloodletting. Inventive deaths and kinetic chases only serve to undermine the sense of dread and impending doom that threatens to swallow the characters as they attempt to piece together the puzzle of the ghost's motivations.

The same goes for nudity and sex. These are scenes typically presented as salacious behaviors for which the participating characters will inevitably be punished. Or, they can be presented so that the audience can feel the character's vulnerability as they are stalked by some deranged, voyeuristic madman. Or in their basest form, the scenes are included as a cheap thrill for an audience of teenage boys who have yet to crack the parental controls on their parents' internet.

None of the above is a concern for audiences who crave jump scares and the startling revelations of a malicious spirit's origins. If the primary thrill of a ghost's existence is watching me shower, I would be more inclined to feel pity than fear. After all, I am pretty sure watching a forty-seven year old, bald man staring wistfully at a bottle of shampoo is the difference between purgatory and Hell.

Ghost films are ruled by inventive jump scares and twisted tales of past events. The key to their formula is that *there is no escape.* Bound by no physical limitations, poltergeists can reveal themselves anywhere at any time.

Is it in the shadows behind the character?

Is it in front of them or behind them?

Encountering mysteriously locked doors or slamming windows, characters panic as they seek to avoid the simple *touch* of the murderous specter.

These elements are essential conditions of the genre contract for these films. Eerie faces emerging from shadows, unexplained noises, campfire tales of innocence twisted and metaphoric situations where sympathetic characters, usually young women, struggle to overcome real life tragedy are what audiences pay to see. Ignoring these conditions or drastically altering them is a violation of that unspoken agreement. It will end in disappointment for both parties.

The diametric opposite of that contract is the slasher film.

These films need to embrace the *exact opposite* of the rules outlined above. Young women in revealing and compromising positions is not only expected, it is *required*. As are wildly elaborate death scenes designed to showcase gruesome effects. Most importantly, gore-hounds are hoping to witness the birth of the next iconic horror villain. Some masked entity vying to join the ranks of the unholy trinity of Michael Myers, Jason Vorhees and Freddy Krueger.

In addition, slasher audiences are not looking for layered, multi-faceted characters. They are looking for archetypes: the jock jerk, the slutty sorority girl, the awkward dork, the likable stoner and, of course, the innocent virgin. Again, make no mistake, these still need to be *well written* versions of these known quantities, but veer too far into artistic interpretations of these standards and you risk losing your core audience. And producers know that because losing the fans translates into losing money.

Because in the end, it is all about money.

Global box office stands at *38 billion dollars* as I write this. In two years, it is projected to reach *50 billion*. Factor in television content (*The Walking Dead, American Horror Story* and every third series on Netflix) and Internet based content and you could use the resulting number to feed one billion people for one year with enough money left over to keep you in scotch and hookers for the rest of your life.

But I digress . . .

Those were only two examples of the genre contract. There are a multitude of tomes chronicling the various sub-genres of horror and any one of them can be used as a template for audience expectations. As writers, we are tempted by the idea of reinventing the wheel. We want to be the engineers of the defining moments of the genre as a whole. We want our work to be recognized, quoted and endure for decades.

What we do is important to us and we hope it will be as equally important to the world at large. However, like anything in nature we have to learn to crawl before we can stand and we have to learn to walk before we run.

If the above adage were a hard and fast rule that would mean that a writer would generate his masterpiece upon completing his fourth script. Of course, nothing is that concrete in an industry that relies on a strong synergy between creativity and commerce. If there is a better example of the Ouroboros than the film industry, I have yet to see it.

However, I have found that most screenwriters hit their stride around their third script. It was certainly true for me. A rare few knock it out of the ball park with their first offering, a few more with their second. Others do not find their voice until the fifth or sixth. However bear in mind, we are discussing *produced screenplays*. We are discounting the innumerable discarded, unfinished and abandoned scripts stashed in folders with names like: *Revisit And Polish, Needs Something More* and *What The Fuck Was I Thinking*.

You would be surprised how thick that last folder becomes after a few years of late nights and hefty bar bills.

A word of advice, *do not* delete those folders. The amount of gold buried beneath the overwritten clichés, unintentional plagiarisms, stilted lines of dialogue and *Deus ex Machina* endings is incalculable.

You may have stopped writing because you did not know where to take the story. You may have stepped away because the foundation of the story was flawed. You might have taken a break because you wrote yourself into a corner and the idea of tearing months of work to pieces and rebuilding was too daunting and depressing. The reasons can be numerous and all are equally valid.

For example, I once abandoned a script after two months of work because I took a night off, went to the movies and saw a trailer for *the movie I was writing*. To make matters worse, I went to opening of said movie and it really was the story I had been toiling over for months. However the fatal blow was that the movie was great *and* a huge success.

The bar bill that night was not hefty, it was *crushing*.

So, why not exile these failed works to digital oblivion? The answer lies in our own behavioral patterns. If you started writing it, there must have been something that attracted you to the material in the first place. The core concept, a character, a few scenes your brain could not shake . . . *something* that prompted you to dare walking that lesser taken path in the midnight hour.

Whatever *it* was it is still there. I can assure that if you revisit those forgotten works years later, armed with the combination of experience and fresh eyes, you will discover a treasure trove of great lines, effective scares and engaging characters you had long forgotten. Those elements might not work within the confines of its original context, but some of them might be well suited for a current project.

After several years working as private investigator and bounty hunter while attending university part-time, I decided to return to school full-time to study filmmaking. During that time I wrote a seemingly endless amount of scripts. To say the earliest works were bad would be an oversimplification. Losing your wallet is bad. Forgetting your mother's birthday is bad. Getting skin caught in your zipper is bad.

Those scripts were on the level of drunkenly crawling into your girlfriend's bed only to discover you have the wrong room and that her roommate is a rather humorless man.

However, each script was a little better than the last and with each screenplay I learned a lesson. What worked, what did not work, what elicited a positive response and what elicited a, *It makes me want to know more,* response were all necessary stepping stones to writing my first truly successful screenplay. The reason it was a success came down to it being built on the foundation of noble failures.

But were those early works truly failures?

The answer is *no.* Not only did they pave the way for eventual success, but years later when I reviewed them, I found there were a fair amount of concepts, characters and scenes that actually *worked.* Granted those elements were lost in a forest of pretensions themes, stilted expository dialogue and paper thin revelations, but once removed and refined, many of those moments proved useful within the framework of a more seasoned, and coherent, story.

The above is collection of tips, suggestions and

tactics offered to fill any gaps in a fledgling writer's bag of tricks. This anthology is full of wisdom imparted from veteran authors, screenwriters and many others who all share one commonality; their passion for the genre of horror. Horror has put food on their tables, sent their children to college and in some cases, bought mansions or small islands. Or in my case, I refer you to the before-mentioned scotch and hookers. However, there is one vital ingredient that cannot be imparted verbally or in print.

Je ne sais quoi.

It all comes back to that indefinable quality. No one knows what it is or how you capture it. However for reasons that are equally as cryptic, we all know it when we see it. Even if we are not exactly sure what we are seeing.

Though there is no scientific or mathematical formula capable of quantifying the essence of successful writing, there are signs that can alert us when that essence is missing.

If you are bored writing it, people will be bored reading it. Seems simple, but you would be stunned at the number of established writers who unintentionally lead themselves down the primrose path. Sometimes, it is that they have put so much time and effort into the project that they refuse to admit that is failing. Or, it is a matter of pride.

The story is not working, but the author believes that if they continue to push hard enough, something will give. In other cases, the writer keeps blindly typing in hopes that true inspiration will blindly strike them or that through the unproven process of word processing alchemy, the whole messy affair will coalesce into a brilliant story before they reach page ninety-five.

Take this piece, for instance. I contributed a piece to the first anthology of which I was very proud. The subject was about the origin of story ideas that would eventually become screenplays. I opted to recount an evening of surreal circumstances that would become the catalyst for the film, *Keepsake,* as the framework for exploring how the seeds of a successful script are planted.

When invited to contribute to the sophomore edition, I wanted to expand upon cultivating and nurturing those seeds. In addition, I wanted to make some adjustments to the casual tone and loose style that were prevalent in the early work.

I tried an academic voice and that lasted for about fifteen-hundred words. Scrapped it. Then I attempted to construct something with a sort of *question and answer* format. That iteration made it to around twenty-five hundred words before it was jettisoned. I even endeavored to fabricate a fictional conversation between a prospective producer and a hopeful screenwriter. That one died in the womb.

Many nights of notes and revisions, hours of shining my forehead with my palm and a few empty bottles of scotch later, I finally found a voice that worked.

A casual tone and loose style.

Why did I trash the earlier versions?

Because they did not speak to me.

Were they bad?

One of them, absolutely. The other two, not so much. But in the end, none of them resonated. They felt workmanlike, pedestrian . . . serviceable, but not special. If they felt that way to me, the author, I know they would have fallen flat with you, the reader.

So I swallowed my pride, sopped up my tears and did what I should have done from the beginning. I did what came naturally. I wrote what I wanted to write the way I wanted to write it and let nature take its course.

I was attempting to construct something serious or clever or even ground breaking. The key word in that last sentence is, *construct*. I was trying to fabricate not *originate*. If I had allowed those seeds to grow *organically* I would have saved myself a lot of time, heartache and hangovers. In essence, I was attempting to reinvent my own wheel.

Be true to yourself. Be true to your own voice. It is unique to you. No one can tell you how to harness that *indefinable quality*, but I can tell you this, if you are not passionate about what you are writing, it will be already forgotten before the reader reaches the last page. We are writers and there are times we have to take dull, cookie-cutter jobs to pay the bills. I can almost guarantee that every author in this anthology has experienced that scenario at least once in their careers. I can also guarantee that they downplay or dismiss those works whenever possible. I certainly do.

At the risk of sounding like a motivational speaker, avoid those jobs. Avoid anything does not excite you. Avoid emulation. Most importantly, avoid the naysayers, the doomsayers and anyone else who refuses to recognize your commitment or your appetite for storytelling.

Embrace the bizarre addiction that is writing.

Embrace your voice whether it be conventional or unconventional. Embrace the rules and requirements of your chosen genre while seeking new ways to subtly subvert or improve them.

Take every, *no,* you hear from producers as a challenge. If neither of you find the other's argument convincing enough to change or alter the script, find a producer willing to listen. There are few things more rewarding than working with a producer that is creatively collaborative. Just remember, that you have to be willing to give in order to receive.

Whatever you do, be true to yourself. If you are not, you will be fundamentally unhappy and that unhappiness will show in your work. Anyone who enters any aspect of the film industry for the express purpose of becoming rich and famous will find their careers a bitter disappointment. We all have to make a livable wage, but that is not why we embark on these journeys.

We choose these roads because there is something inside us that cannot be ignored, an itch or a voice that we cannot scratch or silence unless we are in front of our laptops typing furiously. We have stories inside of us, both good and bad, struggling and pleading to escape. Heed those urges. You may not become wealthy, but you will be happier for it.

It is my sincerest hope that some of the people reading this found the above information useful or comforting. Failing that, I hope they at least found it entertaining. The only thing I can say with any certainty is that it was written in my voice my way. I invite you to do the same and I look forward to privilege of reading it when you are done.

Artwork by Luke Spooner

NOW WHAT?

THE TALE OF THE PERFECT SUBMISSION

JESS LANDRY

MUCH LIKE THE Illuminati, the world of publishing consists of underground clubs, secret handshakes, symbols hidden in bank notes, and Nicolas Cage's never-ending quest to steal the Declaration of Independence. Yes, it's *really* that exciting—pinky swear!

But I'm about to let you in on a little secret, one that will sully my name and force me to live with the cave dwellers, eating plump and juicy creepy crawlers, never to see the light of day again (it's cool, I'm already pretty pale): there are several ways to stand out from the crowd, to make your manuscript shine brighter than all the other amazing stories in the slush pile. And, oh boy, I'm about to spill those beans.

So, submitted for the approval of the Midnight Society, I call this article "The Tale of the Perfect Submission."

But first, a few precursors:

A-S-S-H-O-L-E

Before you even sit down to write your novel or short story or obvious masterpiece, please ask yourself, "Am I an asshole?"

If you're unsure, answer these questions:
- Do I enjoy watching others suffer?
- Do I like to bully people over the internet and/or in real life?
- Do I think the world is owed to me?
- Do I hate kittens?

If you answered "yes" to any of these, you are, indeed, an asshole (and quite possibly a psychopath, in which case, please don't murder me for calling you an asshole, thanks).

The horror community is a tight network—everyone knows one another in a six-degrees-of-Kevin-Bacon kind of way, word often travels fast when someone acts out in a counterproductive way, and in this day and age of social media, your reputation can be put through the ringer faster than I spend my bi-weekly paycheck (mortgages, right?). If you tarnish your name before (or even after a few sales), well, that's not going to do anybody any good. Please, keep your ego in check and work on your craft instead.

So when you send out your manuscript and cover letter to a publisher or agent, please don't be like, "Here's my work, now where's the contract?" It's perfectly fine to feel confident about your project (though I think most writers would argue that when they send off a manuscript, "confident" isn't the word they would use to describe their emotions), but nothing is ever guaranteed. Ever. Not even after you sign on the dotted line.

Your cover letter is, more often than not, your first meeting between you and the company you're trying to sell your work to—don't assume that just because you love it, they will, too.

If a publisher rejects your manuscript, don't send them an email back reaming them out. No, that is what assholes do. In fact, if you get that rejection, don't do anything (except eat a whole container of Ben & Jerry's Cherry Garcia and binge-watch all nine seasons of *The Office*). For a non-asshole, as tempting as it is to send an email back to the publisher thanking them for their time, don't do it—they've likely sent out several hundred rejections already and, believe me, they know it sucks when things don't work out as planned. Just leave it at that, and go onto the next.

The Social Network

Did you know that the internet isn't all porn and cat videos? Turns out there are other like-minded individuals out there with goals and hobbies similar to yours. It's true! Seek these kindred spirits out: join writing groups, follow your favorite writers and publishers on social media, volunteer your time (or score yourself a sweet-paying gig) with organizations, magazines, websites, whatever. Just get your name out there and get your voice heard.

Bear with me here, the same can be said for doing stuff in person—yes, actually putting on pants and leaving the house.

Pants are the gateway to great things.

Pants make miracles happen.

PANTS.

Join an in-person writing group that meets up once a week, volunteer with a local writer's organization, get to know the people around you. Talking with your fellow enthusiasts could lead to exciting possibilities and unmatched opportunities. You never know unless you put yourself out there. So do it. Just do it. (I'm screaming at you like Shia LaBeouf right now.)

Now that you've established that: a.) you're not an asshole; and, b.) people kinda sorta know who you are, we can get into the good stuff:

Guidelines Exist For a Reason

Similar to the, "Maybe don't be an asshole," rule, I always thought this one went without saying. Instead, it bears repeating until you've said it so much that the words start to sound weird.

In a nutshell, if the guidelines ask for a collection submitted in one Word document, don't send each story as a separate piece.

If the guidelines ask for novel submissions only, don't send a short story.

If the guidelines ask for your best, most polished work, don't send in a thrown-together manuscript, then say, "I've only lightly edited this, but I assume your editors will do what needs to be done in the end." (See previous point on being an asshole.)

All of these have happened to me (and so much more). When I receive things like this, it tells me two things: 1.) You don't listen; and, 2.) You don't listen.

If you can't follow simple steps to send in your

work, something you should be proud of, why would I waste my time reading it?

A little miss of one guideline is a-okay. You underlined some words instead of italicizing them; you forgot to add the word count to the title page—but a blatant disregard of the submission process is not cool, bro. If a publisher's guidelines ask for a double-spaced manuscript in 12 pt. Times New Roman, then give the people what they want. Don't send a single-spaced 500-page epic in 16 pt. Comic Sans. When a publisher sees an abomination such as this, they'll often delete your entire submission without a second thought (and shame on you if you think Comic Sans is a nice font. Shaaaame).

Ramble On (Don't Do It)

When it comes to your cover/query letter, give the people what they want: the basics. Who you are, what your story is about, the word count, the genre, the end. As much as we would all love to engage in some friendly chatter, now is not the time for that. Publishers are busy people, and the smaller the press, the more hectic the workload.

After you submit your manuscript, one of two things will happen: you'll either receive a submission confirmation, or you'll hear nothing at all. Every press is different when it comes to things like that, but the one thing they all have in common is the response time. So once you've sent your masterpiece off into the great unknown, all you can do now is wait.

Juicy Fruit is Gonna Move Ya

Heading back to that fancy schmancy cover letter of yours, be sure to give us all the juicy details of your story. For the most part, publishers want a full synopsis, so here's your chance to leave 'em wanting more. Hook them with the beginning, write up a tight and clean middle, and finish 'em off with that spectacular, no holds barred end. Make the people reading your synopsis feel as though you understand your story completely, that you know your characters inside-out, that the story poured out of you like vomit after an all-night kegger. It's okay to spoil any pertinent surprises you may have in your query. This letter is the slush readers' first introduction to you, so make it stand out, make it flashy, make it all about your story and how awesome it is. You got this.

Do Your Due Diligence

Make sure that your manuscript is in the best possible condition it can be. Don't send in an unedited hot mess under the assumption that all the editing will be done when the publisher accepts it. HELLS NO. This is your work, take some pride in it, put effort into it, show us that you care. If you send in an unsolicited manuscript that jumps fonts, that isn't double-spaced, that looks like you just copy and pasted everything without going over it with a fine-toothed comb, it just shows that you couldn't give two shits about your work. And why should we care when you clearly don't?

Title Me

Your title is just as integral as the story itself, so don't skimp on it when it comes time to naming your little precious. If your story is about a pretty princess who watches the *Jurassic Park* trilogy all day, I would suggest not calling it, "The Pretty Princess Who Watches *Jurassic Park* One and Two (But Skips Three Because, Let's Face It, That Was A Terrible Movie) All Day."

Think hard—what's your story about? What sort of fancy wordplay can you use? What sort of imagery do you want to portray?

Naming your book or story is just like naming a baby: don't leave it with something that you'll regret later on (like Nevaeh or Britney Shakira Beyoncé, which I wish was not true, but yes, apparently someone decided to name their child that).

Patience, Obi-Wan

If the guidelines give you an average wait time, then by god, wait it out. Do not send a query before the allotted time. We know you're excited, we know that you want an answer right away—hell, we'd love to give you one as soon as possible, but publishers receive hundreds (possibly thousands) of manuscripts every year. It takes time and effort (and a risk of going cross-eyed) to give the worthy ones the look-over they deserve.

Read, Read, Read

If you get to that magical moment when the publisher accepts your manuscript, read the contract. Don't be afraid to ask questions. Legal jargon is not a lingo that everyone speaks. It's okay to feel like you don't understand. That's why asking questions is so important. A good publisher will take time to answer any question you may have. And always, always, always keep a signed copy for yourself.

There are a lot of conditions that go into finding a good home for your manuscript, and the journey may feel long and unrewarding, but as long as you keep at it, then there's no stopping you.

And, in truth, there's no such thing as a perfect submission. There is no formula, no Hogwarts-worthy potion that'll get you that book deal or acceptance letter or even help you finish that short story. All there is, is your drive, your commitment, and all the asses you can kick when you make your dreams come true.

So . . . what are you waiting for?

TURNING THE NEXT PAGE: GETTING STARTED WITH THE BUSINESS OF WRITING

JAMES CHAMBERS

AS A WRITER you put your heart and soul into your words. You breathe life into your characters, refine your plot, polish your prose, revise it, maybe with feedback from beta readers or a workshop group—and one glorious day you write, "The End." Some stories come easily, some fast, some like pulling teeth.

Whatever path you followed it feels good to complete a new piece of work. You lived with the story for the time you wrote it. You rallied your creativity to bring it to life and tell it the best way you know how. Scribing a bit of your soul onto the blank page is hard work, but finishing a story only marks the end of one chapter and the beginning of another. To share what you've written with readers means taking on a task almost as daunting as writing the first words of a new piece on an empty white screen.

Now it's time to navigate the business side of publishing.

Bringing a story to publication involves many factors. For those only starting out it's a daunting list:

networking with editors, locating a suitable publisher, negotiating contracts and rights, understanding what editors and publishers expect of you and what you should expect of them. Then there is planning how to publicize, promote, and sell your work.

In the publishing partnership, author and publisher must unite to present work to the public. This arrangement of mutual obligations and commitments can vary widely from work to work, publisher to publisher, even book to book. The path to publication often goes smoothly, but authors must always watch out for the bumps, detours, and dead ends that come along the way. Preparing to publish your work includes honing your knowledge of the publishing business, and there are many resources available to help you do so.

An excellent place to begin are writing communities, which offer essential support for authors making their first forays into the business of writing.

The horror community holds a well-earned reputation for being especially welcoming and generous in this regard, but writers can find camaraderie and help in any genre. Whether you attend writing workshops, join professional writing associations, or simply get together for coffee with local authors once a month, these groups can help you get a handle on business issues. "Talking shop," enables you to share experiences and information. If you're on your own writing alone before deciding to take the next step with your work, joining a writing community might seem challenging. In actuality, all it takes is communicating with other writers, and most writers are glad to talk a little shop now and then.

Even overcommitted, best-selling authors may take a few minutes at a convention or a book signing to answer a question or two, offer some words of encouragement, or introduce you to other writers. It's unlikely, though, that you'll be able to ask those busy authors questions on a regular basis—or pick their brains about what rights a market you're considering wants, or if a contract is fair, or what you can realistically expect to earn in royalties. That takes a deeper connection, a mentor committed to lending you a hand over the long haul.

Many professional writing groups facilitate mentorships through formal programs. The Horror Writers Association, for example, offers a popular mentoring program that pairs new writers with seasoned authors in a framework designed to help writers advance their career. Other writing groups, such as the International Thriller Writers Association, the Mystery Writers of America, and the Romance Writers Association offer similar programs.

Mentors can offer you advice and feedback for improving your writing, but they can also coach you on marketing and selling your work, protecting your rights, reading contracts, and on how to earn money as a writer. No formal program is required. You can find a mentor on your own by networking, whether online, at conventions, or through other channels.

As much as a writer's work requires the solitary labor of creating and putting words on the page for readers to enjoy via the solitary act of reading, navigating the publishing business takes personal interactions and often runs on personal connections. Networking paves the way for publishing success.

Getting to know established authors face-to-face can lead naturally to mentoring relationships. Many successful authors recall their struggles starting out and take joy in the success of up-and-coming writers they like. They won't do the work for you, of course, but they may offer you the tips and encouragement you need to lay the groundwork for your career and steer clear of risks.

This applies to editors, agents, and publishers too. A personal connection with an editor can lead to openings to submit your work that may not reach the writing community at large. Making a good impression on an agent in a friendly conversation can grease the wheels down the road when you ask them to consider your novel. Many of these professionals want to see new writers succeed and take an interest in those who impress them.

The reverse also holds true. Rub an agent or editor the wrong way, and they may choose not to work with you. There are always more authors hoping to sell their books and stories to a given market than the market can accept. Agents, editors, and publishers say, "No," much more often than they say, "Yes."

That's the nature of publishing. It makes only good business sense to give your work its best chance to speak for itself by maintaining a polite and professional attitude.

Doing good business can mean not talking business at all. Professional relationships, like personal relationships, grow from common interests, positive interactions, and enjoying each other's company.

Meeting an editor for the first time?

Don't pitch them your half-finished novel or all six short stories you wrote last summer first thing as you shake their hand.

Instead, ask them what new projects they're excited about or what some of their favorite books are. Find out if you have anything common, such as a shared hometown or an interest in cooking, gaming, music, or anything else in general. There are times to talk business and times to simply talk. Knowing the difference goes a long way toward building a good professional reputation to serve you well for years to come.

Forge a positive personal connection with an editor, and they may ask about your work out of genuine interest. Even if they don't, you'll still be in a better position to pitch them down the road. Should nothing work out, you've still made a strong professional contact who might put in a good word for you with other editors. Editors and publishers enjoy working with people they feel comfortable with and consider reliable. For writers starting out, these relationships lay the foundation for future business. You may spend a fair amount of time building them before you really start selling your work, but it's time well spent, a long-term investment in your career.

While building your publishing network, you should also do your homework and make sure you understand how publishing functions. This involves mastering what different types of rights mean, how different publishing agreements and models work, the fundamentals of contracts, and what's required to successfully publish a book or story. Many online resources offer great information about this. Most professional writing groups offer reference information or forums where members can ask questions and share knowledge.

Some, such as the Authors Guild, even offer contract review services for their members. Panels about the ins and outs of contracts are a staple at conventions and writing workshops. You can learn much by listening to veteran authors talk about the ups and downs of their experiences. If you've found a mentor, they can probably answer many of your questions, and if not, they may point you in the right direction to do your research.

When getting started with the business of writing, concentrate on learning the basics. Understand how publishers pay authors—whether through advances and royalties, royalties only, or work-for-hire fees, and whether royalties are paid as a percentage of list price or net receipts, and how often you will receive royalty statements. All of these mean different things to your bottom line.

Learn publishing rights, how publishers exploit them, and how they generate income for you. Rights are the heart of your copyright, your intellectual property. What rights you grant to an editor or publisher can have ramifications that last years.

Consider, for instance, that you sold film rights to your novel to a small press with no contacts in the film industry. If a producer later expresses interest to you directly, you still need to work through your publisher to negotiate any possible option or sale. A good agreement can generate nice income while a misstep can lose it or tie up your work in limbo. Think about which rights you're willing to grant to a publisher and which you want to withhold.

Learn about rights reversions, the process by which a publisher returns your rights to you. Know the difference between contracts limited to a specific term, such as three or five years, and those based on the availability or sales of your book. This determines how long a publisher holds the rights you grant them. Many publishing contracts prevail for as long as the publisher keeps a work in print, either physically or digitally. Without the right safeguards that can result in a publisher holding onto your work long after their sales of it slow to a trickle.

Publishing involves a great deal of trust on the part of both author and editor or publisher. They trust you're providing original work, your best work, and will cooperate with editing and preparing your story as well as supporting and promoting its publication. You're trusting they'll do their best to prepare and edit your work, distribute it, promote and sell it, and pay you fairly and on-time.

Your contract codifies that trust. You should expect your publisher to live up to its terms and commit yourself to doing likewise, and to do so you need to thoroughly understand the language and practices involved.

When considering all this, don't lose sight of your larger publishing goals. Where do you hope to be a few years from now? Writing novels? Publishing a short fiction collection?

Many authors, especially early in their careers, worry more about simply getting their work published than about how it is published or what their next steps should be. That urgency and excitement to see one's work in print is understandable, but it can lead to bad business decisions. It can pay to have patience and let the publishing wheels turn, and they do turn quite slowly at times, rather than to go for a fast acceptance. That may seem counterintuitive. After all, authors write stories to be read. What's the point of holding back from an opportunity to put your work in front of readers?

The business of writing is a cross-country road trip, not a milk run. Your choices of what and where you publish now can affect your career in the future. Selling a story to a semi-pro market that may reach one hundred readers means that story won't be available when a pro market with the right theme and a bigger readership opens up a few months later. You can always write another story, sure, and there's no guarantee you'd have sold the first one to the pro market, but pursuing lesser markets means you're putting energy into sales with less potential for return, and taking more time away from writing.

A bad business proposition all around.

Accumulating the knowledge you need to publish successfully takes time. It's important to become part of a writing community. You need people to turn to for insight and advice as you weigh publishing deals, find new wrinkles in contracts, or run into issues with publishers. Online resources explain much of the basics, but there are endless ways to modify a contract for a book or a short story, let alone the subsidiary rights that could see your work adapted for audiobooks, films, translations, new print editions, and more.

In one regard, the business of writing is straightforward. Authors should be paid for their published work. But the mechanics of how that work is published and how the author is paid can be complex enough to keep a room full of lawyers grinning. Most genre press deals won't be so intricate. Selling a story to an anthology or magazine is often simple. Established publishers tend to use regular boilerplate contracts that become well-known in the business.

For novels, the contracts become more involved and require more consideration. They can always be negotiated. Most publishers expect authors, and certainly agents, to ask for at least some changes, whether it's to strike an option clause, increase the number of author copies, or omit selected subsidiary rights. That's when knowledge gained from your writing community and research comes into use, enabling you to understand the pros and cons of any deal and how to improve it.

Most importantly, though, when stepping into the business side of writing, make sure to keep up your creative momentum. Don't become bogged down in the sale of a single story or book. One successful sale can ease the way for others. Keep writing!

You're building a career.

Always keep an eye on the future, your next project, your next story, your next inspiration. Don't lose faith if a sale falls through or a story is declined. Have confidence in your creativity, forge ahead. Write the next story and the next until you write the story that's be accepted, and then make sure you know what you're agreeing to when you sign on the dotted line.

Artwork by Luke Spooner

BIOGRAPHIES

Linda D. Addison grew up in Philadelphia and began weaving stories at an early age. She currently lives in Arizona and has published over 300 poems, stories and articles. Ms Addison is the first African-American recipient of the world renowned Bram Stoker Award® and has received four awards for collections: "Four Elements" written with Charlee Jacob, Marge Simon and Rain Graves (Bad Moon Books 2013); "How To Recognize A Demon Has Become Your Friend" short stories and poetry (Necon EBooks, 2011), "Being Full of Light, Insubstantial" (2007), "Consumed, Reduced to Beautiful Grey Ashes" (2001). "Dark Duet" (Necon EBooks, 2012), a collaborative book of poetry written with Stephen M. Wilson, was a 2012 finalist for the HWA Bram Stoker Award(R). She co-edited Sycorax's Daughters, an anthology of horror fiction & poetry by African-American women (publisher Cedar Grove Publishing, 2017) with Kinitra Brooks and Susana Morris, which was a HWA Bram Stoker finalist in the Anthology category. In 2018 she received the HWA Lifetime Achievement Award.

http://www.cith.org/linda/index.html

Award-winning author **Maria Alexander** is a novelist, short story writer, screenwriter, poet and virtual world designer. Her novel *Mr. Wicker* won the Bram Stoker Award (2014) for Best first novel and her book *Snowed* (2016) received a Stoker for Best Young Adult Novel. Her short story *Though Thy Lips Are Pale*, which appeared in the anthology *Dark Delicacies III: Haunted*, was singled out for an honorable mention by Editor **Ellen Datlow** in *Best Horror of the Year, Vol. 2*.

Kevin J. Anderson is the author of 140 novels, 56 of which have appeared on national or international bestseller lists; he has over 23 million books in print in thirty languages. Anderson has coauthored fourteen books in the DUNE saga with Brian Herbert, over 50 books for Lucasfilm in the Star Wars universe. He has written for the *X-Files*, *Star Trek*, *Batman* and *Superman*, and many other popular franchises. For his solo work, he's written the epic SF series, The Saga of Seven Suns, a sweeping nautical fantasy trilogy, "Terra Incognita," accompanied by two progressive rock CDs (which he wrote and produced), and alternate history novels *Captain Nemo* and *The Martian War*, featuring Jules Verne and H.G. Wells, respectively. He has written two steampunk novels, *Clockwork Angels* and *Clockwork Lives*, with legendary drummer and lyricist Neil Peart from the band Rush. He also created the popular humorous horror series featuring Dan Shamble, Zombie P.I., and has written eight high-tech thrillers with Colonel Doug Beason.

Michael Bailey is the multi-award-winning author of *Palindrome Hannah*, *Phoenix Rose*, and *Psychotropic Dragon* (novels), *Scales and Petals,* and *Inkblots and Blood Spots* (short story/poetry collections), *Enso* (a children's book), and the editor of *Pellucid Lunacy, Qualia Nous, The Library of the Dead*, and the *Chiral Mad* anthologies published by Written Backwards. He is also an editor for Dark Regions Press, where he has created dark science fiction projects like *You, Human*. He is currently at work on a science fiction thriller, *Seen in Distant Stars*, and a new fiction collection, *The Impossible Weight of Life*.

Jessica Marie Baumgartner Jessica's motto is: Adventure first, then write! When not running around exploring nature she chases after multiple versions of herself and feeds furry babies. In addition, she is the award winning author of the *Embracing Entropy* series and a current member of the Missouri Writer's Guild. Her work has been featured in a wide variety of publications including: *Fantastic Tales of Terror, Bards and Sages, Aurora Wolf, The Society of Misfit Stories, The Lorelei Signal,* and many more.

Born and raised in Ireland, **Kealan Patrick Burke** is the Bram Stoker Award-Winning author of *The Turtle Boy, Kin,* and *Sour Candy*. Visit him on the web at www.kealanpatrickburke.com or follow him on Twitter at @kealanburke

The Oxford Companion to English Literature describes **Ramsey Campbell** as "Britain's most respected living horror writer". He has been given more awards than any other writer in the field, including the Grand Master Award of the World Horror Convention, the Lifetime Achievement Award of the Horror Writers Association, the Living Legend Award of the International Horror Guild and the World Fantasy Lifetime Achievement Award. In 2015 he was made an

Honorary Fellow of Liverpool John Moores University for outstanding services to literature.

Mort Castle, deemed a "horror doyen" by Publishers Weekly, has won three Bram Stoker Awards®, two Black Quills, a Golden Bot, and has been nominated for an Audie, the International Horror Guild Award, the Shirley Jackson Award, and the Pushcart Prize. He's edited or authored 17 books; his recent or forthcoming titles include: *New Moon on the Water*; *Writer's Digest Annotated Classics: Dracula*; and the 2016 Leapfrog Fiction contest winner *Knowing When to Die*. More than 600 Castle authored "shorter works," stories, articles, poems, and comics have appeared in periodicals and anthologies, including *Twilight Zone*, *Bombay Gin*, *Poe's Lighthouse*, and *Tales of the Batman*. Castle teaches fiction writing at Columbia College Chicago and has presented writing workshops and seminars throughout North America.

James Chambers is the Bram Stoker Award-winning author of the original graphic novel *Kolchak the Night Stalker: The Forgotten Lore of Edgar Allan Poe* as well as the Lovecraftian novella collection, *The Engines of Sacrifice*, described in a Publisher's Weekly starred-review as " . . . chillingly evocative . . . " He has also written the story collection *Resurrection House* and the dark, urban fantasy novella, *Three Chords of Chaos*. His story, *A Song Left Behind in the Aztakea Hills*, published in Shadows Over Main Street 2, was nominated for a Bram Stoker Award. His tales of crime, fantasy, horror, pulp, science fiction, steampunk, and more have appeared in numerous anthologies and magazines. He has also edited anthologies—most recently A New York State of

Fright—as well as comics and graphic novels and hundreds of non-fiction books in a wide range of subjects. His website is www.jameschambersonline.com.

Greg Chapman is the Bram Stoker Award®-nominated and Australian Shadows Award-nominated author of *Hollow House* and the author of five novellas: *Torment, The Noctuary, Vaudeville, The Last Night of October*, and *The Followers*. His debut collection, *Vaudeville and Other Nightmares*, was published in 2014.

His short stories have appeared in numerous publications, including Dark Eclipse, DevolutionZ, SQ Mag, Midnight Echo, and several anthologies. His short story, *The Bone Maiden*, was an Australian Shadows Award finalist in 2015, as was his novella, *The Followers,* in 2016.

His debut novel *Hollow House* was nominated for a Bram Stoker Award® in 2016 and he also received the Richard Laymon President's Award for services to the Horror Writers Association in 2017.

He is also a horror artist and his first graphic novel *Witch Hunts: A Graphic History of the Burning Times*, written by authors Rocky Wood and Lisa Morton, won the Superior Achievement in a Graphic Novel category at the Bram Stoker Awards® in 2013. He also illustrated the one-shot comic, Bullet Ballerina, written by Tom Piccirilli.

His second novel, *The Noctuary: Pandemonium*, the sequel to his acclaimed 2011 novella, was published by Bloodshot Books in late 2017.

Greg is also the current President of the Australasian Horror Writers Association.

Visit www.darkscrybe.com

Richard Chizmar is a *New York Times, USA Today, Wall Street Journal, Washington Post*, Amazon, and *Publishers Weekly* bestselling author.

He is the co-author (with Stephen King) of the bestselling novella, *Gwendy's Button Box* and the founder/publisher of *Cemetery Dance* magazine and the Cemetery Dance Publications book imprint. He has edited more than 35 anthologies and his fiction has appeared in dozens of publications, including multiple editions of *Ellery Queen's Mystery Magazine* and The Year's 25 Finest Crime and Mystery Stories. He has won two World Fantasy awards, four International Horror Guild awards, and the HWA's Board of Trustee's award.

Chizmar (in collaboration with Johnathon Schaech) has also written screenplays and teleplays for United Artists, Sony Screen Gems, Lions Gate, Showtime, NBC, and many other companies. He has adapted the works of many bestselling authors including Stephen King, Peter Straub, and Bentley Little.

Chizmar is also the creator/writer of Stephen King Revisited, and his third short story collection, *A Long December*, was published in 2016 by Subterranean Press. With Brian Freeman, Chizmar is co-editor of the acclaimed *Dark Screams* horror anthology series published by Random House imprint, Hydra.

Chizmar's work has been translated into many languages throughout the world, and he has appeared at numerous conferences as a writing instructor, guest speaker, panelist, and guest of honor.

Please visit the author's website at: Richardchizmar.com

After graduating from Edinboro University of Pennsylvania with his Bachelor's Degree in Communications, and obtaining his Master's Degree in Demonology from Miskatonic University, **Tim Chizmar** has written for various magazines, newspapers and websites including Fangoria, First Comics News, Girls and Corpses, and many others. He has sold short stories to such popular collections as Halloween Tales, Hell Comes to Hollywood 2, 18 Wheels of Horror and even Chicken Soup for the Soul. This dark writer has written various screenplays for Hollywood production companies and even appeared in films from Full Moon Features. He launched his own publishing house in 2018 called SpookyNinjaKitty and currently they put out seven brand new titles a year including the popular *Modern Madness* collections and his bizarre demon tale, *Soul Traitor*. Tim has been a proud member of various writers' organizations and is currently the co-chair for the Las Vegas Chapter of the prestigious Horror Writers Association. Aside from the darker topics, it has not all been a career of terror as his lighter credits to date include ABC, FOX, Showtime, Playboy, NBC, and even The Hallmark Channel. He has produced various television pilots including once he developed a comedy/action series for CMT with wrestling superstar Rob Van Dam. As a headlining comedian Tim Chizmar was a favorite at The World Famous Hollywood IMPROV, The Jon Lovitz Comedy Club, has toured all over the world playing sold-out casinos, clubs and colleges. To date he has worked with such standup legends as Jeff Foxworthy, Gabriel Iglesias, Jon Lovitz, Daniel Tosh, and many others. When he's not inspiring fellow writers and artists by appearing on various panels such as at San Diego Comic-Con,

WonderCon, Scare LA, or speaking at Hollywood Success events, he's constantly working on his next project. Because for Tim Chizmar . . . There's always a next project!

Rachel Autumn Deering is an Eisner and Harvey Award-nominated writer, editor, and book designer from the hills of Appalachia. She has worked for Titan Books, DC/Vertigo Comics, Blizzard Entertainment, Cartoon Network, and more. She is a rock and roll witch with a heart of slime.

Robert Ford is the author of the novels *The Compound*, and *No Lipstick in Avalon*, the novellas *Ring of Fire, The Last Firefly of Summer, Samson and Denial, Bordertown*, and the short story collection *The God Beneath my Garden*. He can confirm the grass actually is greener on the other side, but it's only because of the bodies buried there.

Print and ebook versions of his work are available through Amazon and various other vendors.

Writer/Director **Mick Garris** was an easy choice for this roundtable. Creative artist in several areas Mick's first forays into writing were in journalism, reviews, and as a press agent. In the late 1970's he created and served as the on-screen host for a Los Angeles cable access interview program show called "Fantasy Film Festival," that aired on L.A.'s legendary Z-Channel which was a early precursor of what was to come. His big break came through Steven Spielberg in 1985 as one of the writers and story editors for the television series *Amazing Stories*. Mick's first book was a short story collection *A Life in the Cinema* in 2000. Mick also joined Heather Graham in writing a story for *Dark*

Delicacies III: Haunted by treating us all to the gruesome short story *Tyler's Last Act.*

Christopher Golden is the *New York Times* bestselling, Bram Stoker Award-winning author of such novels as *Of Saints and Shadows, The Myth Hunters, The Boys Are Back in Town,* and *Strangewood.* He has co-written three illustrated novels with Mike Mignola, the first of which, *Baltimore, or, The Steadfast Tin Soldier and the Vampire*, was the launching pad for the Eisner Award-nominated comic book series, *Baltimore*. He is currently working on a graphic novel trilogy in collaboration with Charlaine Harris entitled *Cemetery Girl*. His novels *Snowblind* and *Tin Men* were released in 2014. Golden was born and raised in Massachusetts, where he still lives with his family. His original novels have been published in more than fourteen languages in countries around the world. Please visit him at www.christophergolden.com

Cody Goodfellow has written five novels, and co-wrote three more with New York Times bestselling author John Skipp. His first two collections, *Silent Weapons For Quiet Wars* and *All-Monster Action*, each received the Wonderland Book Award. He wrote, co-produced and scored the short Lovecraftian hygiene film *Stay At Home Dad*, which can be viewed on YouTube. He is also a director of the H.P. Lovecraft Film Festival-San Pedro, and cofounder of Perilous Press, an occasional micropublisher of modern cosmic horror. He lives in Burbank, California, and is currently working on building a perfect bowling team.

Michael Paul Gonzalez is the author of the novels *Angel Falls* and *Miss Massacre's Guide to Murder and Vengeance*. His newest creation is the audio drama podcast *Larkspur Underground*, a serialized horror story. A member of the Horror Writers Association, his short stories have appeared in print and online, including *Drive-In Creature Feature, Gothic Fantasy: Chilling Horror Stories, Lost Signals, Seven Scribes— Beyond Ourselves, 18 Wheels of Horror, the Booked Podcast Anthology*, HeavyMetal.com, and the *Appalachian Undead* Anthology. He resides in Los Angeles, a place full of wonders and monsters far stranger than any that live in the imagination. You can visit him online at MichaelPaulGonzalez.com

Stephen Graham Jones is the author of sixteen novels and six story collections. Most recent is the novella *Mapping the Interior*, from Tor.com, and the comic book *My Hero*, from Hex Publishers.

Stephen lives and teaches in Boulder, Colorado.

Del Howison is a journalist, writer, and the Bram Stoker Award-winning editor of the anthology *Dark Delicacies: Original Tales of Terror* and the *Macabre by the World's Greatest Horror Wri*ters. His short story, *The Lost Herd* was turned into the premiere (and highest rated) episode, *The Sacrifice*, for the series *Fear Itself*. He has been nominated for over half a dozen awards. He is the cofounder and owner of Dark Delicacies, a book and gift store known as "The Home of Horror," located in Burbank, California.

Tonya Hurley is the New York Times best-selling author of the highly acclaimed "ghostgirl" book series;

creator, writer and producer of animated and live action hit television series; writer and director of independent films; writer and director of commercials for Playstation, Gameboy and Warner Home Video; and creator of ground-breaking videogames. Her young adult trilogy, *The Blessed*, was released by Simon and Schuster in 2012.

Hurley has written and directed several acclaimed independent films, which have been selected for film festivals around the world including the LA Independent, TriBeca and Edinburgh and have also been broadcast on ABC, PBS and IFC.

Hurley was nominated for the prestigious Rockefeller Foundation Award in Film and made the semi-finals of the Sundance Institute's Writer's Lab with her feature film script. She studied writing, music and filmmaking at The University of Pittsburgh, screenwriting at New York University, and stop motion animation at The School of Visual Arts in New York City. Currently her film "Baptism of Solitude: A Tribute to Paul Bowles" is being distributed through the United Nations.

Her first book "ghostgirl" was released in 2008 and instantly hit the New York Times bestseller list. The sequel "ghostgirl: Homecoming" was released in 2009. Both have become international bestsellers available in over 22 languages around the world. The audiobooks for both are narrated by Parker Posey with original music by Vince Clarke The third book in the "ghostgirl" trilogy—"ghostgirl Lovesick" was released in July 2010.

Hurley began her career in New York City as a personal publicist for such artists as John "Rotten" Lydon, Prince, George Michael, Morrissey, The Cure, Mary-Kate and Ashley Olsen, Larry McMurtry, RL

Stine, The Three Tenors, Erasure, Depeche Mode, Paul Westerberg, Bush, and John Cale.

Visit her "ghostgirl" website at www.ghostgirl.com.

Eugene Johnson is a writer and Bram Stoker nominated editor who has written and edited in various genres. His anthology *Appalachian Undead*, co-edited with Jason Sizemore, was selected by FearNet, as one of the best books of 2012. Eugene's articles and stories have been published by award winning Apex publishing, The Zombiefeed, Evil Jester Press, Warrior Sparrow Press and more. Eugene also appeared in *Dread Stare*, a political theme horror anthology from Thunder Dome press. Eugene's anthology, *Drive-in Creature Feature*, pays homage to monster movies, features New York Times best-selling authors Clive Barker, Joe R. Lansdale, Christopher Golden, Jonathan Maberry and many more. He was nominated for the Bram Stoker award for *Where Nightmares Come From: The Art Of Storytelling In The Horror Genre* along with his co-editor Joe Mynhardt.

As a filmmaker, Eugene Johnson worked on various movies, including the upcoming *Requiem*, starring Tony Todd and directed by Paul Moore. His short film *Leftovers*, a collaboration with director Paul Moore, was featured at the Screamfest film festival in Los Angeles as well as Dragoncon.

Eugene is currently developing fun projects at EJP, he spends his time working on several projects including *Brave*, a horror anthology honoring people with disabilities; the *Fantastic Tales of Terror* anthology; and his children's book series, Life lessons with Lil Monsters. Eugene is currently a member of the Horror Writers Association. He resides in West Virginia with his fiancé, daughter, and two sons.

Todd Keisling is the author of *A Life Transparent*, *The Liminal Man*, and the critically-acclaimed novella, *The Final Reconciliation*. His most recent release is the horror collection, *Ugly Little Things: Collected Horrors*, available now from Crystal Lake Publishing. He lives somewhere in the wilds of Pennsylvania with his family where he is at work on his next novel.

Brian Kirk is an author of dark thrillers and psychological suspense. His debut novel, *We Are Monsters*, was a Bram Stoker Award finalist for Superior Achievement in a First Novel. His second novel, *Will Haunt You*, will be released in March 2019.

His short fiction has been published in many notable magazines and anthologies. Most recently, *Gutted: Beautiful Horror Stories* and the Bram Stoker Award-winning *Behold! Oddities, Curiosities and Undefinable Wonders*, where his work appears alongside multiple New York Times bestselling authors.

Visit briankirkblog.com for writing news and ways to connect. Don't worry, he only kills his characters.

From the day she was born, **Jess Landry** has always been attracted to the stranger things in life. Her fondest childhood memories include getting nightmares from the *Goosebumps* books, watching *The Hilarious House of Frightenstein*, and reiterating to her parents that there was absolutely nothing wrong with her mental state.

Since picking up a pen a few years ago, Jess's fiction has appeared in anthologies such as Crystal Lake Publishing's *Where Nightmares Come From*, Unnerving's *Alligators in the Sewers*, Stitched Smile's *Primogen: The Origins of Monsters*, DFPs *Killing It*

Softly, and April Moon Books' *Ill-Considered Expeditions*, as well as online with SpeckLit and EGM Shorts.

She currently works as Managing Editor for JournalStone and its imprint, Trepidatio Publishing, where her goal is to publish diverse stories from diverse writers. An active member of the HWA, Jess has volunteered as Head Compiler for the Bram Stoker Awards since 2015, and has most recently taken on the role of Membership Coordinator.

You can visit her on the interwebs at her sad-looking website, jesslandry.com, though your best bet at finding her is on Facebook and Twitter (facebook.com/jesslandry28 and twitter.com/jesslandry28), where she often posts cat memes and references Jura

Joe R. Lansdale is the author of 48 novels and over 20 short story collections. He has written and sold a number of screenplays, has had his plays adapted for stage. His work has been adapted to film; *Bubba Ho-Tep* and *Cold in July* among them. His best-known novels, the Hap and Leonard series has been adapted for television with Lansdale as co-executive producer with Lowell Northrop under the title, *HAP AND LEONARD*. He has also edited or co-edited numerous anthologies.

Kasey Lansdale, first published at the tender age of eight by Random House, is the author of several short stories and novellas, with stories from Harper Collins and Titan Books, as well as the editor of assorted anthology collections, including Subterranean Press' *Impossible Monsters*. She is best known as a Singer/Songwriter. Most recently, you can hear

Lansdale as the narrator of various works, including Stan Lee's *Reflections,* George R.R. Martin's *Aces Abroad,* and George A. Romero's latest installment, *Nights of the Living Dead*, among others. Her new collection, *Terror is our Business*, was lauded by Publisher's Weekly as "storytelling that delightfully takes on a lighter and sharper.

Vince Liaguno is the Bram Stoker Award-winning editor of *Unspeakable Horror: From the Shadows of the Closet* (Dark Scribe Press 2008), an anthology of queer horror fiction, which he co-edited with Chad Helder. His debut novel, 2006's *The Literary Six*, was a tribute to the slasher films of the 80's and won an Independent Publisher Award (IPPY) for Horror and was named a finalist in *ForeWord Magazine's* Book of the Year Awards in the Gay/Lesbian Fiction category.

More recently, he edited *Butcher Knives and Body Counts* (Dark Scribe Press, 2011)—a collection of essays on the formula, frights, and fun of the slasher film—as well as the second volume in the *Unspeakable Horror* series, subtitled *Abominations of Desire* (Evil Jester Press, 2017). He's currently at work on his second novel.

He currently resides on the eastern end of Long Island, New York, where he is a licensed nursing home administrator by day and a writer, anthologist, and pop culture enthusiast by night. He is a member (and former Secretary) of the Horror Writers Association (HWA) and a member of the National Book Critics Circle (NBCC).

Author Website: www.VinceLiaguno.com

Jonathan Maberry is a New York Times bestselling author, 5-time Bram Stoker Award-winner, and comic book writer. His vampire apocalypse book series, V-WARS, is in production as a Netflix original series, starring Ian Somerhalder (*Lost*, *Vampire Diaries*) and will debut in early 2019. He writes in multiple genres including suspense, thriller, horror, science fiction, fantasy, and action; and he writes for adults, teens and middle grade. His works include the Joe Ledger thrillers, *Glimpse*, the Rot & Ruin series, the Dead of Night series, *The Wolfman, X-Files Origins: Devil's Advocate, Mars One*, and many others. Several of his works are in development for film and TV. He is the editor of high-profile anthologies including *The X-Files, Aliens: Bug Hunt, Out of Tune, New Scary Stories to Tell in the Dark, Baker Street Irregulars, Nights of the Living Dead,* and others. His comics include *Black Panther: Doomwar, The Punisher: Naked Kills,* and *Bad Blood*. He lives in Del Mar, California.

Find him online at www.jonathanmaberry.com.

Elizabeth Massie is a Bram Stoker Award and Scribe Award-winning author of novels, short fiction, media tie-ins, poetry, and nonfiction. Her works include Sineater, Hell Gate, Desper Hollow, Wire Mesh Mothers, Welcome Back to the Night, Twisted Branch (under the pseudonym Chris Blaine), Homeplace, Naked On the Edge, Afraid, Sundown, The Fear Report, The Tudors: King Takes Queen, The Tudors: Thy Will Be Done, Dark Shadows: Dreams of the Dark (co-authored with Mark Rainey), Homegrown, Night Benedictions, Versailles, Buffy the Vampire Slayer: Power of Persuasion, the Ameri-Scares series of spooky novels for middle grade readers, the Young Founders series of historical novels for young adults, the Silver Slut superhero adventure series, and more.

Massie spends her spare time knitting, geocaching, and staring mindlessly into space. She lives in the Shenandoah Valley with her husband, illustrator and theremin-player Cortney Skinner.

Lisa Mannetti has won the Bram Stoker Award twice: for her debut novel, *The Gentling Box* and her short story, *Apocalypse Then*. She has also been nominated five additional times in both the short and long fiction categories: Her story, *Everybody Wins*, was made into a short film (BYE BYE SALLY) and her novella, *Dissolution*, will soon be a feature-length film, also directed by Paul Leyden. Her work, including *The Gentling Box*, *1925: A Fall River Halloween*, and *The Box Jumper*, has been translated into Italian.

Her most recently published longer work, *The Box Jumper*, a novella about Houdini, was not only been nominated for a Bram Stoker Award and the prestigious Shirley Jackson Award, it won the "Novella of the Year" award from This is Horror in the UK.

She has also authored *The New Adventures of Tom Sawyer and Huck Finn*, two companion novellas in her collection, *Deathwatch*, a macabre gag book, *51 Fiendish Ways to Leave your Lover*, as well as non-fiction books, and numerous articles and short stories in newspapers, magazines and anthologies. Forthcoming works include several other short stories, a dark novel about the dial-painter tragedy in the post-WWI era, *Radium Girl*, and another dark novel, *Cultus*.

Lisa lives in New York in the 100 year old house she originally grew up in, with two wily (mostly black) twin cats named Harry and Theo Houdini.

Visit her author website: www.lismannetti.com
Visit her virtual haunted house:
www.thechanceryhouse.com

Thomas F. Monteleone has published more than 100 short stories, 5 collections, 8 anthologies, and 30 novels—including the bestseller, New York Times Notable Book of the Year, *The Blood of the Lamb*. A five-time winner of the Bram Stoker Award, he's also written scripts for stage, screen, and TV, as well as the bestselling *The Complete Idiot's Guide to Writing a Novel* (now in a 2nd edition). His latest novels are a global thriller, Submerged, and the conclusion of a YA trilogy, *The Silent Ones* (with F. Paul Wilson). With his daughter, Olivia, he co-edits the award-winning anthology series of imaginative fiction— *Borderlands*. With his wife, Elizabeth, he is a co-founder of the annual Borderlands Press Writers Boot Camp. He is well-known as an entertaining reader of his work, and routinely draws a large, appreciative audience at conventions. Despite being dragged kicking and screaming into his seventies and losing most of his hair, he still thinks he is dashingly handsome—humor him. In the spring of 2017, he received the Lifetime Achievement Award from the Horror Writers Association at StokerCon in Long Beach California.

Paul Moore is a filmmaker who has written and directed four feature films, most recently *Keepsake* and *Requiem*. He is also the co-owner of the movie production studio *Blind Tiger Filmworks,* and his first short story *Spoiled* was published in the well-received anthology *Appalachian Undead*. It was a very rewarding experience and he is happy to follow that effort with *Things,* a homage to both the spirit of B-movie alien invasion films and several of the films that inspired him to pursue a career in filmmaking. He also appeared in *Dread State* and *Where Nightmares Come From*.

Lisa Morton is a screenwriter, author of non-fiction books, award-winning prose writer, and Halloween expert whose work was described by the American Library Association's Readers' Advisory Guide to Horror as "consistently dark, unsettling, and frightening." Her most recent releases include *Ghosts: A Haunted History* and the short story collection *Cemetery Dance Select: Lisa Morton*. Lisa lives in the San Fernando Valley and online at www.lisamorton.com.

Yvonne Navarro is the author of twenty-three published novels and lots of short stories, articles and a reference dictionary. Her most recent published book is *Supernatural: The Usual Sacrifices* (based in the Supernatural Universe). Her writing has won a bunch of awards and stuff. Lately she's been really getting into painting and artwork. She lives way down in the southeastern corner of Arizona, about twenty miles from the Mexican border, and is married to author Weston Ochse. They dote on their rescued Great Danes, Ghoulie, The Grimmy Beast, and I Am Groot as well as a talking parakeet named BirdZilla.

Joe Mynhardt is a three-time Bram Stoker Award-nominated South African publisher, non-fiction and short story editor, and mentor.

Joe is the owner and CEO of Crystal Lake Publishing, which he founded in August, 2012. Since then he's published and edited short stories, novellas, interviews and essays by the likes of Neil Gaiman, Clive Barker, Stephen King, Charlaine Harris, Ramsey Campbell, John Connolly, Jack Ketchum, Jonathan Maberry, Christopher Golden, Graham Masterton, Damien Angelica Walters, Adam Nevill, Lisa Morton,

Elizabeth Massie, Joe McKinney, Joe R. Lansdale, Edward Lee, Paul Tremblay, Wes Craven, John Carpenter, George A. Romero, Mick Garris, and hundreds more.

Just like Crystal Lake Publishing, which strives to be a platform for launching author careers, Joe believes in reaching out to all authors, new and experienced, and being a beacon of friendship and guidance in the Dark Fiction field. In 2018 he started a coalition of small press publishers to support both each other and their authors.

Joe's influences stretch from Poe, Doyle, and Lovecraft to King, Connolly, and Gaiman (and so many more).

You can read more about Joe and Crystal Lake Publishing at www.crystallakepub.com or find him on Facebook.

Gene O'Neill has seen about 200 of his stories and novellas published, several reprinted in France, Spain, and Russia. Some of these stories have been collected in *Ghost Spirits, Computers & World Machines, The Grand Struggle, In Dark Corners, Dance of the Blue Lady, The Hitchhiking Effect, Lethal Birds*, and *Frozen Shadows & Other Chilling Stories*. He has seen six novels published. Gene has been a Stoker finalist twelve times. In 2010 *Taste of Tenderloin* won the haunted house for collection; in 2012 *The Blue Heron* won for Long Fiction. A series of two novels in *The White Plague Chronicles* will come out in 2019—*The Sarawak Virus* in the spring, *Pandemic* in the winter. Also out in 2019, *Entangled Soul*, a collaborative novella, with Chris Marrs. Recently, he finished *The Beast with Two Backs*, a novella with a strong Maya background.

Gene's lives in the Napa Valley with his wife, Kay. He has two grown children, Gavin, who lives in Oakland, and Kaydee who lives in Carlsbad and rides herd on his two g-kids, Fiona and TJ.

When he isn't writing or visiting g-kids, Gene likes to read good fiction or watch sports—all of them, especially boxing.

Writer **Steve Niles** is well known to fans of graphic novels, horror stories, and screenplays. Several of his graphic novels have been optioned for film but he is probably most noted for the film translation of his vampire graphic novel *30 Days of Night*. His character Cal McDonald is featured prominently in the *Criminal Macabre* series of graphic novels. But he has also turned some of those adventures into straight prose novels and short stories two of which, *All My Bloody Things* and *The Y Incision* found homes in the *Dark Delicacies* and *Dark Delicacies II: Fear* anthologies respectively. Steve also had a long relationship with the late **Bernie Wrightson** as friends and partners in many graphic novels.

Kelli Owen is the author of more than a dozen books, including the novels *Teeth* and *Floaters*, and novellas *Wilted Lilies* and *Waiting out Winter*. Her fiction spans the genres from thrillers to psychological horror, with an occasional bloodbath, and an even rarer happy ending. She was an editor and reviewer for over a decade, and has attended countless writing conventions, participated on dozens of panels, and spoken at the CIA Headquarters in Langley, VA regarding both her writing and the field in general. Born and raised in Wisconsin, she now lives in Destination, Pennsylvania. Visit her website at kelliowen.com for more information.

Chuck Palahniuk is the best-selling author of more than seventeen fictional works, including *Fight Club*, *Invisible Monsters*, *Survivor*, *Choke*, *Lullaby*, *Diary*, *Haunted*, *Rant*, *Pygmy*, *Tell-All*, *Damned*, *Doomed*, *Beautiful You*, and most recently *Make Something Up* and *Adjustment Day*. He has also written nonfiction, graphic novels, and coloring books. He lives in the Pacific Northwest.

John Palisano has a pair of books with Samhain Publishing, *Dust of the Dead*, and *Ghost Heart*. *Nerves* is available through Bad Moon. *Starlight Drive: Four Halloween Tales* was released in time for Halloween, and his first short fiction collection *All That Withers* is available from Cycatrix press, celebrating over a decade of short story highlights. *Night of 1,000 Beasts* is coming soon. He won the Bram Stoker Award in short fiction in 2016 for "Happy Joe's Rest Stop." More short stories have appeared in anthologies from Cemetery Dance, PS Publishing, Independent Legions, DarkFuse, Crystal Lake, Terror Tales, Lovecraft eZine, Horror Library, Bizarro Pulp, Written Backwards, Dark Continents, Big Time Books, McFarland Press, Darkscribe, Dark House, Omnium Gatherum, and more. His non-fiction pieces have appeared in *Blumhouse*, *Fangoria* and *Dark Discoveries* magazines.

He is currently serving as the Vice President of the Horror Writers Association. Say 'hi' to John at: www.johnpalisano.com and http://www.amazon.com/author/johnpalisano and www.facebook.com/johnpalisano and www.twitter.com/johnpalisano

Sarah Pinborough is the Sunday Times #1, New York Times and Internationally best-selling author of 25 novels. Published in over 30 territories her work spans a variety of genres from YA thrillers to dystopian/sci-fi crime and historical cross-genre horror. Her recent psychological thriller, *Behind Her Eyes*, was an international hit and is greenlit for a six part series filming in 2019 with Left Bank and Netflix. *Behind Her Eyes* was also shortlisted for the Crime and Thriller book of the year at the British Book Awards. Her YA thriller, 13 Minutes, is also in development with Netflix and Michael De Luca. Her most recent novel, *Cross Her Heart*, was sold to the US in a healthy seven figure deal and is already in development with World Productions. Her *Dog-Faced Gods* trilogy is in development with Lionsgate and Festival. She is also a screenwriter who had written for the BBC and has several original projects in development. She lives in Stony Stratford with her Romanian rescue dog Ted.

Heather Graham Pozzessere is a New York Times best-selling American writer, who writes horror, romance, thriller, and mystery. She writes under, both her maiden name **Heather Graham** and under the pseudonym **Shannon Drake**. She was awarded a Lifetime Achievement Award by the Romance Writers of America along with countless others. When I was a trustee for the Horror Writers Association Heather was the Vice President. In 2009, when Editor Jeff Gelb and I were putting together the anthology *Dark Delicacies III: Haunted*, I asked Heather for a horror story for the book. She blessed me with *Mist on the Bayou*.

Mary SanGiovanni is the author of the *The Hollower* trilogy (the first of which was nominated for the Bram Stoker Award), *Thrall, Chaos, Chills*, and the forthcoming *Savage Woods*, and the novellas *For Emmy, Possessing Amy, The Fading Place*, and *No Songs for the Stars*, and the forthcoming *A Quiet Place at the World's End*, as well as the collections *Under Cover of Night, A Darkling Plain*, the forthcoming *Night Moves* and *A Weirdish Wild Space*. Her fiction has appeared in periodicals and anthologies for the last decade. She has a Masters degree in Writing Popular Fiction from Seton Hill University, Pittsburgh, where she studied under genre greats. She is currently a member of The Authors Guild, The International Thriller Writers, and Penn Writers, and was previously an Active member in the Horror Writers Association.
http://marysangiovanni.com

Mark Savage. Mark hails from Australia where he made and sold his first feature *Marauders* at the age of 24. He has also written and produced for television. His specialty is thrillers, horror, crime, cult, action and exploitation-themed films. His film *Defenceless* won the Best Film, Best Director, and Best Actress awards at the 2005 Melbourne Underground Film Festival. His film *120/80: Stressed to Kill* starring **Bill Oberst Jr**, and **Armand Assante** is a black comedy about middle-age crisis. He is also known for his film documentary of **Jackie Chan** *Beyond Mr. Nice Guy*.

David James Schow was born in Marburg, Germany and was adopted by American parents then living in Middlesex, England. After publishing non-fiction book and film criticism in newspapers and magazines, his first professionally published fiction was a novelette in Galileo Magazine in 1978. He spent the next decade honing his skills in the short fiction form. He won a Dimension Award from *Twilight Zone Magazine* (for most popular short story) in 1985 and a World Fantasy Award (best short fiction) in 1987.

He commenced screenwriting in 1989 with an uncredited dialogue polish on *A Nightmare on Elm Street Part 5: The Dream Child,* after which both his first teleplay and first screenplay were bought and produced (the Freddy's Nightmares episode "Safe Sex" and the feature *Leatherface: Texas Chainsaw Massacre III* respectively).

After inventing the rubric "stalk-and-slash" in 1977 to describe the genre later simplified as "slasher films," Schow similarly coined the notorious neologism "splatterpunk" in 1986. To reflect the shifting climate of the horror aesthetic during the early 1990s, he logged 41 installments of his popular "Raving & Drooling" column for *Fangoria Magazine.* This and other non-fiction op-ed material was collected in the book *Wild Hairs* (2000), which won the International Horror Guild's award for best nonfiction in 2001.

Twitter @DavidJSchow Facebook DavidJSchow

John Skipp is a Saturn Award-winning filmmaker (*TALES OF HALLOWEEN*), Stoker Award-winning anthologist (*DEMONS, MONDO ZOMBIE*), and New York Times bestselling author (*THE LIGHT AT THE END, THE SCREAM*) whose books have sold millions of copies in a dozen languages worldwide. His first anthology, *BOOK OF THE DEAD,* laid the foundation in 1989 for modern zombie literature. He's also editor-in-chief of Fungasm Press, championing genre-melting authors like Laura Lee Bahr, Autumn Christian, Danger Slater, Cody Goodfellow, and

Devora Gray From splatterpunk founding father to bizarro elder statesman, Skipp has influenced a generation of horror and counterculture artists around the world. His latest book is *THE ART OF HORRIBLE PEOPLE*.

Luke Spooner Luke Spooner is a freelance illustrator from the South of England. At 'Carrion House' he creates dark, melancholy and macabre illustrations and designs for a variety of projects and publishers, big and small, young and old.

Jeff Strand is the four-time Bram Stoker Award-nominated author of over forty books, including *Pressure, Dweller,* and *Bring Her Back*. His website is www.JeffStrand.com.

Richard Thomas is the award-winning author of seven books: three novels—*Disintegration* and *Breaker* (Penguin Random House Alibi), and *Transubstantiate* (Otherworld Publications); three short story collections—*Staring into the Abyss* (Kraken Press), *Herniated Roots* (Snubnose Press), and *Tribulations* (Cemetery Dance); as well as one novella in *The Soul Standard* (Dzanc Books). With over 135 stories published, his credits include Cemetery Dance (twice), *PANK, story South, Gargoyle, Weird Fiction Review, Midwestern Gothic, Gutted: Beautiful Horror Stories, Qualia Nous, Chiral Mad 2 & 3,* and *Shivers VI* (with Stephen King and Peter Straub). He has won contests at ChiZine and One Buck Horror, and has received five Pushcart Prize nominations to date. He is also the editor of four anthologies: *The New Black* and *Exigencies* (Dark House Press), *The Lineup: 20 Provocative Women*

Writers (Black Lawrence Press) and *Burnt Tongues* (Medallion Press) with Chuck. He has been nominated for the Bram Stoker, Shirley Jackson, and Thriller awards. In his spare time he is a columnist at LitReactor and Editor-in-Chief at Gamut Magazine. His agent is Paula Munier at Talcott Notch. For more information visit www.whatdoesnotkillme.com.

Marie O'Regan is a British Fantasy Award-nominated author and editor, based in Derbyshire. Her first collection, *Mirror Mere*, was published in 2006; her second, *In Times of Want*, came out in September 2016, and her short fiction has appeared in a number of genre magazines and anthologies in the UK, US, Canada, Italy and Germany. She was shortlisted for the British Fantasy Society Award for Best Short Story in 2006, and Best Anthology in 2010 (*Hellbound Hearts*) and 2012 (*Mammoth Book of Ghost Stories by Women*). Her genre journalism has appeared in magazines like *The Dark Side, Rue Morgue* and *Fortean Times*, and her interview book with prominent figures from the horror genre, *Voices in the Dark*, was released in 2011. An essay on 'The Changeling' was published in PS Publishing's *Cinema Macabre*, edited by Mark Morris. She is co-editor of the bestselling *Hellbound Hearts, Mammoth Book of Body Horror* and *A Carnivàle of Horror—Dark Tales from the Fairground*, plus editor of bestselling *The Mammoth Book of Ghost Stories by Women* and is Co-Chair of the UK Chapter of the Horror Writers' Association. Marie is represented by Jamie Cowen of The Ampersand Agency.

Bev Vincent is the author of some 80 short stories, including appearances in *Alfred Hitchcock's Mystery*

Magazine, Ellery Queen's Mystery Magazine and two MWA anthologies. His work has been nominated for the Bram Stoker Award (twice), the Edgar (for *The Stephen King Illustrated Companion*) and the ITW Thriller Award, and he was the 2010 winner of the Al Blanchard Award. He is a contributing editor of *Cemetery Dance* magazine, where his Stephen King: News from the Dead Zone column has appeared since 2001. His most recent book is *The Dark Tower Companion*. He lurks around various corners of the internet including Twitter (@BevVincent), his book review blog (OnyxReviews.com) and website (bevvincent.com). In the "real world," he lives in Texas, where he is trying to ignore the news while working on a novel.

Tim Waggoner has published close to forty novels and three collections of short stories. He writes original dark fantasy and horror, as well as media tie-ins, and his articles on writing have appeared in numerous publications. He's won a Bram Stoker Award, been a finalist for the Shirley Jackson Award and the Scribe Award, and his fiction has received numerous Honorable Mentions in volumes of Best Horror of the Year. He's also a full-time tenured professor who teaches creative writing and composition at Sinclair College in Dayton, Ohio.

David Wellington got his start serializing his zombie story *Monster Island* online in 2003. Since then he has written more than twenty novels, including the 13 Bullets series, the Jim Chapel thrillers, the standalone novel *Positive,* and most recently a science fiction trilogy beginning with *Forsaken Skies* (as D. Nolan Clark). He has also worked in video games, comic books and other media. He lives in New York City.

F. Paul Wilson is the award-winning, NY Times bestselling author of fifty-plus books and numerous short stories spanning medical thrillers, sf, horror, adventure, and virtually everything between. More than 9 million copies of his books are in print in the US and his work has been translated into 24 languages. He also has written for the stage, screen, and interactive media. He is best known for his urban mercenary, *Repairman Jack*. He was voted Grand Master by the World Horror Convention and received Lifetime Achievement Awards from the Horror Writers of America, the Libertarian Futurist Society, and the RT Booklovers Convention. His works have received the Stoker Award, the Porgie Award, the Prometheus and Prometheus Hall of Fame Awards, the Pioneer Award, and the prestigious Inkpot Award from San Diego ComiCon. He is listed in the 50th anniversary edition of Who's Who in America.

Stephanie M. Wytovich is an American poet, novelist, and essayist. Her work has been showcased in numerous anthologies such as *Gutted: Beautiful Horror Stories, Shadows Over Main Street: An Anthology of Small-Town Lovecraftian Terror, Year's Best Hardcore Horror: Volume 2, The Best Horror of the Year: Volume 8*, as well as many others.

Wytovich is the Poetry Editor for Raw Dog Screaming Press, an adjunct at Western Connecticut State University and Point Park University, and a mentor to authors with Crystal Lake Publishing. She is a member of the Science Fiction Poetry Association, an active member of the Horror Writers Association, and a graduate of Seton Hill University's MFA program for Writing Popular Fiction. Her Bram Stoker Award-winning poetry collection, *Brothel*, earned a home with Raw Dog Screaming Press alongside *Hysteria: A Collection of Madness, Mourning Jewelry,* and *An Exorcism of Angels.* Her debut novel, *The Eighth,* is published with Dark Regions Press.

Her next poetry collection, *Sheet Music to My Acoustic Nightmare,* is scheduled to be released late 2017 from Raw Dog Screaming Press.

Follow Wytovich at http://www.stephaniewytovich.com/ and on twitter @JustAfterSunset.

Mercedes M. Yardley is a dark fantasist who wears poisonous flowers in her hair. She is the author of *Pretty Little Dead Girls, Nameless,* and the Bram Stoker Award-winning *Little Dead Red.* Mercedes lives in Las Vegas and can be reached at www.abrokenlaptop.com.

THE END?

Not quite . . .

Dive into more Tales from the Darkest Depths:

Novels:
House of Sighs (with sequel novella) by Aaron Dries
Beyond Night by Eric S. Brown and Steven L. Shrewsbury
The Third Twin: A Dark Psychological Thriller by Darren Speegle
Aletheia: A Supernatural Thriller by J.S. Breukelaar
Beatrice Beecham's Cryptic Crypt: A Supernatural Adventure/Mystery Novel by Dave Jeffery
Where the Dead Go to Die by Mark Allan Gunnells and Aaron Dries
Sarah Killian: Serial Killer (For Hire!) by Mark Sheldon
The Final Cut by Jasper Bark
Blackwater Val by William Gorman
Pretty Little Dead Girls: A Novel of Murder and Whimsy by Mercedes M. Yardley
Nameless: The Darkness Comes by Mercedes M. Yardley

Novellas:
Quiet Places: A Novella of Cosmic Folk Horror by Jasper Bark
The Final Reconciliation by Todd Keisling
Run to Ground by Jasper Bark

Devourer of Souls by Kevin Lucia
Apocalyptic Montessa and Nuclear Lulu: A Tale of Atomic Love by Mercedes M. Yardley
Wind Chill by Patrick Rutigliano
<u>*Little Dead Red*</u> by Mercedes M. Yardley
Sleeper(s) by Paul Kane
Stuck On You by Jasper Bark

Anthologies:
C.H.U.D. Lives!—A Tribute Anthology
Tales from The Lake Vol.4: The Horror Anthology, edited by Ben Eads
Behold! Oddities, Curiosities and Undefinable Wonders, edited by Doug Murano
Twice Upon an Apocalypse: Lovecraftian Fairy Tales, edited by Rachel Kenley and Scott T. Goudsward
Tales from The Lake Vol.3, edited by Monique Snyman
Gutted: Beautiful Horror Stories, edited by Doug Murano and D. Alexander Ward
<u>*Tales from The Lake Vol.2*</u>, edited by Joe Mynhardt, Emma Audsley, and RJ Cavender
Children of the Grave
The Outsiders
Tales from The Lake Vol.1, edited by Joe Mynhardt
Fear the Reaper, edited by Joe Mynhardt
For the Night is Dark, edited by Ross Warren

Short story collections:
Frozen Shadows and Other Chilling Stories by Gene O'Neill
Varying Distances by Darren Speegle
The Ghost Club: Newly Found Tales of Victorian Terror by William Meikle

Ugly Little Things: Collected Horrors by Todd Keisling
Whispered Echoes by Paul F. Olson
Embers: A Collection of Dark Fiction by Kenneth W. Cain
Visions of the Mutant Rain Forest, by Bruce Boston and Robert Frazier
Tribulations by Richard Thomas
Eidolon Avenue: The First Feast by Jonathan Winn
Flowers in a Dumpster by Mark Allan Gunnells
The Dark at the End of the Tunnel by Taylor Grant
Through a Mirror, Darkly by Kevin Lucia
Things Slip Through by Kevin Lucia
Where You Live by Gary McMahon
Tricks, Mischief and Mayhem by Daniel I. Russell
Samurai and Other Stories by William Meikle
Stuck On You and Other Prime Cuts by Jasper Bark

Poetry collections:
WAR by Alessandro Manzetti and Marge Simon
Brief Encounters with My Third Eye by Bruce Boston
No Mercy: Dark Poems by Alessandro Manzetti
Eden Underground: Poetry of Darkness by Alessandro Manzetti

If you've ever thought of becoming an author, we'd also like to recommend these non-fiction titles:

Where Nightmares Come From: The Art of Storytelling in the Horror Genre, edited by Joe Mynhardt and Eugene Johnson
Horror 101: The Way Forward, edited by Joe

Mynhardt and Emma Audsley
Horror 201: The Silver Scream Vol.1 and *Vol.2*,
edited by Joe Mynhardt and Emma Audsley
*Modern Mythmakers: 35 interviews with Horror
and Science Fiction Writers and Filmmakers* by
Michael McCarty
Writers On Writing: An Author's Guide Volumes
1,2,3, and 4, edited by Joe Mynhardt. Now also
available in a Kindle and paperback omnibus.

**Or check out other Crystal Lake Publishing
books for more Tales from the Darkest
Depths.**

Hi, readers (or should I say authors?). It makes our day to know you reached the end of our book. Thank you so much. This is why we do what we do every single day.

Whether you found the book good or great, we'd love to hear what you thought. Please take a moment to leave a review on Amazon, Goodreads, or anywhere else readers visit. Reviews go a long way to helping a book sell, and will help us to continue publishing quality books. You can also share a photo of yourself holding this book with the hashtag #IGotMyCLPBook!

Thank you again for taking the time to journey with Crystal Lake Publishing.

We are also on . . .

Website:
www.crystallakepub.com

Be sure to sign up for our newsletter and receive two free eBooks: http://eepurl.com/xfuKP

Books:
http://www.crystallakepub.com/book-table/

Twitter:
https://twitter.com/crystallakepub

Facebook:
https://www.facebook.com/Crystallakepublishing/
https://www.facebook.com/Talesfromthelake/
https://www.facebook.com/WritersOnWritingSeries/

Pinterest:
https://za.pinterest.com/crystallakepub/

We strive to know each and every one of our readers, while building personal relationships with our authors, reviewers, bloggers, pod-casters, bookstores and libraries.

Crystal Lake Publishing is and will always be a beacon of what passion and dedication, combined with overwhelming teamwork and respect, can accomplish: Unique fiction you can't find anywhere else.

We do not just publish books, we present you worlds within your world, doors within your mind, from talented authors who sacrifice so much for a moment of your time.

This is what we believe in. What we stand for. This will be our legacy.

Welcome to Crystal Lake Publishing—Tales from the Darkest Depths